Roman Ingarden's Aesthetics and Ontology

Also available from Bloomsbury:

Human Beings and Their Images, by Christoph Wulf
Husserl's Phenomenology of Natural Language, by Horst Ruthrof
New Realism and Contemporary Philosophy, edited by Gregor Kroupa and Jure Simoniti
Philosophy, Literature and Understanding, by Jukka Mikkonen

Roman Ingarden's Aesthetics and Ontology

Contemporary Readings

Edited by
Leszek Sosnowski and Natalia Anna Michna

BLOOMSBURY ACADEMIC
LONDON • NEW YORK • OXFORD • NEW DELHI • SYDNEY

BLOOMSBURY ACADEMIC
Bloomsbury Publishing Plc
50 Bedford Square, London, WC1B 3DP, UK
1385 Broadway, New York, NY 10018, USA
29 Earlsfort Terrace, Dublin 2, Ireland

BLOOMSBURY, BLOOMSBURY ACADEMIC and the Diana logo are trademarks of
Bloomsbury Publishing Plc

First published in Great Britain 2023
This paperback edition published 2025

Copyright © Leszek Sosnowski, Natalia Anna Michna and Contributors, 2023

Leszek Sosnowski and Natalia Anna Michna have asserted their right under the Copyright,
Designs and Patents Act, 1988, to be identified as Editors of this work.

Cover image © Mina De La O/Getty Images

All rights reserved. No part of this publication may be reproduced or transmitted in
any form or by any means, electronic or mechanical, including photocopying, recording,
or any information storage or retrieval system, without prior permission in writing
from the publishers.

Bloomsbury Publishing Plc does not have any control over, or responsibility for, any third-
party websites referred to or in this book. All internet addresses given in this book were
correct at the time of going to press. The author and publisher regret any inconvenience
caused if addresses have changed or sites have ceased to exist, but can accept no
responsibility for any such changes.

A catalogue record for this book is available from the British Library.

A catalog record for this book is available from the Library of Congress.

ISBN: HB: 978-1-3503-2150-2
PB: 978-1-3503-2154-0
ePDF: 978-1-3503-2151-9
eBook: 978-1-3503-2152-6

Typeset by Deanta Global Publishing Services, Chennai, India

To find out more about our authors and books visit www.bloomsbury.com and sign up
for our newsletters.

Contents

List of Illustrations — vi

Introduction: Roman Ingarden, The Life of a Philosophical Work
Natalia Anna Michna and Leszek Sosnowski — 1

Part I Ontology

1. Modes and Moments in Ingarden's Ontology *Peter Simons* — 33
2. Logical Modalities, Existential Moments, and Modes of Being: Some Reflections on Ingarden's Existential Ontology *Jan Woleński* — 51
3. Questions Concerning Reality: Ingarden's Erotetical Path Toward Realism *Giuditta Corbella* — 68
4. Sounds and/or Tones? Scruton, Ingarden (. . . and Levinson) on Musical Aesthetics and Ontology *Edward M. Świderski* — 84

Part II Aesthetics

5. Lipps, Stein, and Ingarden on Empathy and the Coexperiencing of Value in the Aesthetic Experience *Jeff Mitscherling* — 103
6. 8-Bit Mystique: An Ingardenian Aesthetic Analysis of the Appeal of Retro Computer Games *Matthew E. Gladden* — 121
7. Roman Ingarden on Aesthetic Attention *Harri Mäcklin* — 138
8. Roman Ingarden on Fictional Times *Charlene Elsby* — 150

Notes on Contributors — 163
Index — 166

Illustrations

Figures

1.1	Concept lattice of modes and moments	43
1.2	Teardrop diagram of regions, modes, and moments	44
6.1	Technical limitations of historical 8-bit game systems' graphics	126
6.2	8-bit and 8-bit-style games often present critical information using brief text that possesses a high degree of indeterminacy	126
6.3	When representing objects visually, 8-bit-style games employ formats ranging from (a) the maximally indeterminate, which requires more extensive acts of concretization in a player's mind, to (h) the moderately indeterminate, which possesses fewer visual "gaps" that must (or can) be concretized	128

Tables

1.1	Occurrence Table of Modes and Moments	41
1.2	Abbreviations for Modes and Moments	42

Introduction

Roman Ingarden, The Life of a Philosophical Work

Natalia Anna Michna and Leszek Sosnowski

The philosophy of Roman Witold Ingarden still inspires researchers, who explore its academic potential and apply Ingarden's ideas and concepts to contemporary philosophical research. The book now in your hands is not only proof of the vitality of Ingarden's philosophy but a tribute to this Polish thinker, whose original and, in many respects, innovative thought exerted a significant impact on twentieth-century phenomenological reflections, as well as (from a broader perspective) on contemporary Western philosophy. The present publication is a collection of articles on Ingarden's ontology and aesthetics. It is worth emphasizing, however, that its individual chapters are not limited to discussions or presentations of the views of the Polish philosopher. Their authors, coming from various traditions and schools of philosophizing, have undertaken the difficult task of careful analysis and development of the various threads present in Ingarden's philosophy. The book is therefore a source of knowledge about his most important philosophical achievements. However, first and foremost, it testifies to the unflagging timeliness and contemporary character of his philosophy. In other words, this publication is proof of the "life" of an academic work, by way of an analogy to the "life" of a work of art. Ingarden introduced this metaphorical term as a result of adopting a conceptual opposition: schematicity as an element of the structure of a work and its concretization as an element of subjective reception. These two relational elements form the basis of the actualization of the work as a result of successive readings. These new readings/concretizations "enliven" the work at each encounter (Ingarden 1973b: 346–7).

Ingarden also adopts an extra-aesthetic approach to a work of art, that is, an approach without concretization. This is a researcher's approach, in which it is possible to obtain a pure reconstruction of the work, during which special attention is paid to "the meaning of the semantic units, the syntactic structure of the sentences, the possible ambiguity of words and groups of words, and syntactic-logical functions present among sentences" (Ingarden 1973a: 341). This attention, supported by the phases of analytical and synthetic research in the cognition of the work, enables the avoidance of errors in its reconstruction. This type of cognition can seemingly be transferred to an academic work, which is subject to the process of reconstruction in terms of meaning and sense while retaining features such as purely intentional propositional correlates or presented items. Regardless of similarities, the essential difference lies in the function of an academic work, since "[i]t consists of establishing cognitive results attained and transmitting them to other conscious subjects" (Ingarden 1973b: 329). Experience in the reading of academic works indicates that they are subject to reconstruction, just as works of art are subject to concretization. Their quantity, quality, or absence thereof depends, in Ingarden's opinion, on the cultural atmosphere of the epoch in question. This conclusion cannot be fully applied to academic works, since the issue will appear differently with reference to works of philosophy as opposed to those of particular sciences. Certainly, however, the issue of the "life" of an academic work is worthy of further analysis, and the chapters presented in this book conclusively prove the "vitality" of Ingarden's philosophical work.

Here it is worth adding some background information on Ingarden and his philosophy, particularly on his studies in Lviv and subsequent education in Germany, where he met Edmund Husserl and—as one of Husserl's most outstanding students—acquired sophisticated philosophical knowledge as a phenomenologist. Ingarden began his studies at the University of Lviv in 1911. There, he attended classes taught by Kazimierz Twardowski, who suggested that Ingarden should relocate to Göttingen in Germany in order to study under Husserl's direction. Ingarden highly appreciated the time he spent studying at the Georg August University, emphasizing again and again the atmosphere of freedom and creativity that prevailed there, and recalling studies which provided "a wide variety of educational stimuli, both within and outside the lectures themselves," where "new academic results, those of both the students and their professors, were reciprocally communicated and contentious matters discussed" (Ingarden 1998: 16). This atmosphere provided incentive to work, and afforded a sense of participation in the creation of knowledge: "It felt as if one was taking part in emerging new knowledge, meeting people with divergent scientific interests, in the most diverse fields of learning, with divergent views" (Ingarden 1998: 16). From the beginning of his stay in Göttingen, Ingarden was part of an informal student group centered around Husserl, referred to as the "Göttingen circle," consisting of about thirty individuals and including students not only from European countries but also from the United States and Canada.

The outbreak of the First World War forced Ingarden to leave Göttingen—on October 14, 1914, to be exact. The philosopher returned to the University of Lviv in Vienna, where Twardowski had relocated it for the duration of the war. At a meeting of the Polish Philosophical Society on December 19, 1914, Ingarden presented, in connection with Husserl's philosophy, "certain central issues of so-called phenomenology" (Ingarden 1914), wishing to clear up misunderstandings that were arising with regard to phenomenological reflections at that time and to refute the accusations directed against those reflections. Additionally, Ingarden, aiming at an explanation of the nature of the originality inherent in phenomenology, stated in his lecture that the purpose of this trend was "to know the very subject of study. To endeavor to perceive this object and to directly perceive its ultimate quality is the path of cognition" (Ingarden 1914).

In order to continue his studies and work under Husserl's supervision, Ingarden returned to Göttingen for two short periods, from May to August 1915 and from February to April 1916, then followed his teacher to Freiburg im Breisgau for two periods, from May 1916 to January 1917 and from the end of September of that year to January 1918. The latter period concluded with Ingarden's defense of his doctoral thesis. The philosopher passed his doctoral examination in philosophy, mathematics, and physics under Husserl on January 16, 1918. In his memoirs, he recalled the last moments he spent with Husserl before returning to Poland: "On the evening before my final departure from Freiburg following my doctoral examination, I visited Husserl's hospitable home to say goodbye to the Master and his wife Malwina [Malvine Husserl]. Of course, we soon began to philosophize as usual" (Ingarden 1981a: 23). For both of them, philosophy was as inevitable as breath, as life.

The war was still going on; the contrast "between philosophy and the reality of war was shocking" (Ingarden 1981a: 23). Philosophy thus became both a shield and a space that wartime events could not penetrate. Husserl needed this shield, especially following the death of his son, Wolfgang. For Husserl, Ingarden recalled, it was always a good time to philosophize, to hold an inspiring conversation with someone who understood both him and (his) philosophy:

> Around eleven o'clock in the evening there was an air raid. Husserl lived on the second floor, so we all went down to the apartment on the ground floor, where we stood in the hall with the landlord's family. Husserl, however, continued the philosophical dispute, somewhat oblivious to what was happening. Then

we said goodbye [. . .] I was hoping to return soon. It took almost ten years, however, before I could resume those philosophical evenings with Husserl. (Ingarden 1981a: 23)

Personal contact with Husserl and his assistant Adolf Reinach turned out to be important for the development of Ingarden's thought, as it brought out in him a firm faith in philosophy—its purpose, object, and method of study. Therefore, the Polish philosopher enthusiastically accepted Husserl's statement (in May 1912) that the main object of philosophy is the study of essence. However, the most important thing for Ingarden was contact with the Master, as he called Husserl. Two features, essential for the reciprocal contacts between the Master and the apprentice, can be seen here: Ingarden was one of the last students belonging to the Göttingen phenomenological circle, and for a long time he maintained constant and close contact with Husserl. With good reason, Husserl cited him, in a letter dated December 2, 1929, as the "dearest and most faithful among my older students" (Spiegelberg 1982: 223).

As a result of his studies with Husserl, Ingarden acquired the ability to ask fundamental questions and to conduct thorough, profound analyses of philosophical problems. During their final meeting in Freiburg, Ingarden read to Husserl excerpts from his doctoral dissertation, which revealed problems concerning the philosophy of Henri Bergson and triggered intense discussion. Ingarden later recalled that their conversations from this period were important to Husserl because they enabled him to conduct a real dialog in which the interlocutor, thinking for himself, offered surprising arguments and objections, following his own independent line of thought: "When I now recall all of those conversations with Husserl, I must say that not only were they rich in terms of content, but they also constituted precious moments in which Husserl's important intuitions came to life and brought him closer to a number of important problems" (Ingarden 1981a: 22).

Clearly, Husserl found a philosophical partner in Ingarden: "Husserl needed someone with whom he could assume an understanding, someone in front of whom he could think aloud and develop his own discoveries" (Ingarden 1981a: 22). This could not be a passive listener, but rather someone capable of criticism and of undertaking polemics with the Master. If this condition was met, then "the powers of insight and verbal expression were revived within him, powers, however, which could not be so easily aroused when he worked alone" (Ingarden 1981a: 22). Lively conversation was necessary to stimulate his mind and to develop thoughts, problems, and themes "without unnecessary distance, as well as without the adverse effect of digressions" (Ingarden 1981a: 22). Ingarden also preserved an image of Husserl working without the "aid" described earlier:

> I once saw Husserl through the glass door of his office, working all alone. I saw how he paced the room restlessly, how he gesticulated in lively fashion, sitting down at the desk from time to time to jot down a few words, then breaking off and pacing around the room as if trying to overcome certain obstacles. He created the impression that thinking, with reference to gaining insights, cost him a great deal. In conversation this didn't occur at all. (Ingarden 1981a: 22–3)

The current perspective enables us to state unequivocally that without Göttingen, without the atmosphere prevailing there, without the acquaintances and friendships with students and university lecturers he established there, and finally without Husserl himself, Ingarden, as he is understood today, would not exist. This means, moreover, that the academic legacy of this philosopher— which is, we do not hesitate to state, the most important Polish element of philosophical intellectual culture, including, in particular, the phenomenological movement—would not exist either. Ingarden was indeed a Polish philosopher, but also undoubtedly a philosopher of the world—Κόσμου φιλόσοφός [*Kosmou filosofos*], as Władysław Tatarkiewicz wrote when remembering Ingarden a year after his death (Tatarkiewicz 1972: 56).

Ontology as the First Area of Study

The starting point of Ingarden's philosophical considerations is the issue of the controversy over the existence of the world, which is the origin of all of the threads found therein. The systematic thought of the Polish philosopher is combined with complex structuring and precise analysis of philosophical issues, representing fundamental problems of the basic disciplines of philosophy, creatively elaborated. Within this whole, Ingarden's considerations create a network of closely intertwined problems, characterized by varying degrees of generality and specificity. As a result, the reader is presented with a thoroughly and profoundly presented philosophical system; however, this fact makes it no easier to follow Ingarden's thoughts. An additional difficulty is presented by the philosopher's language, which describes eidetic insights into the subject under study. His masterfully controlled phenomenological style of inquiry, descriptive, "visual," and analytical down to the tiniest details, is at the same time "meandering." The potential reader or student of his thoughts should take this into account in making study plans, as only a holistic approach to Ingarden's views can ensure orientation in terms of perspective and detail.

Ontology is, for Ingarden, the first area of study, free from any assumptions or premises derived from other teachings. In this area, he distinguished between existential, formal, and material ontology, referring thereby to Aristotle and distinguishing himself from Husserl, who failed to account for the existential aspects of ontological investigations. Ingarden dealt mainly with existential and formal issues, devoting less attention to material questions. Ontology is possible due to the fact that the cognizing subject encounters the content of an idea as the domain of an object, within which pure possibilities occur (Ingarden 2013: I, 72). Ontology is therefore free from all existential assumptions concerning the factual existence of the object of its research.

Ontology, taken in its methodological aspect, is an *a priori* science, founded upon an eidetic view, that is, regardless of factual claims. In the objective aspect of research, ontology is an *a priori* analysis of the contents of an idea, pure ideal qualities, and necessary relationships between them, as well as the pure possibilities determined by these relationships. Ontological deliberation

> has its ultimate foundation in the pure apprehension of the most primitive ideal qualities (of "pure *Wesenheiten*") and of the necessary interconnections binding them. On the other hand, it proceeds to an analysis of pure possibilities that follow for the individual being from the interrelations ascertained to obtain within ideas' contents. (Ingarden 2013: I, 61–2)

In the next portion of *Controversy over the Existence of the World* Ingarden reduces these distinctions to a single form of analysis of the content of an idea. The realm of ideas is therefore the only assumption required by Ingarden in his ontology, for it is ideas that constitute the condition that makes them possible. Ontology is limited strictly to the analysis of ideas, omitting the question of their existence. To reinforce and highlight this conviction, Ingarden uses what, in his opinion, is a good example of a similar approach to an object of research occurring in geometry or set theory, which are also *a priori* sciences.

Ingarden was aware of the problem associated with a potential accusation directed at an ontology as thus understood: specifically, the previously adopted (even in implicit form) assumption of the existence of an idea, which undermines ontology's supposed lack of assumptions. Ingarden addressed this issue twice in his habilitation lecture, *Stanowisko teorii poznania w systemie nauk filozoficznych* [The position of the theory of knowledge in the system of philosophical sciences] (1924), as well as in *Controversy*. In the first case, he stated that "at the basis of every ontology lie existential judgments, stating the existence of an idea of a given domain" (Ingarden 1971: 402). He confirmed this in the second case, extending the justification: "Three fundamentally different realms of being have to be distinguished in the totality of what exists [*im All des Seienden*]: the realm of individual entities, the domain of ideas, and the sphere of pure qualities (Jean Héring called them *Wesenheiten*)" (Ingarden 2013: I, 67). This "metaphysical inventory" transcends ontology, which assumes nothing and makes no judgment concerning the existence of the object of its research. Thus Ingarden understood ontology as an autonomous science, which, as a result of a meticulous, intuitive analysis of the possible ways in which ideas and their contents exist, establishes the necessary relationship between pure ideal qualities and pure possibilities, as determined by those previously revealed relationships. Research as thus understood is detached from the real world, objective facts, and the particular sciences researching those facts.

That Ingarden, in his method of conducting research, was decidedly closer to analytical philosophy, even if understood in a particular way, is not an uncommon notion. According to one moderate position, even if Ingarden implements Husserl's program of phenomenology in his philosophy, "it is also close to analytical philosophy, although, unlike the latter, it analyzes not the creations of language but the content of ideas" (Strózewski 1993: 10). A more extreme position concerns the analytical nature of Ingarden's considerations, which becomes more profound the more he frees himself from Husserl's influence (Jadacki 1981: 6). This enables both of these Polish researchers to define Ingarden's philosophy as analytical phenomenology. Thus, the phenomenological method is a type of analysis that is supposed to lead to recognition of a visually analyzed object or some of its aspects. This method, understood as a faithful description of what is given, is supported by the analytical method from three perspectives: ontological (existential, formal, material), in terms of studying contradictions in the content of the idea; comparative-historical, in terms of evaluating consistency with previous systems of views and the concepts contained therein; and, finally, metaphysical, in terms of the consistency of judgments with reality.

Ingarden, following the publication of *Das literarische Kunstwerk* in German in 1931, appeared within the international academic community as a philosopher of art whose considerations were deeply embedded within his ontology. This picture of Ingarden was expanded and consolidated following his successive publications abroad, especially in the fields of epistemology and ontology. It was to the latter discipline that he owed his exceptional reputation as a phenomenologist, with ontology as the basis of all of his philosophical inquiries. Thus it might be believed that we are dealing here with a philosophical system formed by Ingarden on the Cartesian model. This should come as no surprise if we keep in mind how important Descartes was to Husserl. The Cartesian system is illustrated by the metaphor of the tree of sciences, which Descartes himself expresses as follows:

> Thus the whole of philosophy is like a tree. The roots are metaphysics, the trunk is physics, and the branches emerging from the trunk are all the other sciences, which may be reduced to three principal ones, namely medicine, mechanics, and morals. (Descartes 1985: 186)

Despite the obvious differences between the French and Polish philosophers, this modified schema appears applicable to Ingarden's considerations, which could be described as a tree of philosophy. The foundation (the roots) is general ontology and particular ontologies, which are then transformed into metaphysics (the trunk), of which the crown (the branches) is equivalent to a critique of cognition, encompassing specific sciences such as physics, ethics, aesthetics, and anthropology.

The image created by the tree metaphor appears inviting; the question remains open as to whether it is justified. Ingarden's considerations, while certainly systematic as well as systemic in nature, do not constitute a system in the Hegelian sense. Ingarden understood systems in two ways: as summative and as organic wholes. In the former case, the whole is made up of the sum of the parts, which can be disconnected *in concreto*. In the latter case, the whole is formed by the organic union of the parts, which can be disconnected only mentally (Ingarden 1966b, 485; 1970: 83; 2016: 248). The difference between them is fundamental, since it depends on the nature of the relationship between the elements that make up these wholes. Ingarden's systematically constructed philosophy partakes of a systemic character, even though it is not itself a system. Within it, ontology has a special place, since it is on ontological results that the problems formulated and solutions obtained in all other philosophical disciplines and specific sciences depend. Thus ontology is closely related to the other philosophical disciplines important to Ingarden, serving them as a theoretical foundation.

Particular Ontologies

General ontology, as understood by Ingarden, constitutes the foundation of the philosophical disciplines in which he is interested and is transformed into particular ontologies whose objects of research are ideas fundamental to individual disciplines. The chief task of the theory of cognition, which Ingarden called pure or absolute, is to discover the content "of the main idea of overall cognition in general, regardless of the type of subject through which it would be achieved, in what acts of consciousness it was obtained, or to which object it would apply" (Ingarden 1971: 382). The next step would be to "explore less general ideas, falling under the main overall idea of cognition in general, and to establish the relationships between these ideas" (Ingarden 1971: 382). In a detailed approach, it is necessary to examine the elements of the general idea of cognition, and thus the general ideas of the cognitive act of consciousness, followed by the subject of consciousness, the object of cognition, and finally the idea of the relationships between the content of the cognitive act of consciousness and the object of cognition (Ingarden 1971: 389n). This methodological approach avoids the limitations associated with the dogmatic nature of individual sciences.

Ontology is also the basis for anthropological and ethical research. Ingarden considered ethics as pure theory (theoretical ethics), which he distinguished from one of the branches of ethics (applied ethics or ethical technology), considered "practical science (philosophy)." The former field concerns the study of moral values, their mode of existence, their mutual relations, and, finally, the conditions of their occurrence within the framework of a single whole. Moreover, the scope of these studies includes objects possessing (or capable of possessing) moral values in a double sense. On one hand, this may concern a subject considered as a bearer of ethical values, with a question addressing the "object of moral evaluation"; on the other hand, it may concern "features of certain objects, which—themselves differing from 'good'—condition the attribution of 'good' to these objects, with a question addressing the 'moral criterion'" (Ingarden 1989: 12–15). In *Man and Value* Ingarden raised fundamental ethical and anthropological issues, such as the ontological foundation of responsibility, formed by objectively existing values, the identity of the subject of responsibility, the personal "I," freedom of will, and the causal and temporal structure of the world (Ingarden 1983: 53–118).

Ontology is also of fundamental significance in considerations of language, especially with reference to names as elements thereof. Ingarden analyzes the content of the nominal significance of names and the structure of the object to which a given name refers. As a result of these analyses, he determines the structure of the significance of the name, within which he highlights several points, of which the first three are particularly important: (1) the individual indicator of direction, which is a feature of every meaning and "expresses" its "being directed to" an intentional object, "created" in terms of its content by the material and formal contents of the significance of the name (Ingarden 1973b: 64–5; 1982: 47–8); (2) material content, which is made up of "constants" and "variables" of the name in question, and performs the function of qualitative determination of the object's endowment (Ingarden 1973b: 66–7; 1982: 49), and formal content, which determines the formal structure of a given object and thus performs the function of determining "something" as the subject of features, the ownership of that something, or the state of that something (Ingarden 1973b: 69–71; 1982: 50); (3) points of existential characterization and position.

Ingarden's analysis of questions, posed in his habilitation dissertation *Essentiale Fragen. Ein Beitrag zu dem Wesensproblem* (On Essential questions: A contribution to the essence problem), must also be situated within the context of linguistic issues. The erotetic issues contained therein, constituting an important element in the development of Ingarden's philosophical research, are also linked with ontological issues. The subtitle of the dissertation indicates this relationship by directing the analyses toward cognition of the nature of being, that is, the realism-idealism problem. The considerations contained in the dissertation concern questions about the mode of existence of individual beings and ideal entities and qualities. These remarks, derived from the introduction to Ingarden's book *Z teorii języka i filozoficznych podstaw logiki* (From the theory of language and the philosophical foundations of logic), can be summed up in one unequivocal statement: "In accordance with the scope of my research, this dissertation significantly transcends the mere analysis of questions, for it extends into the field of formal ontology and outlines the theory of the essence of an individual object" (Ingarden 1982: 7). Thus formulated, the goal determines the way questions are understood, because for Ingarden the interrogative sentence is important not as an act of interrogation, but as "a product of the act of inquiry, possessing a semantic unity" (Ingarden 1982: 327–8). In his search for its structural points, Ingarden ignored the very fact of the question and thus its mental aspect. As a result, the question, as a form of linguistic expression, leads to ontological conclusions.

The earlier paragraph directs our attention to the question of how these general statements by Ingarden concerning ontology and their relationships to particular philosophical disciplines are related to the materials gathered in this volume. The chapters in this book will enable readers to orient themselves regarding their constructive character in relation to Ingarden's research, signifying their function as creative continuations of a polemical or systematic nature. The first approach implements a historical and the second a subjective position, with a clear tendency to verify the theses of the Polish philosopher.

One more issue, related to the thematic scope of the chapters presented in the book and, consequently, to the form of this introduction, requires clarification. The volume placed in the reader's hands is devoted entirely to ontological and aesthetic issues. Confinement to these issues is not accidental but primarily the result of substantive considerations. Ingarden took a systematic approach to the study of aesthetic problems, which constituted the starting point for his ontological and epistemological considerations. These considerations, in turn, supplied this research with the phenomenological method, which entailed a focus on the essence of the object and the content of its general idea. Thus, the relationship between Ingarden's ontology and his aesthetics appears to be not merely significant or important but fundamental to his entire philosophy. In the individual chapters of this book, the reader will find various approaches to and justifications of this significant relationship between Ingarden's aesthetics and his ontology. Of course, the issues contained therein are not limited to ontology and aesthetics; numerous references can be found to other specific areas of Ingarden's system, including epistemological, logical, and axiological issues.

Simons and Woleński: Reflections on Ingarden's Existential Ontology

The first two chapters introduce us to the issue of existence. As we recall, Ingarden considered the problem of existence, based on existential ontology, in terms of pure possibilities, corresponding to the content of ideas. In the opening segments of *Controversy*, he poses existential questions of a metaphysical nature concerning factual existence and questions of an ontological nature concerning the possibility of existence, making the latter the subject of his subsequent considerations. In this context, the essential question is expressed as follows: "Which mode of being is it that is proper to it; that is to say, is prescribed by its essence—irrespective of whether it actually exists that way or not?" (Ingarden 2013: 88). To answer this question, Ingarden analyzes the idea of existence in general, the idea of individual modes of being, and, moreover, the idea of an object in the aspects of form and matter. Existence is always, Ingarden states, the existence of something, which means that it possesses the form of a particular mode of existence.

Ingarden distinguishes four such modes of being and, at the same time, four domains of being, namely, absolute (transient), ideal (nontemporal), real (temporal), and intentional (purely intentional). The indicated modes of being are subject to expansion when moments characterizing existence in time, and thus related to reality, are taken into account. Existential moments, as abstractions of a higher order which play the role of constituting modes of being, are helpful in understanding these modes. Ingarden distinguishes four pairs: ontic autonomy (self-existence)—ontic heteronomy (non-self-existence); ontic originality—ontic derivativeness; ontic self-sufficiency—ontic self-sufficiency; ontic independence—ontic dependence (Ingarden 2013: 108). After excluding contradictory combinations of existential moments, Ingarden obtained eight admissible concepts of being. These issues are addressed by the next two authors: Peter Simons in the chapter "Modes and Moments in Ingarden's Ontology" and Jan Woleński in the chapter "Logical Modalities, Existential Moments, and Modes of Being: Some Reflections on Ingarden's Existential Ontology."

At the outset of his analyses, Simons declares his interest in the issue of how Ingarden arrived at the division of modes of being, as outlined earlier. Importantly, while the author agrees with this division, he does not accept the way in which the Polish philosopher made these distinctions. Simons expresses his skepticism regarding the potential for extracting ontological categories through examining the content of objective ideas whose source lies in Platonic ideas. In contrast to Ingarden, the author lacks this epistemic certainty concerning the method used by the Polish philosopher and the advantages of his classification. He believes that ontology is often misled by (as he expresses it) certain features of the empirical world and the shortcomings of our linguistic-conceptual apparatus. These doubts enable him to express the view that as a result of these weaknesses we are dealing with an a posteriori ontology, which nullifies its priority regarding questions about what actually exists. In conclusion, Simons does not accept Ingarden's view of different modes of being, arguing that there are no such modes—which does not preclude the existence of things of different kinds. However, his greatest resistance (as he points out) is provoked by Ingarden's treatment of time, and more precisely the temporality of beings, although these critical remarks do not prevent him from proceeding to interesting analyses of Ingarden's views.

In several paragraphs, Simons remarks on existential ontology in order to present his own position, different from Ingarden's, against this background. The object of his interest is Ingarden's use of existential moments to distinguish between categories or modes of being, referring to the summary contained in §33 of *Controversy*. Following a discussion of existential moments and the families to which they belong—in Ingarden's language, modes of being—Simons refers critically to the definition of certain existential moments, asking whether they are always exhaustive and mutually exclusive. To clarify the issue, he gives various examples of ordering (e.g., library catalogs, biological taxonomies, table occurrences, concept lattices), while indicating his own, called The Teardrop, as the best among those mentioned for capturing the innovative nature of Ingarden's ontological proposition.

The conclusion of Simons's chapter may serve as a good introduction to the following chapter by Woleński, "Logical Modalities, Existential Moments, and Modes of Being: Some Reflections on Ingarden's Existential Ontology." As Simons writes:

> I must say, a source of some regret to myself, that because of the antagonism between Ingarden and the more logically inclined members of the Lvov–Warsaw School, he was not able to profit from their formal expertise and they were not able to profit from his ontological sophistication. Advanced ontology requires both sets of skills. (Simons 2023: 49)

Woleński, an acknowledged expert on Ingarden and the philosophers of the Lvov–Warsaw School alike, combines both approaches in his considerations. In the present case, Woleński considers the problems concerning Ingarden's existential ontology, regarding them as logical formalizations. This leads to an isolated approach to concepts and to their investigation in a state of certain reciprocal independence, which enables this exposition to be understood with greater clarity. In the case of Ingarden's existential-ontological analyses, the danger resulting from the very general nature of his considerations is reduced.

In his considerations, Woleński employs a logical square (D1) representing the elementary principles of modal logic and its two generalizations in the form of a logical hexagon (D2) and octagon (D3). The aim of this research is to compare Ingarden's ontological theorems with the principles of modal logic, for which analyses of the concepts of possibilities, necessities, and their variants are essential. Woleński therefore accepts the position that modal logic is useful in ontology, despite a problem involving the compatibility of ontological modalities with the rules of logical modalities. Therefore, he assumes that both types of modality are subject to the same formal rules.

Woleński uses a logical square in a segment devoted to presenting the core of modal logic (and its generalizations) through interpreting the logical consequences of categorical sentences. Following a detailed analysis of modal functors, he proceeds to consider Ingarden's modes of being and existential moments. Here he notes that Ingarden offered no definition of them in his writings; hence the researcher, in order to gain understanding of them, must make use of the examples and comments provided by the philosopher. On the basis of the fragments quoted from *Controversy*, Woleński presents an analysis of selected modes of being such as possibility or reality and of existential moments such as originality and derivativeness. In these analyses, the author uses a logical octagon (D3), since, as it turns out, some types of existential moments (modes of being) are present within it. Hence, it may be assumed, two questions emerge to guide further research: (1) whether Ingarden would accept all the categories present in (D3) as modes of being; (2) whether is necessary to study the separation of possibilities and realities, which contradicts (D3).

Corbella: Questions and the Problem of Reality

It is precisely this systematic continuation of research that characterizes the next chapter by Giuditta Corbella, "Questions Concerning Reality: Ingarden's Erotetical Path Toward Realism." Corbella takes up the theory of questions presented by Ingarden in his habilitation thesis, treating it as a tool to solve the problem of the existence of an independent reality. Ingarden analyzed essential questions concerning knowledge of the essence of an object, and thus ontological and epistemological issues. He included systematic considerations and, as can be judged from his subsequent publications, based his entire exposition on them. The dissertation was the first step along the path of Ingarden's research as an ontologist and epistemologist. Ingarden considered the problem of questions within the broader context of the nature of being and its cognition, which was intended to serve as an introduction to subsequent analyses of the issue of realism-idealism.

Ingarden's habilitation thesis, *Essentiale Fragen. Ein Beitrag zum Problem des Wesens*, was an ontological preparation for solving the problem of an independent, external reality, toward which the eidetic-ontological analyses contained in Chapters 2–5, on which Ingarden's researchers generally focus, were directed. These chapters are devoted to three questions, concerning the nature of the existence of individual beings, essences, and ideal qualities, respectively. Corbella believes, however, that the theory of questions is a methodological preparation for ontological considerations, and that Ingarden's ontological theorems should be treated as a whole. Therefore, in her chapter "Questions concerning reality," the author links the first and the last chapters of Ingarden's treatise, obtaining in this way an overview of the basic problems of the theory of questions, which is important in subsequent analyses.

Corbella precisely outlines the problem area of her considerations; namely, she intends to investigate Ingarden's theory of questions as a means by which to tackle the controversy over the existence of an independent reality in *Essentiale Fragen*. Her chapter aims to consider Ingarden's erotetical legacy and connect it to the realism-antirealism problem addressed by the philosopher throughout his academic life. Corbella divides her considerations into three parts, of which the first is historical, and the next two are theoretical, with reference to erotetic and ontological issues. In the first part, the author discusses the circumstances surrounding the publication of the text in German and the tasks and aim of the dissertation, placing it against the background of Ingarden's later publications, especially *Controversy over the Existence of the World*. She aptly observes that Ingarden's aesthetic analyses are also the result of a strategic choice, which marked the entire path of his philosophical research and in which he demonstrated a realistic attitude. Hence, as well, the ontological problem of the realism-idealism dispute is present as well in aesthetics, concerning, for example, the distinction between intentional and real objects.

Corbella clearly indicates her goal: to Ingarden's eidetic-ontological intentions, she wishes to add his erotetic and ontological considerations, which she implements in a few steps. Despite methodological differences, the first and the last chapter are linked in terms of their anti-skeptical character. Moreover, she draws attention to the consequences connected with the scope of ontological research, as it results in a "reversal" of the hierarchical order of judgments and questions; a question sentence is placed on a higher level than a declarative sentence. As Corbella argues, the act of questioning not only relates to reality but does so more visibly than an assertive judgment, as a result of the question's intensification of the directional component of the act of consciousness: "The questioner is not only saying something about reality; he rather interrogates reality about itself, demanding it to give him a proper answer" (Corbella 2023: 79).

Świderski: Sounds, Tones, and the Ontology of Music

Edward M. Świderski broadly indicates the area of his analyses, designating as their subject the views of Roger Scruton, Ingarden, and Jerrold Levinson (who is polemical with regard to the others) concerning the musical work. This author, in a chapter entitled "Sounds and/or Tones? Scruton, Ingarden (. . . and Levinson) on Musical Aesthetics and Ontology," raises at the outset important questions which provoke consideration of the differences between their theories. The essential question is whether musical aesthetics requires an ontology of music and therefore a definition of musical "objects." Generally speaking, these objects can be tones or sounds that shape the musical experience. This distinction in the context of the nature of the tones is crucial in subsequent analysis.

According to Scruton, tones, whose characteristics (pitch, timbre, harmony, rhythm) affect the quality of the musical experience, are important in music. Hence, in his opinion, musical ontology is irrelevant to musical aesthetics, because it is imaginative and not cognitive abilities that influence the perception of tones and their features. Based on this claim, Scruton concludes that the content and justification of a musical experience come from within the listener; hence philosophical reflection on music is a question of aesthetics, not of ontology. Levinson, through proclaiming that tones are properties of sounds and public objects in the world, makes serious allegations against Scruton: first, he cannot explain the public nature of this experience. Consequently, although access to a work of music exists through organized sounds, the work itself—its inner meaning as an aesthetic object—has no significant connection to an artifact outside the mind. Scruton is interested in a description of the understanding of music "which conceives of the philosopher's task as making perspicuous the structures of experience and its intentional objects" (Świderski 2023: 85). On this basis, Levinson accuses Scruton of phenomenological musical aesthetics and characterizes his "phenomenology" as dependent on the belief that works of art persist only in the mind and are only accidentally linked to some type of artifact.

Ingarden based his musical aesthetics on tonal experience, expressing his conviction, important in this context, concerning the difference between tones and sounds. He also recognized the importance of the ontology of music, which enabled him to place this experience on an objective basis, namely, on a musical work understood as a structured tonal formation of a higher order. The objectivity of this structure depends on the consideration of a musical work not as a physical, mental, or ideal but as a purely intentional object. In his conception, Ingarden attaches particular importance to ideal (pure) sound qualities, which the listener experiences as a musical structure, and thus as formations of sound organized in time, thematically. However, in order to have such an experience, the listener, in Ingarden's opinion, must adopt an aesthetic attitude. Świderski points out the weakness of this view of Ingarden's, indicating the controversial nature of the concept of attitude. The difficulty is related to its lack of definition, as it is not clear whether the listener consciously changes attitudes, from practical to aesthetic, or is perhaps forced to make this change as a result of the "musical frisson" caused by these qualities. Another problem, arising from Ingarden's concept of creativity and metaphysical qualities, concerns the specific purposefulness of a musical work within his understanding. It is not without reason that Świderski states, in relation to Ingarden, that the philosopher "spoke almost mystically about the reasons why we create cultural entities such as artworks: we do so to bring 'down to earth,' so to speak, values that we do not create but sense their transcendent presence" (Świderski 2023: 98).

The characteristics of the views of the aestheticians mentioned here are for Świderski a pretext for the presentation of contemporary discussions on the understanding of music. In presenting the views of individual philosophers, he brings out their arguments, showing how they intersect or undermine or support one another. Many problems arise during the discussion, such as acousmatic experience in the context of musical experience; the importance of the relationship between musical features, such as timbre, harmony, or rhythm, for the reception of a work; accusations of phenomenological idealism resulting in specific philosophical and aesthetic consequences; understandings of and attitudes toward intentionality in the context of mental conceptions; the role of musical imagination and understanding of hearing in the context of musical culture; understandings of a purely aesthetic attitude; the identity of a musical work. As a result, the reader learns in detail about the contemporary understanding of a musical work.

Aesthetics as Cognition of a Work of Art

Ingarden, wrote Peter McCormick, "was probably one of the most thoughtful students of aesthetics in the twentieth century" (McCormick 1985: 7). One should concur with this opinion for substantive, not patriotic, reasons. Ingarden treated aesthetic problems systematically, meaning that they remained closely related to his ontology and epistemology. Aesthetic research was the point of departure for his considerations of both disciplines, in which he initiated research with significant philosophical consequences. As he wrote in his programmatic article "On Philosophical Aesthetics," the task of aesthetics

> is seen as consisting in explaining basic concepts and providing insights into the basic ontic connections and relations between certain experiences and certain objects (particularly works of art) as well as their values. (Ingarden 1985: 17)

Thus understood, aesthetics

is not only an essential supplement for other branches of philosophy but also itself needs their material and methodological support. Especially when explaining the mode of being and the structure of works of art, it must turn to the result reached by general ontology and the philosophical theory of values. (Ingarden 1985: 17)

Aesthetics as an independent philosophical discipline includes, in Ingarden's case, a system of specific disciplines such as the history of aesthetics, philosophy of art (i.e., knowledge of literature), philosophy of aesthetics, and aesthetic research. In the case of the philosophy of art, Ingarden distinguished three divisions: the philosophy of literature, the study of literature, and literary criticism. The philosophy of aesthetics comprises methodological considerations concerning the method, program, and tasks set for aesthetics (Ingarden 1970: 56–94). Aesthetic research, which covers a wide range of research into art, constitutes the core of Ingarden's aesthetic analyses, to which he devoted the greatest attention.[1] This area of research was particularly important to him because these analyses were intended to form his own systemic proposition for phenomenological aesthetics. The last two areas of research are important for the remarks that follow. It is worth adding here that Ingarden, despite including numerous historical references, did not deal with the de facto history of aesthetics.

The objective scope of aesthetic research included the ontology and phenomenology of works of art, the aesthetic object, the creative process, artistic and aesthetic values, the aesthetic experience, the theory of cognition of a work of art, the aesthetic object, and the value of both types. The aesthetic study of the relevant objects is served by the phenomenological method, which enables a given object to be grasped directly, by means of a "suitably shaped experience," and to be described faithfully. Consequently, this method enables the acquisition of "studies focused on the *essence* of given facts and a search for the content of general ideas involved in the studied objects" (Ingarden 1970: 41). Ingarden was convinced that the use of this method yielded results which could not be ensured by research in aesthetics organized in other ways. He also had no doubt that this research had to assume the character of an eidetic analysis of the general idea of a work of art, or works of specific types of art. He stated that "[f]rom the start the work of art was assumed to be purely intentional product of an artist's creative acts," and that, at the same time, "as a schematic entity having certain potential elements, it was contrasted with its 'concretions'" (Ingarden 1970: 29). This approach to a work of art emphasizes the importance of the artist and the recipient. The former is necessary for the creation of the work; the latter, due to the differing courses of experience of the psychological subject, for the life of the work of art and thus the conditions of its existence and its mode of manifestation (Ingarden 1985: 29). And finally, Ingarden distinguished and contrasted philosophical with empirical aesthetics, rejecting empirical research of a generalizing nature.

Ingarden attributed particular significance to the concept of the aesthetic situation, which unites—as revealed in phenomenological analysis—ontological, epistemological, aesthetic, and anthropological dimensions. He considered this concept exclusively from the model side, and thus in the first two dimensions, apart from two additional aspects: typologizing and specific. Ingarden defined the aesthetic situation as "an encounter, whether of the creator with the object he produces [. . .] or, on the other hand, an encounter between the created object [. . .] and the recipient" (Ingarden 1985: 17). The structure of the aesthetic situation appears to consist of three elements, as it is created by the artist, the object of his work, and the recipient of this creation; however, it is impossible to ignore the initiating and superior fourth element in the situation, aesthetic value, which intrinsically colors the entire relationship.

Ingarden accepted the category of *situation* for objective and methodological reasons. In the former case, this was a response to the one-sided concepts of "objective" aesthetics—limited to the work of art—and "subjective"—limited to the experiences of the subject (Ingarden 1985: 17). In the latter case, it was a question of, first, separating out all elements inherent in such a situation; second, considering them in terms of reciprocal connections; and third, avoiding their artificial isolation in excess of the actual need resulting from the objectives of the research (Ingarden 1981b: 173–5). Consideration of the role of the concept of the aesthetic situation in Ingarden's system implies the necessity to capture the recipient's encounter with the work of art on one hand and with its creator on the other. The first of these aspects, essential for Ingarden, is connected with the problems of "concretization," "aesthetic experience," "artistic and aesthetic values," and, finally, "metaphysical qualities." Thus, the aesthetic situation is the encounter of a certain subject (creator, recipient) with a certain object (a work of art), leading, as a result of the interaction of the former with the latter, to the constitution of an aesthetic object. This short introduction enables questions to be posed concerning the problems discussed in the chapters contained in the second part of the book.

Mitscherling: Empathy and Aesthetic Experience

Jeff Mitscherling, in his chapter entitled "Lipps, Stein and Ingarden on Empathy and the Coexperiencing of Value in the Aesthetic Experience," devoted to the concept of aesthetic experience as considered in the context of empathy, emotional experience, and aesthetic encounters with value. The author compares Ingarden's views with the conceptions of Theodor Lipps and Edith Stein, placing at the starting point of his considerations the thesis that, in addition to Stein, the Polish philosopher also "adopted significant features of Lipps's account in his own description of what he called the 'emotional coexperiencing of psychological occurrences of portrayed persons' in our cognition of the literary work of art" (Mitscherling 2023: 103). This view is interesting, as it differs from the interpretation generally accepted in the literature of Ingarden's position on this issue.

Empathy, as of the beginning of the twentieth century, was considered to be one way of knowing other people. As an issue, it became prominent thanks to the philosophizing German psychologists of the time, such as Theodor Lipps, Johannes Volkelt, and Friedrich Vischer, who extended the problem of empathy to aesthetic research. The question of empathy was then taken up by phenomenologists such as Husserl, Stein, and Ingarden. This question was especially important for phenomenology, since, in placing the awareness of the philosophizing subject at the center of the discussion, it made it possible to face the danger of solipsism. Ingarden expressed this problem with the aid of a question: "how to extricate oneself from solipsism when speaking of the pure 'I' and the pure consciousness of the philosopher?" (Ingarden 1988: 171). He then answered unequivocally, stating that for Husserl, during the period of *Méditations Cartésiennes*, avoidance of this danger was connected with reference to the *Einfühlung*, "which supposedly provides us with a path to other subjects" (Ingarden 1988: 171).

In Lipps's theory, empathy, which precedes intellectual understanding, fulfills important functions in the contacts of the individual with other people and in communing with art. Thus we are dealing here with two ways of understanding empathy: that related to everyday life and that related to a work of art. An individual's observed behavior evokes a specific reaction in the recipient, whether positive or negative. It is possible to experience this reaction thanks to one's innate ability to imitate the emotions of others. These "feedback" emotions are expressed externally in the form of emotionally meaningful content. This imitation is so strong that in the act of empathy the "I" of the person experiencing this act disappears, uniting with the other "I." What follows from this is Lipps's conviction that the experience of our act of empathy has the same object as that of the experience of the person with whom we are empathizing.

Stein was critical of Lipps's view, although she accepted a part of it which indicated that empathy is an internal sharing of the experience of others. Nor did she follow Husserl's path concerning empathy, although here too she adopted his views of the subject's constitution of the world of values (as a result of empathy) as a "new kingdom of objects," as well as of the other person (Stein 1988: 121–2, 126). This thread was highlighted by Ingarden, who wrote that "the most painful thing [for her] was the question of how to explain the possibilities of understanding between people, the possibilities of creating a human community" (Ingarden 1988: 172). The way to consider this problem was to analyze the constitution of the individual in terms of his or her relationship to another individual or community of individuals. From this perspective, the act of empathy enables us to know the experience of another subject, but not the object of that experience. Hence, Stein also states that empathy has a dual character: it is source cognition as a present experience and at the same time non-source in relation to its content. Thus, in the act of empathy, the subject experiences the other person's consciousness in general, but not its object (Stein 1988: 23).

Ingarden, while accepting certain findings of both Lipps and Stein, at the same time enriches them with his own thoughts. Cognition of the mental states of others is a fact for Ingarden; therefore, he directs his research efforts toward an explanation of the way in which this happens. He accepts two types of cognition of the mental states of another human being: direct and indirect. In the first type, there is the problem of cognizing the psyche of another person. As a result of his analyses, he rejects empirical theories: of inference *per analogiam*, of associative, of imitation, and of empathy as understood by Lipps. Moreover, he criticizes Lipps's theory of empathy, based on the belief that we do not have the experience of feeling something within another human being. This does not mean, however, that we do not "learn . . . about the mental state of another human being in a direct and visible way" (Ingarden 1971: 420). In the second type of cognition, however, we deal with cognition "of the psychological properties of a certain human being on the basis of the products of his or her activity," which might be "letters, literary works, works of art, products of technology and industry, social facilities, and institutions of all kinds" (Ingarden 1971: 408).

In analyzing the perception of a work of art, Ingarden speaks of a moment of breakthrough in the aesthetic experience, which takes place in the "process of building a new subject of features onto qualities that are given to us" (Ingarden 1966a: 143). In this process empathy plays various roles in different types of works of art: smallest in a musical work, greater in a literary work, and greatest in the reception of a painting or sculptural work. In addition to that of the

Polish translation of Stein's doctorate,[2] Ingarden gives the examples of *Bacchante couchée* by Augustin Moreau and portraits by Rembrandt, while posing important questions:

> In the former Luxembourg Museum in Paris, there was a sculpture by Moreau entitled *Bacchante*. This is a reclining woman, undoubtedly—this is visible—in erotic ecstasy. Her smile is such that it actually says everything; it is a smile of delight, of some extraordinary delight. Very well, one says, but that's a stone in front of you. Where exactly does this strange phenomenon come from? How is it that I see a woman, and a woman in a certain mood, having a certain experience, moreover, a certain psychological type of a person, character, etc.?

And he replies: "*das wird alles eingefühlt*—it's all cut into this stone." And finally Ingarden concludes: "this is the starting point of aesthetics, leading to the first concept of 'empathy' as empathizing with one's own moods, one's own feelings" (Ingarden 1988: 173–4).

Gladden: Ingarden and the Aesthetics of Computer Games

Ingarden began his aesthetic research with literary works, in order to move on to research concerning other traditional areas of art, comprising analyses of the structure of works in the fields of paintings, music, film, or theater. However, he avoided many avant-garde trends in contemporary art that were already in existence in his lifetime. Nor did he pay any attention to computer games, for obvious reasons: these appeared only after his death. Thus Matthew Gladden has taken up an interesting challenge, using Ingarden's aesthetic tools to evaluate retro computer games, that is, 8-bit games, created in the 1980s. The artistic austerity, simplicity of plotting, and technological primitivism of these single-level games condemned them, seemingly, to their being preserved exclusively in historical memory. However, it happened otherwise, and the reasons for this state of affairs constitute the topic of considerations in this chapter.

Gladden expresses the view that the 8-bit game is an organic artistic whole, created by elements of literary, musical, visual, architectural, and motion imaging. The attractiveness of the whole, conceived in this way, results from the "qualitatively differentiated schematic constructions" of its elements, resulting in a number of layers representing the sum of the elements of this whole. However, the crowning glory of these games is their interactivity, a feature absent from traditional works—in this case, the resistance of artificial intelligence to the player. All of this creates completely unique conditions for the recipient in the process of concretizing an 8-bit work. This results from the very nature of these games, which retain a much greater degree of indeterminacy than today's games, due to, for example, the abbreviation of verbal messages, which forced the player to be more independent within the story than at present. As a result, concretization forced the recipient's full engagement in the game, using all of his or her knowledge and experience and making the game more individualized and better adapted to the expectations of the player.

Gladden has introduced a few screenshots to illustrate his theses, relating to the textual and visual aspects of the games in question. In its simplicity, the 8-bit game does not impose a specific visualization of the game fragment on the recipient, allowing him or her a great deal of freedom of imagination, which the author associates with a form of indeterminacy that possesses rich artistic value and can give rise to singularly meaningful aesthetic experiences, rather than with nostalgia theory. This fact translates into the attractiveness of games of this type and, consequently, into their life as works of art. Gladden refers directly to the category of the life of a literary work that Ingarden discussed in *Das literarische Kunstwerk*. Each new concretization enlivens a work, making it more dynamic through bringing out a new aspect, while a lack of concretizations leads to its disappearance, so that in the end it will "die a natural death" (Ingarden 1973b: 354). This description is carried over to the "life" of 8-bit games over the last several decades, which is the result not of nostalgia but of their artistic and aesthetic value. The author strongly emphasizes that the revival of 8-bit games results from the fact that many of them were true works of art, even masterpieces (e.g., *The Legend of Zelda*, *Metroid*, and *Ultima IV: Quest of the Avatar*). For this reason as well, Gladden evokes Ingarden's phenomenological aesthetics—to make use of his tools, such as concretization, combined with the life of a work of art, in order to explain the aesthetic value of 8-bit games, their charm, and even mystique.

Mäcklin: Art, Attitude, Experience

Ingarden thoroughly elaborated issues in the area of aesthetic experience. From his first works to his last, this area is linked to the concept of the aesthetic situation that arises as a result of encountering and communing with a work of art. Analysis of the concept of this situation led Ingarden to a detailed description of its objective and subjective conditions, which enabled him to avoid reduction of the aesthetic experience to one of its elements.

It is to these specifically aesthetic issues that the chapter "Roman Ingarden on Aesthetic Attention" is devoted. Its author, Harri Mäcklin, draws attention at the outset to the fact that Ingarden does not use the term "aesthetic attention" but favors the more traditional term "aesthetic attitude" while recognizing that while the terms may differ, the meaning of the latter encompasses the meaning of the former. Mäcklin uses Ingarden's theories of aesthetic attention and experience to defend the uniqueness of the aesthetic experience. Ingarden had no doubt that these concepts included the cognitive potential inherent in encountering, receiving, and experiencing a work of art. Following a period of criticism in the second half of the twentieth century, to which George Dickie contributed, these concepts have been reintroduced into aesthetic considerations in the current century. At the center of these discussions was Bence Nanay, who, starting from a naturalistic philosophy of perception, defends the specificity of aesthetic attention, claiming that it simultaneously encompasses several properties of one object, thus differentiating it from other types of attention. It is in regard to these particular theses that Mäcklin polemicizes with Nanay, devoting his chapter to the problem of the role of attention in aesthetic experience and making use, in his considerations, of the results Ingarden obtained in his phenomenological aesthetics.

In Nanay's understanding, aesthetic attention has several important features: first, it is disinterested and can be focused on several properties of the object for their own sake; second, it can be provoked by an aesthetic object, although not necessarily as a result of the activity of the subject; third, it is distinguished by long-lasting effects, transcending the aesthetic experience itself; finally, it may include not only works of art but also natural objects or customs. Whereas Mäcklin appreciates Nanay's proposal, which has enlivened the discussion around the concept of aesthetic attention, introducing it into the mainstream of aesthetic considerations, he criticizes it for its narrow scope within the context of the phenomenological approach. It is for this reason as well that he compares Nanay's proposal with Ingarden's concept of aesthetic attitude, focusing on their understandings of the role of attention in aesthetic experience.

Mäcklin compares similarities in the views of both philosophers, such as the structuring of the aesthetic attitude, its existence as a necessary condition of aesthetic experience, the disinterestedness of its attention/attitude, and, finally, its inactive character. However, generally speaking, their similarities are of limited importance compared to their differences, which are more numerous and of greater gravity. First, then, Nanay's definition of aesthetic attention as focused-but-diffused is insufficient, in Mäcklin's opinion, to explain the aesthetic nature of experience. This is not the case with Ingarden, who, Mäcklin believes, would argue that this understanding of attention does not explain the aesthetic experience, but constitutes only one aspect of the recipient's encounter with a work of art; the other aspects comprise reflective (pre- and post-aesthetic) phases. Second, the transition from a natural to an aesthetic attitude, according to Nanay, is not clear. According to Ingarden, the impetus for this transition is a preliminary emotion that produces desire so as to deepen contact with the work and thus to constitute an aesthetic object. Third, Nanay, unlike Ingarden, possesses a simplified understanding of the intentional nature of aesthetic attention, one which does not enable its clear distinction from nonaesthetic attention. Fourth, Nanay, unlike Ingarden, never fully recognizes the power of concentration—which narrows the field of consciousness, shifting other objects to its periphery—on a work of art. Fifth, Nanay, unlike Ingarden, fails to explain how aesthetic attention is simultaneously distributed over the momentous aspects of the work. Lastly, Nanay, unlike Ingarden, does not treat aesthetic experience as an active activity which leads to the concretization of the aesthetic object. These observations enable Mäcklin to conclude that Ingarden's phenomenological aesthetics contains valuable propositions not to be overlooked in the contemporary aesthetic debate.

Elsby: Aesthetics and Time

Ingarden never developed a theory of time, although he occupied himself with this problem many times at various periods of his academic activity. Danuta Gierulanka, Ingarden's assistant during the period of his university work, presented a detailed register of articles with a brief description of each. In the introduction, she states that these multifaceted considerations of the issue of time can be reduced to two forms: multiple interconnected and mutually conditioned threads considered by Ingarden within a single work, or, conversely, a single problem discussed in many articles. In this case, Ingarden distinguished between aspects of time, thus creating "a peculiar network of threads unexpectedly binding works from fields that are sometimes distant from each other" (Gierulanka 1972: 88). It is this approach that is particularly interesting here, as Gierulanka discusses Ingarden's works, characterizing the type of research carried out:

> Perhaps we obtain the most striking example of the latter form of multi-facetedness by attempting to grasp what in Ingarden's research is said about

time, and in which papers. Here is a compilation of the relevant works and the definition of aspects in which the theme of time is treated in each of them:

Spór (Controversy)—time as a moment of the mode of real existence and its role in determining the formal type of an object (event, process, object enduring in time);

Das Kausalproblem (The causal problem)—temporal relationship of cause and effect;

Das literarische Kunstwerk (The literary work of art)—the time presented in a work, the quasi-temporal structure of the literary work, changes in the concretization of the work over time (the so-called "life of the work");

O poznawaniu dzieła literackiego (On the cognition of a literary work)—temporal abbreviations and perspectives in the reception of a literary work;

Utwór muzyczny . . . (The musical work . . .)—music as organization of time;

Kilka uwag o sztuce filmowej (Some remarks on the art of film)—the issue of the organization of time in the film *Człowiek i czas* (Man and time): two different experiences of time and their relationship with the sense of "I";

O odpowiedzialności (On responsibility)—preservation of a subject's identity over time as a condition of responsibility; the temporal structure of the world as the foundation of responsibility;

Intuicja i intelekt u H. Bergsona (Intuition and intellect in Henri Bergson)—so-called duration tensions, geometrized time vs. pure duration;

Rozważania dotyczące zagadnienia obiektywności (Considerations of the issue of objectivity)—varieties of ontic objectivity for objects from different phases of time. (Gierulanka 1972: 88)

The quotations show the research methods used by Ingarden, which were phenomenological descriptions (arising out of direct experience), eidetic insights (based on these experiences), and, finally, anthropological-ethical and/or aesthetic analyses. These reflections, as broadly understood, did not lead Ingarden to form a general theory of time, and thus he took no position on behalf of any of the parties to the dispute then in progress between the Kantian position that time is merely a phenomenon or transcendental appearance and the position proclaiming the reality of time and its presence in the real world. Hence also the not uncommon statements that "the problem of the actual essence and role of time remained open for Ingarden" (Bielawka 1991: 109–17). Ingarden was aware of this, as well as of the originality of his own proposal, as illustrated in his remark in *Controversy*:

> [T]here seems to be a kernel in the conception I am presenting here that does not appear in any of the other authors. This involves, first of all, the intimate relation

between time and mode of being, as well as the various modes of "being-in-time." (Ingarden 1987: 232)

This remark raises a question concerning the reasons which inclined Ingarden to deal with the problem of time.

In her chapter entitled "Roman Ingarden on Fictional Times," Charlene Elsby extends Ingarden's research on the metaphysics of time in relation to his concept of a literary work. The author introduces the thesis that literary time is "completely different" from real time, which results from their differing ontologies: the first purely intentional, the second real. In both literary and actual realities, however, there is a past, a present, and a future. The author offers additional comments on Kurt Vonnegut's novel *Slaughterhouse Five*, with the intention of achieving three aims: to show the particular difference between the real and literary present, to undermine the views of 4D space-time theorists, and to show how Vonnegut's depiction of an atemporal present is rendered comprehensible thanks to Ingarden's concept of literary time.

Two understandings of the present result from the different ontologies of literary and real time: literary time is plastic, as it "exemplifies a malleability that real time does not, because it embraces a 'neutral' present" (Elsby 2023: 151), whereas real time is not, because it is limited by a privileged and active present. A good illustration of this difference is the situation of the reader who concretizes the literary hero while reading. In the reader's case, we are dealing with the real, active present of the reader; in the case of the hero, with a fictional and diverse present defined by the literary text, presented from various temporal perspectives. The intentional nature of this time and of the work itself does not mean, however, that the events presented in it elude temporality by taking place in a neutral present. Such an impression may result from the "leveling" of temporal moments in the work, though they are also captured in the three temporal aspects of a fictional world.

Elsby distinguishes between three different understandings of time: real time, the time of the work of art as a physical object, and the time represented in the work. The last mentioned may be the subject of an experiment by its author, who manipulates the course of time through, for example, its inversion or the equalization of all of its aspects. We are then dealing with the temporal ordering of that which is presented in the work and that which exerts an influence on the concretization of the literary work. Despite the modification of time depicted in the work, it is still, says Ingarden, "a time in which the basic structures of present, past, and future, even if modified, are present" (Ingarden 1973b: 312).

Elsby agrees with this opinion, concluding that the atemporal ordering of events in a literary work becomes temporal in its aesthetic concretization.

* * *

The editors wish to thank the authors of these chapters for their contributions and commitments to the creation of this book. Thanks are also due to the reviewers who subjected individual texts to a thorough and critical reading, resulting in the best possible form. The editors also thank Suzie Nash, editor at Bloomsbury Publishing, whose support and assistance in the process of preparing the book were invaluable. Thanks are likewise due to Richard Erickson, linguistic editor, for his careful work on the linguistic aspects of the publication.

Notes

1 For the sake of clarity, it should be added that this also includes research on nature in its aesthetic aspect; Ingarden, however, did not consider this area of inquiry.
2 It is worth adding here that the text at the end of Stein's book *On the Problem of Empathy* was presented by Ingarden at a conference devoted to Stein on April 6, 1968, in Cracow, at the invitation of Cardinal Karol Wojtyła. The Polish translation of the book was published twenty years later.

References

Bielawka, M. (1991), "The Mystery of Time in Roman Ingarden's Philosophy," in *Analecta Husserliana*, ed. A.-T. Tymieniecka, vol. XXXIII, 109–17. Dordrecht: Reidel/Kluwer Academic Publishers.

Descartes, R. (1985), *The Philosophical Writings of Descartes*, vol. I, trans. J. Cottingham, R. Stoothoff, and D. Murdoch, Cambridge: Cambridge University Press.

Gierulanka, D. (1972), "Filozofia Romana Ingardena. Próba wniknięcia w całość dzieła" (The Philosophy of Roman Ingarden: An Attempt to Penetrate the Whole *Oeuvre*), in *Fenomenologia Romana Ingardena* (Roman Ingarden's Phenomenology), ed. Z. Augustynek and J. Kuczyński, 70–90, Warsaw: IFIS PAN.

Ingarden, R. (1914), "Odczyt w Polskim Towarzystwie Filozoficznym we Lwowie z 19.12.1914" (A Lecture at the Polish Philosophical Society in Lviv 19.12.1914), in *The Roman Ingarden Digital Archive*. Available online: http://ingarden.archive.uj.edu.pl/archiwum/odczyt-w-polskim-towarzystwie-filozoficznym-we-lwowie-z-19-12-1914 (accessed December 20, 2022).

Ingarden, R. (1966a), *Studia z estetyki* (Studies in Aesthetics), vol. I, Warsaw: PWN.

Ingarden, R. (1966b), *Studia z estetyki* (Studies in Aesthetics), vol. II, Warsaw: PWN.
Ingarden R. (1970), *Studia z estetyki* (Studies in Aesthetics), vol. III, Warsaw: PWN.
Ingarden, R. (1971), *U podstaw teorii poznania* (Foundations of the Theory of Knowledge), Warsaw: PWN.
Ingarden, R. (1973a), *The Cognition of the Literary Work of Art*, trans. R. A. Crowley and K. R. Olson, Evanston: Northwestern University Press.
Ingarden, R. (1973b), *The Literary Work of Art*, trans. G. G. Grabowicz, Evanston: Northwestern University Press.
Ingarden, R. (1981a), "Moje wspomnienia o Edmundzie Husserlu" (My Recollections of Edmund Husserl), trans. Z. H. Mazurczak and St. Judycki, *Studia Filozoficzne* 2(183): 3–24.
Ingarden, R. (1981b), *Wykłady i dyskusje z estetyki* (Lectures and Discussions on Aesthetics), Warsaw: PWN.
Ingarden, R. (1982), *Z teorii języka i filozoficznych podstaw logiki* (From the Theory of Language and the Philosophical Foundations of Logic), Warsaw: PWN.
Ingarden, R. (1983), *Man and Value*, trans. A. Szylewicz, Munich: Philosophia Verlag.
Ingarden, R. (1985), *Selected Papers in Aesthetics*, ed. P. McCormick, Washington: The Catholic University of America Press.
Ingarden, R. (1988), "O badaniach filozoficznych Edith Stein" (On the Philosophical Research of Edith Stein), in E. Stein, *O zagadnieniu wczucia* (On Empathy), 155–80, Cracow: Znak.
Ingarden, R. (1989), *Wykłady z etyki* (Lectures on Ethics), Warsaw: PWN.
Ingarden, R. (1998), "Wspomnienia z Getyngi" (Memories from Göttingen), *Pismo Artystyczno-Literackie* 5–6(75–76): 11–17.
Ingarden, R. (2013), *The Controversy over the Existence of the World*, vol. I, trans. A. Szylewicz, Frankfurt am Main: Peter Lang.
Ingarden, R. (2016), *The Controversy over the Existence of the World*, vol. II, trans. A. Szylewicz, Frankfurt am Main: Peter Lang.
Jadacki, J. J. (1981), "Spór między Romanem Ingardenem a Edmundem Husserlem" (The Controversy Between Roman Ingarden and Edmund Husserl), *Archiwum Historii Filozofii i Myśli Społecznej* 27: 191–225.
McCormick, P. (1985), "On Ingarden's Selected Papers in Aesthetics: An Introduction," in *Roman Ingarden, Selected Papers in Aesthetics*, ed. P. McCormick, 7–17, Washington: The Catholic University of America Press.
Spiegelberg, H. (1982), *The Phenomenological Movement. A Historical Introduction*, The Hague: Martinus Nijhoff Publishers.
Stróżewski, W. (1993), "Fenomenologia analityczna Romana Ingardena. Zarys problematyki" (Roman Ingarden's Analytical Phenomenology: An Outline of the Problem), *Kwartalnik Filozoficzny* XXI(1): 5–11.
Tatarkiewicz, W. (1972), "Roman Ingarden," in *Fenomenologia Romana Ingardena* (Phenomenology of Roman Ingarden), 55–7, Warsaw: *Studia filozoficzne* (special edition).

Part I

Ontology

1

Modes and Moments in Ingarden's Ontology

Peter Simons

Introduction

Ingarden's *Spór o istnienie świata* (Controversy about the Existence of the World; hereafter: *Spór*) is not only his largest and most ambitious work; it is a major contribution to ontology and metaphysics. While the ontology that Ingarden develops is more conservative than many other major metaphysical systems of the same era, such as those of Samuel Alexander, Alfred North Whitehead, and Donald Cary Williams, it does succeed in its primary objective, which is to provide a thorough and reasoned realist alternative to the transcendental idealism of his teacher Edmund Husserl. Its considerable length, and the fact that it was incomplete, has to some extent hindered its reception, especially outside Ingarden's native Poland, and outside the phenomenological tradition. Analytic philosophers, both within and outside Poland, have paid it little attention, which is a pity, since it repays analytical attention.

While I have many substantive disagreements with Ingarden over ontology, which I shall briefly mention later, there is one aspect of his work which I consider is highly commendable and which is found far too infrequently in ontological treatises. This is his use of what he calls *existential moments* to distinguish and delimit the basic kinds of entity. Ingarden takes these collectively to divide objects into fifteen pairwise exclusive and jointly exhaustive kinds or *categories*, which themselves fall into five major areas or realms of being: absolute, real, ideal, empirically possible, and purely intentional. This chapter examines how Ingarden achieves this partition of being and commends it in spirit while disagreeing in matters of execution.

Ontology and Metaphysics

Ingarden distinguishes ontology from metaphysics. Ontology is concerned with the elaboration of a system of categories of possible entities, whether or not each of the categories is actually filled or instantiated by anything, while metaphysics deals with the question as to which of these categories is in fact instantiated. Ingarden considers that the ontological categories can be excogitated by examining the content of objective ideas, which is his version of the essential intuition practiced in the realist Göttingen school of phenomenology before the First World War. In other words, ontology is *a priori*. I am deeply skeptical about both the possibility of such *a priori* excogitation and even more skeptical about the view that its source is in platonic ideas. What this means is that I cannot claim the kind of epistemic certainty about the merits of such a classification that Ingarden's method assures him can be attained. I think by contrast that the often recalcitrant features of the empirical world and the insecurity of our linguistic and conceptual apparatus for dealing with it render even ontological investigations thoroughly fallible and shot through with uncertainty and provisionality. This renders ontology in good part a posteriori and undoes its supposed priority over questions of what there in fact is. For this reason, I shall avoid as far as possible making use of the term "metaphysics" and will stay with the term "ontology," it being understood that, in contrast to Ingarden, I make no modal claims about how things must be.

Existential Ontology

Ingarden divides ontology into three parts: existential, formal, and material. In this, he outdoes Husserl, who has only formal and material ontology. While they broadly agree on material ontology, Ingarden's account of the nature of formal ontology differs from Husserl's. Husserl regards formal ontology as concerning those concepts and kinds of thing that are ontologically ubiquitous, that is, that are found in all domain or realms of being. Ingarden takes formal ontology to be concerned with the forms of possible objects. Existential ontology is about neither the form nor the matter of objects but about the ways in which they exist. Ingarden follows Aristotle in taking objects in the different categories to exist in different ways, or to have different *modes of being*. Tempting though this idea has been to many, I think it can and should be resisted. There are not different ways of existing, though there are of course existing things of fundamentally different kinds. In any case, my focus will not be on the thesis that objects from different categories have different ways of existing, mistaken though I think it is, but on the basic classes or categories of object themselves, and how Ingarden distinguishes them. This can be pursued independently of the question whether or not the objects in the different categories have different modes of being.

Existential ontology in Ingarden is theoretically prior to formal ontology, which is why it is placed first in *Spór*. Within ontology I do think there is some scope for distinguishing a part which is more fundamental than others, and that is precisely the delimitation of a series of categories, which are the classes of objects that in Ingarden are claimed to have different modes of being. Assuming that our ontology is not monocategorial, that is, that we recognize two or more categories of object, the question then arises as to how the categories are distinct from one another. There are three basic approaches to this. The first is to claim that there is no reasonable account to be given and that we should recognize that categorial distinctions are surd or brute. This is not only rationally unsatisfying, but it also flies in the face of over two millennia of philosophy, where philosophers from Plato and Aristotle through to the present attempt to say in what respects the different categories differ. The second approach is to derive the categories from linguistic and/or logical divisions, for example, the distinction between nouns, verbs, and sentences, or names, predicates, functional expressions, and sentences, or different kinds of answers to questions. There have been many attempts along these lines, and some have claimed that Aristotle and many scholastics were led by linguistic considerations in their schemes of categories. It certainly applies to many modern analytic philosophers, such as Frege, Russell, Wittgenstein, and Armstrong. The difficulty with this approach is that it threatens a relativism of categories, based on the variety of languages employed to guide the division, but also that it too does not take sufficient account of the fact that the fit between language and the world is not a perfect one, that there is no preestablished harmony. The third way is to look for objective features of a special kind that divide the categories. This has been very much a minority option. Brentano claimed that Aristotle did this; more recent exponents are Jonathan Lowe and myself. But by far the most prominent exponent of this approach in modern times is Ingarden in *Spór*. The objective features in question, which Ingarden calls *existential moments* and I call ontic *factors*, are—counterintuitive though it may initially seem—not themselves entities within a category. The reason for this—though I do not find this stated in Ingarden—is that if they were, we would be caught in a vicious infinite regress.

It is Ingarden's use of these moments to differentiate the categories or modes of being that is my concern in this chapter. Ingarden's discussion of the modes and moments occupies the whole first volume of *Spór* and that is far too much on which to comment in detail. Fortunately for us, Ingarden compresses and summarizes his position in just one section of *Spór*, namely §33, and it is this *thumbnail* summary that will form the basis of my discussion.

The Moments and Their Families

Rather than simply list different modes of being, however these have been arrived at, Ingarden seeks to break down the ways in which different modes of being—and the objects that occupy them—differ from one another by employing the existential moments. Modes of being arise through the consistent combinations of existential moments. Existential moments come in seven families of opposites or mutually exclusive contraries, six of two members and one of four members. Were all the combinations of existential moments that Ingarden lists consistent, there would be $2^6 \times 4 = 256$ modes of being, but there are dependencies among them, that is, some families only apply if a certain member of another family is selected, which reduces the number of consistent combinations to fifteen modes of being. As an ontologist, Ingarden does not commit to there being objects for each mode, but it is clear from his views elsewhere that he thinks nearly all of the modes are actually exemplified in the world. The five major families are concerned with different kinds of (in)dependence, and with time, so it is these which we examine.

Ingarden started with the question whether the world we know exists dependently on us or independently of us, but he considers there to be four different kinds of (in)dependence, and these form the first four families.

The first and most fundamental division is between objects that are (existentially) autonomous (pol. *autonomiczny, samoistny*) and those that are heteronomous (pol. *heteronomiczny, niesamoistny*). Normal objects are autonomous: they are what they are in themselves and because of themselves. Some things, however, such as the unreal things we dream about or future objects that may or may not come to exist, derive their being from other things, in the first case from the dreamer, in the second case from past and present things that make them possible. A special case of heteronomous objects are fictions, such as Hamlet or Harry Potter, which derive their existence from minds and owe their persistence to texts, films, and so on. Ingarden famously dealt with these at length in his first book *Das literarische Kunstwerk* (*The Literary Work of Art*, 1931), and in his view Husserl's idealism downgraded the real world to just such a fictitious status.

An object is original (pol. *pierwotny*) if it cannot be created by any other object, while it is derivative (pol. *pochodny*) if it can be so created. Original objects are rare: only ideal objects such as those of mathematics, ideal universals and states of affairs, and absolute objects, such as God, are original: everything else is derivative, and in particular, nothing in time is original. One species of derivation is causation, but Ingarden regards this as a matter of material ontology and it occupies the unfinished third volume of *Spór*. As no original object can be heteronomous, these two families result in three rather than four groups of modes of being.

An object is self-sufficient (pol. *samodzielny*) if it can exist on its own without being part of a larger whole, and non-self-sufficient (pol. *niesamodzielny*) if this is not the case, that is, if it *cannot* exist independently but only in a whole with something else. This form of (in)dependence had been discussed at length in Husserl's *Logical Investigations* of 1901, and Ingarden acknowledges Husserl's influence. Self-sufficient objects are very like Aristotle's substances. A tomato is self-sufficient, but its particular quality of redness or mass is not. Other non-self-sufficient objects are boundaries, such as the equator.

The final kind of (in)dependence concerns self-sufficient objects only: some require others in order to exist, but not as joint parts of a whole, while others do not. The former are dependent (pol. *zależny*), the latter independent (pol. *niezależny*). Ingarden's examples involve relations: a child is a child only because it has one or more parents, but they do not form a whole (except in pregnancy), and the child typically survives the parents.

Applying these distinctions to Ingarden's primary concern, the real world of stars, wars, and guitars, they are (if past or present) autonomous, derived, and self-sufficient, whereas Husserl's world constituted by consciousness is heteronomous, derived, and non-self-sufficient.

The only family of four existential moments is mainly about time. Present things are active or *actual*,[1] past things are *post-actual*, possible future things are *empirically possible*, while the purely intentional products of consciousness (things we merely think about) are *non-actual*.

Finally, there are two families concerned with how objects that are actual (active), which comprise present things and the absolute, pass through time, and are endangered or not by this passage. Objects are *fissurated* if they pass from one present to another, are as it were continuously "squeezed" between the future and the past. That applies only to present objects, as past ones are no longer squeezed and future ones are not yet squeezed. One conception of the Absolute is fissurated, but there is another (and Ingarden thinks, nobler) conception of the Absolute which is *non-fissurated*, that is, we might say, eternally present, or, as Ingarden says, *durable*. Objects that (can) change are always in danger of going out of existence: Ingarden calls this their *fragility*, and he highlights it as characterizing organisms, but it applies more widely. Non-fragile and active beings have the moment of *persistence*, and this comprises only absolute beings.

Taken together, these combinations generate fifteen consistent modes of being, but they fall into five broad families: we have the real (past and present things, events and processes), the ideal (objects, relations, states of affairs), the absolute (roughly, God, in one of two possible guises), the empirically possible, and finally, intentional objects. It is notable that Ingarden, despite his training as a phenomenologist, finds intentional objects of thought to be the least "substantial" of beings.

Factored Classification

There are serious critical questions that can be asked about the definitions of some of the existential moments and whether they are always exhaustive and mutually exclusive. I have previously discussed these for the four pairs of moments involving dependence (Simons 2005). For the present, however, I am assuming for the sake of argument that the moments are all right as they are, because I am more interested in *how* they delimit the modes and categories. In terms of the way they do this, they function as *differentia* but not in a classical Aristotelian manner. In Aristotle, differentia divides a pre-given genus into two or more species. In the case of Ingarden, it is not single moments but consistent *combinations* of moments that divide the domain of all possible beings. Individual moments do divide at least part of the domain, sometimes all of it. The opposition autonomous/heteronomous divides everything into two superclasses, as does the opposition original/derived. On the other hand, the opposition independent/dependent only applies among things that are self-sufficient. But each of the fifteen modes and categories is given by a unique combination of moments.

The situation is not so different from that facing a library cataloguer. Suppose, without external help, you have to classify a book called *Political Cartoons in 18th Century England*. There are many places where it could end up in the library:

History of England in the 18th Century, History of Political Cartoons, Cartoons, Political Art, Politics in the 18th Century, History of Satire, and so on. Each of those features applying to the subject matter of the book is what library scientists call a *facet*. Faceted classification is the invention of one man: the father of modern library science, S. R. Ranganathan (1892–1972), a person whose name and achievements deserve to be much more widely known among philosophers. The use of facets overcomes the most serious problem for classifying documents: cross-classification. They do not overcome all difficulties of information storage, but they are an immeasurable improvement over numerical or hierarchical schemes.

Another area where facets are used, but not under that name, is biological taxonomy. Modern cladistic taxonomy is based on the examination of properties of organisms—living and fossilized—that are called *characters*. These are nothing more than properties (absolute or relative) which serve to distinguish one kind of organism from another. Examples might include the presence or absence of a notochord, distinguishing chordates from others, or the number and position of openings or fenestrae in an animal's skull, helping to distinguish mammals from birds. Their use, in conjunction with modern computing techniques, allows systematists to conjecture the likely genealogy of classes of organisms. Unlike library science, evolutionary biology requires the classification to match a temporal ordering of development and speciation. Again, this kind of use of characters to determine classes is largely due to one man, the German biologist Willi Hennig (1913–76), the founder of modern phylogenetic systematics, and another person who deserves to be better known among philosophers.

To have a neutral name for the features which in combination serve to divide objects in a complex classification, I call them *factors*, and a classification based on them a *factored* classification or factored taxonomy. Although hierarchical (dendritic, tree-like) classification has been the dominant strand, factored classifications are not unknown in philosophy. Empedocles classified the elements by combining factors from two families: the temperature family (hot/cold) and the humidity family (wet/dry). In pairs, these produce four classes of basic material: earth (cold, dry), air (hot, wet), fire (hot, dry), and water (cold, wet). There is no hierarchy in this classification, and neither of the factor pairs has priority over the other. Likewise, in the *Categories* Aristotle classified things "said without combination" according to the predication family (± said of a subject) and the inherence family (± in a subject), giving the fourfold classification of substances (– said of, – in), kinds or second substances (+ said of, – in), properties (+ said of, + in), and individual accidents (– said of, + in).

But, to my knowledge, the most sustained and sophisticated use of factored classification in philosophy is that of Ingarden in Volume I of *Spór*.

Ingarden's existential moments are factors, and they come in their seven families. Their consistent combinations result in the fifteen modes of being and the fifteen categories of object that could exist with these modes. I do not claim that Ingarden first came up with the moments and then examined their combinations to see which categories they produced. I think it is much more likely that Ingarden already had a pretty fair idea, from other considerations, about what kinds of object he wanted to include in his ontology, and retro-fitted the existential moments to line up with these and to give structure to the classification. As a heuristic, this cannot be impugned. Maybe the factors did lead to some refinement of the classification, for example, the fissuration factor family may have led him to distinguish the two kinds of absolute being. No matter: it is the completed system that concerns me.

Depicting the Taxonomy

Because a factored classification is not hierarchical, a simple tree structure is not appropriate, as it ranks the factors. The question can therefore be posed as to how best to depict the classification. In the §33 thumbnail, Ingarden does this by lists and prose, but this is not compact. A better, if still slightly flat-footed way to do this, is by an *occurrence table*. This is a matrix whose rows are given by the categories (modes) and columns are given by the factors (moments). That objects in a certain category row have the moment given by the factor column is depicted by the occurrence of a cross. The absence of a cross indicates that the object does not have that factor. Table 1.1 is an occurrence table for Ingarden's §33.

The first column refers to Ingarden's Table Index in §33. To save space we have abbreviated the names of modes and moments according to the following keys (Table 1.2).[2]

We have omitted the very minor factors *persistent* and *fragile*, because the former coincides with the absolute modes and the latter with the present modes. Excepting this omission, while the occurrence table does present all the information, it is not especially perspicuous.

There is another way of representing such information, which is that of *formal concept analysis* (FCA). It was developed by the German mathematician Rudolf Wille (1937–2017) (see Wille 1982; Ganter and Wille 1999). It treats concepts

Table 1.1 Occurrence Table of Modes and Moments

Index	Modes	Aut	Het	Or	Der	Fi	NFi	Ac	PAc	Iac	EP	SS	NSS	Ind	Dep
I	A	X		X			X	X				X		X	
Ia	a	X		X		X		X				X		X	
Iia	O	X		X						X		X		X	
Iib	R	X		X						X		X			X
Iic	S	X		X						X			X		
IIIaa	on	X			X	X		X				X			
IIIab	pn	X			X	X		X				X		X	X
IIIac	en	X			X	X		X					X		
IIIba	op	X			X				X			X			
IIIbb	pp	X			X				X			X		X	X
IIIbc	ep	X			X				X				X		
IIIca	of		X		X						X	X			X
IIIcb	pf		X		X						X		X		
Iva	ia		X		X					X		X			
Ivb	ib		X		X					X			X		X

© Peter Simons

Table 1.2 Abbreviations for Modes and Moments

Modes		Moments	
Absolute	A	Autonomous	Aut
Absolute a	a	Heteronomous	Het
Ideal Object	O	Original	Or
Ideal Relation	R	Derived	Der
Ideal State of Affairs	S	Fissurated	Fi
Real Present Object	on	Non-Fissurated	NFi
Real Present Process or Property	pn	Active	Ac
Real Present Event	en	Post-active	PAc
Real Past Object	op	Inactive	IAc
Real Past Process or Property	pp	Empirically Possible	EP
Real Past Event	ep	Self-Sufficient	SS
Empirically Possible Object	of	Non-Self-Sufficient	NSS
Emp Possible PPE	pf	Independent	Ind
Purely Intentional Type a	ia	Dependent	Dep
Purely Intentional Type b	ib		

© Peter Simons

in the traditional manner as comprising an *extension*, given by the objects that fall under the concept, and an *intension*, given by the *attributes* that the concept ascribes to the objects falling under it. This can be given for groups of interrelated concepts over a domain, forming what is called a *formal context*, consisting of objects and attributes. A formal context can be given by an occurrence table. In Ingarden's case, the domain of the formal context is the widest possible: that of all possible objects. Usually, formal contexts have a much narrower domain.

To overcome the partiality of occurrence tables, Wille developed *concept lattices*. A concept lattice is generated from an occurrence table or formal context, and each node in the lattice represents a concept having both an extension and an intension. The nodes include not just those presented by the rows and columns of the occurrence table but in addition all those that are logically generated from these by a specific method. The nodes are related or connected by *edges* which, in lattice diagrams, go up and down. An edge represents that the extension of the higher node immediately includes that of the lower node, and the intension of the higher node is immediately included in the intension of the lower node. Where a node is a join of two or more lower nodes, it represents the union of their extensions and the intersection of their intensions, and where a node is a meet of two or more higher nodes, it represents the intersection of their extensions and the union of their intensions. Every lattice has a supremum, which is the set of all the objects in the domain (in Ingarden's case, all possible modes of being), and an infimum which represents the conjunction (intersection) of all the attributes, which in nontrivial cases is contradictory, and so has a null extension.

When we subject the occurrence table of Ingarden's §33 to this procedure, it generates the concept lattice with the following diagram (Figure 1.1).[3]

Here, labels above a node represent objects (categories, modes of being) and those below a node represent attributes (existential moments). It may be noted that only one node is labeled both above and below: that is the non-fissurative Absolute.

Despite the fact that we have dealt with only six of the seven families, that is, fourteen rather than sixteen moments, there are fifty-nine nodes, of which more than half are unlabeled (thirty-one as against twenty-eight). While this is logically unexceptionable, and some of these unlabeled nodes do represent natural classes, for example, the two absolutes, or present entities, the plethora of unlabeled nodes as well as edges (I counted 122) renders the whole less perspicuous than the occurrence table with which we started: it contains *too*

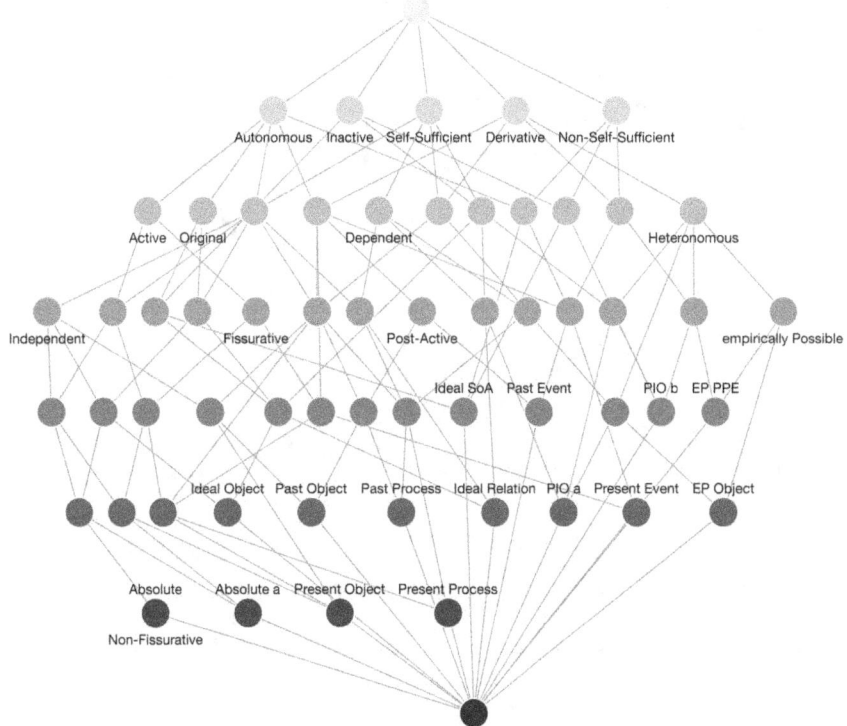

Figure 1.1 Concept lattice of modes and moments © Peter Simons.

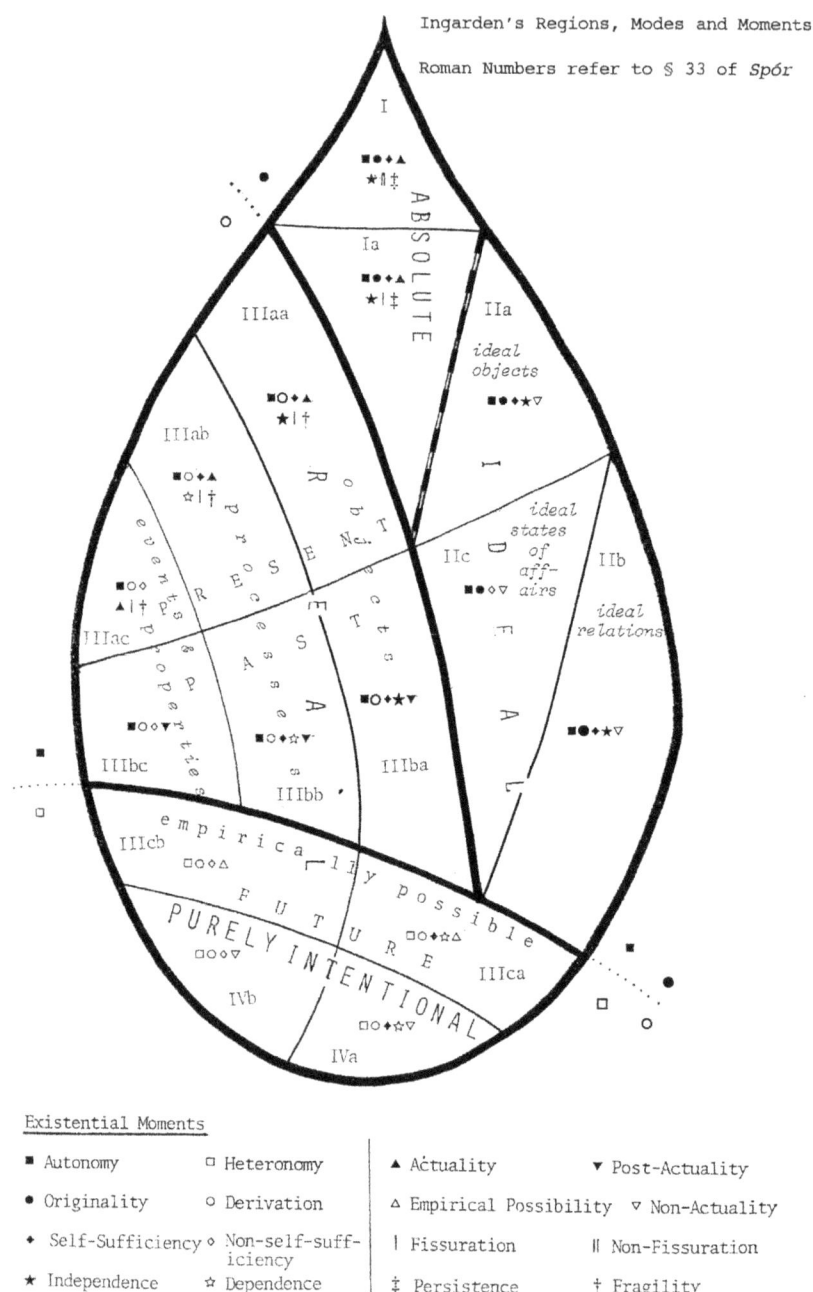

Figure 1.2 Teardrop diagram of regions, modes, and moments © Peter Simons.

much information for our purposes. Whether this is a general feature of FCA or just an artefact of this particular case is not something on which I care to pronounce.

Fortunately, there is a better way to present Ingarden's scheme in graphical or diagrammatic form (Figure 1.2).

This is a typed version of a hand-drawn diagram that I first produced in 1977.[4] Among friends, it is known, for obvious reasons, as *The Teardrop*. The existential moments are represented by non-alphanumeric symbols, as given by the key at the bottom. Each mode of being occupies one of the fifteen smallest sub-regions and is labeled with its Ingarden Index from §33. The combination of moments that delimit it is given by a cluster of the symbols for the moments. Broader classes are labeled across more than one region. Thicker lines divide the major subdomains: the Absolute, the Ideal, the Real, and the Heteronomous. Both I and my Ingardenian friends think that this is a much more perspicuous representation of Ingarden's classification in §33 than either of the others and, apart from reflecting the solidity and innovativeness of Ingarden's ontological work, it has, if I may say so, a certain aesthetic appeal.[5]

Concerns

While this is an ontology, and the question as to which of the categories is actually filled is a metaphysical one, I have no doubt that Ingarden believed that almost all of the categories, with the possible exception of one of the Absolutes, was indeed represented by objects that exist (in their respective modes). Why else would he go to the trouble of finding them a place in his ontology? Now I happen to be an atheist and a nominalist, so as far as I am concerned the Absolute and Ideal regions of Ingarden's ontology are empty. Anti-platonists tend not to try and argue that platonism is *impossible*,[6] but that it is unnecessary: they seek to show that the phenomena that platonism is meant to explain can be explained without abstract (ideal) objects, and then wield Ockham's Razor. If you believe for broadly Fregean or Quinean reasons in mathematical entities, then you have ideal objects. If, for probably different reasons, you believe in the existence of universals (properties and relations), then you may wish to accept the state of affairs to account for contingency among the real things, to knit real individuals and universals together. That these states of affairs should be ideal is not so obvious. Suppose an infant has swallowed a nut and it has stuck in the throat so the child is choking. That is an urgent situation, calling for quick action. If by hitting, shaking, inversion, or whatever action, you dislodge the nut, the situation is no longer there. States of affairs are often called situations, and such situations are temporary. As for the Absolute, while the argument from evil is a serious challenge for those who believe in a benevolent God, I suppose there might be a colder Absolute that is indifferent to suffering. So again, I will simply leave Ingarden's region empty. I also have reservations about the purely intentional, but that is a much too complex issue to discuss in this chapter, so I shall simply note and pass on.

More serious worries concern Ingarden's treatment of time and the objects in it. I have no quarrel with Ingarden's division of real entities into objects (continuants) and processes. I do disagree with Ingarden's terminology of calling instantaneous temporal entities *events* (ger. *Ereignisse*). A football match or the launching of a ship is an event, and they are not instantaneous: Ingarden would consider them processes. Events in Ingarden's sense are best understood as temporal boundaries, and if there are temporal boundaries, there are spatial boundaries as well, such as the equator. Whether boundaries require their own mode of being is unclear. Boundaries depend on what they bound, and cannot be apart from this, so they might be considered to occupy the modes Ingarden assigns to events, so it looks as though they have a home, though spatial boundaries may endure, which temporal boundaries cannot.

My greatest disagreement, however, is with Ingarden's treatment of time, or rather, the temporality of entities. This follows the traditional division into past, present, and future, though Ingarden regards potential future things as heteronomous while present and past things are autonomous. Let us consider a particular event (as I would say) or process (as Ingarden would say). Since Ingarden, unlike modern presentists, accords past and future events some ontological status, he is prepared to accept such things. Any event that actually takes place is present when it is happening, and past when it is finished. But (I claim) it is the same event. What this means is that, though Ingarden vehemently denies such a possibility (Ingarden 2013: 104),[7] *it* must migrate from one mode of being to another, because it loses the moment of actuality and gains that of post-actuality, whereas presentists would say it ceases to exist at all (which is close to Ingarden's view, for whom one entity replaces another). Leaving aside possible future events that do not come to pass, consider events that *do* happen. Is an event unreal before it happens? There is a strong inclination to say so, but I resist that inclination because I think we can use the verb "exist" in an untensed manner and because we can make correct predictions. Obviously, a future event is not in existence *now*, because it is future, but it is not nothing, any more than an event that has finished and is now past is nothing.

Many events are unpredictable or only predictable with low probability: ask any meteorologist or seismologist. But some events can be predicted with astonishing precision. Astronomers are able to calculate the precise date, time, length, and location of solar eclipses, to the second, for thousands of years ahead. For example, there will be a total eclipse across north-eastern Russia, northern Canada, and southern Greenland on Monday, May 6, 2999. Such an event, according to Ingarden, is only an empirical possibility, along with untold others, until the moment it starts to happen, when "it" bursts into reality, and this goes for all events that actually happen. All the other events that might have happened but do not, simply cease to be even as possibilities; they slip into the oblivion of non-being when their appointed time has passed. Of course, this is not just a problem for Ingarden: it applies to all who hold that the distinction between past, present, and future is a real ontological one, but his elevation of the distinction between past, present, and future into an existential-ontological one with unpassable barriers between modes of being makes any problems all the more dramatic in his case.

To outline and defend the eternalist of B-theory of time that I consider correct is beyond the scope of this chapter: I am merely registering my dissent from Ingarden's particular version of the real passage or A-theory.

Other Factored Ontologies

My own confrontation with factoring as a method of generating an ontology came as a consultant to a software engineering firm in California in the 1990s.[8] The final version of our system had ten factor families, nine with two factors, one with three, and since we did not rule any combination *a priori* absurd, that led to an ontology with 1,536 categories (earlier versions had many more). Only a few of these were populated when we abandoned the system. One lesson from that enterprise for myself was that combinatorics alone do not guarantee adequacy. The other lesson was that relations as well as properties that should serve as factors: such relations are those of part to whole, being located at a location, being dependent (in more than one sense) on something, being one of a plurality, being a causal determinant of something, and so on.

The other and more fully worked out factored ontology is that of Jonathan Lowe (Lowe 2005). The world divides, according to Lowe, into four categories:

substances, kinds, modes, and properties, a division which traces its pedigree back to the second chapter of Aristotle's *Categories*. These four categories do not simply sit alongside one another: they are related. Substances *instantiate* substantial kinds and modes instantiate properties. Modes *inhere in* or *characterize* substances. As a result, objects *exemplify* properties, which comes about when a mode which instantiates a property characterizes an object. Whereas in Aristotle the corresponding fourfold classification is based on combinations of properties, in Lowe it is based on the pattern of relationships among the objects in the categories, and the latter approach is more flexible, though perhaps a combination of the two should not be ruled out.

Lowe states that the categories and the relationships among them are not themselves in any of the categories (Lowe 2005: 43). This paradoxical-seeming statement is, I think, absolutely justified. If the factors are themselves entities in a category, they cannot serve to differentiate the categories, on pain of regress or incoherence.[9] Where relationships differentiate the categories, the reason they do not fall into any of the categories (the category of relations, or states of affairs, for example) is that the relationships are *internal*. What this means is that if the related objects exist, they cannot fail to be so related. No additional item, such as a relational state of affairs or a relational trope, is needed. If properties are involved, as in Ingarden, they are essential, which means that if the object exists, it cannot fail to be so.

It seems to me that Ingarden's use of the Husserlian term "moment" for the factors that differentiate modes of being, rather than the term "property," is an indication that he also recognized their peculiar status. Moments in Husserl's sense, as individual instances of properties (Lowe's modes, or modern-day tropes), like the individual whiteness of this piece of paper, after all have a place in ontology, as real non-self-sufficient individuals. In this role, they are incapable of extending across several modes of being in the way that existential moments do. And to extend across different modes of being is not something that an ordinary entity can do, which is why Ingarden qualifies them as *existential* moments. They are seriously different from anything else.

Conclusion

Ingarden's use of existential moments as cross-categorial (supramodal) factors differentiating his categories and modes of being is exceptional, sophisticated, and systematic. It contributes greatly to the depth of *Spór*. I have no doubt that it also reinforced the impression among those of his contemporaries who did not sympathize with his project that his work is unduly "scholastic." From the point of view of reism, or the semantics of predicate logic, he does appear to split hairs and worry about fine distinctions for which others do not feel the need. From our more distanced perspective I trust that we can take a less partisan view of both his achievements and those of his critics. It is, I must say, a source of some regret to myself that because of the antagonism between Ingarden and the more logically inclined members of the Lvov–Warsaw School, he was not able to profit from their formal expertise and they were not able to profit from his ontological sophistication. Advanced ontology requires both sets of skills.

Notes

1. The recent translation has "active," "post-active," and "inactive" where the older translation was "actual," "post-actual," and "non-actual." While the newer translation is probably better, I have tended to use the older one, because it figures in the graphical representation, The Teardrop, given further.
2. Here "PPE" abbreviates "Process, Property or Event."
3. Creating the concept lattice and a diagram for it by hand for even a modest-sized occurrence table is a rather daunting task. Fortunately, there is automation available. This lattice and its diagram were created using a friendly website: it can be found at https://fca-tools-bundle.com/view-context/5e8a17d7ce557b14008b45c6.
4. The handwritten version is reproduced in Johansson (2009).
5. It is an odd sign of technological change that it proved much easier to produce this using a combination of drawn lines and an electric typewriter on paper than using computer graphics. No doubt that reflects the obsolescence of my own abilities as well as the cost of suitably powerful graphics software.
6. Perhaps they should.
7. His view is that despite the way we speak, such "transitions" are mental only and not to be taken literally.
8. The first public outline of the approach was given in Simons (1995).
9. This is argued in Simons (2018).

References

Ganter, B. and R. Wille (1999), *Formal Concept Analysis: Mathematical Foundations*, Berlin: Springer.

Ingarden, R. (2013), *Controversy over the Existence of the World*, vol. I, trans. A. Szylewicz, Frankfurt am Main: Peter Lang.

Johansson, I. (2009), "Proof of the Existence of Universals—And Roman Ingarden's Ontology," *Metaphysica* 10: 65–87.

Lowe, E. J. (2005), *The Four-Category Ontology: A Metaphysical Foundation for Natural Science*, Oxford: Oxford University Press.

Simons, P. (1995), "New Categories for Formal Ontology," in *Investigating Hintikka*, ed. R. Haller, 77–99, *Grazer Philosophische Studien* 49, Amsterdam: Rodopi.

Simons, P. (2005), "Negatives, Numbers, and Necessity Some Worries about Armstrong's Version of Truthmaking," *Australasian Journal of Philosophy* 83(2): 253–61.

Simons, P. (2018), "Lowe, the Primacy of Metaphysics, and the Basis of Categorial Distinctions," in *Ontology, Modality & Mind: Themes from the Metaphysics of E. J. Lowe*, ed. A. Carruth, S. Gibb, and J. Heil, 37–47, Oxford: Oxford University Press.

Wille, R. (1982), "Restructuring Lattice Theory: An Approach based on Hierarchies of Concepts," in *Ordered Sets*, ed. I. Rival, 445–70, Dordrecht–Boston: Reidel.

2

Logical Modalities, Existential Moments, and Modes of Being

Some Reflections on Ingarden's Existential Ontology

Jan Woleński

Philosophers have always made frequent use of modal notions, which speak about necessary and contingent beings, possible courses of events, the impossibility of changing the past, and so on. Such considerations belong to ontology or metaphysics.[1] On the other hand, modalities are studied in modal logic, a specialized branch of formal logic. How is ontology related to modal logic?[2] One quite natural answer is that modal logic provides tools for modalities involved in ontological investigations (ontological modalities). Yet this explanation must be regarded as preliminary, as modal logic deals with logical modalities, ontology with ontological modalities. Two questions can be asked concerning this dualism. First, one can ask about the ontology of modalities (see, e.g., Forbes 1985; Żegleń 1990). For instance, it is said that God is a necessary being, but that empirically perceived things are accidental or merely possible. What does it mean when we say that something is necessary, contingent, or possible? Can we consistently say that something is impossible if the word "something" has existential import? Such considerations can be conducted without appealing to modal logic (Ingarden's magnum opus about the existence of the world is a typical example) or the logic of modalities (for details, see the cited works of Forbes 1985, Żegleń 1990, and, particularly, Williamson 2013; the literature on this problem is huge).[3]

This chapter is based on Woleński (1986 and 1990) but with additions and modifications.

If we take the position that modal logic is relevant to ontology (which I accept), a problem arises as to whether ontological modalities obey principles governing logical modalities. The question is not trivial, because the former are *de re*, the latter *de dicto*. Thus, the sentence (a) *a* is necessary and refers to the object denoted by the name *a*, but (b) it is necessary that *A* says something about a linguistic item (a sentence) represented by the letter *A*, for instance that the formula $A \vee \neg A$ (the rule of the excluded middle) is a necessary sentence (proposition, statement, truth). If we remain within propositional calculus, the difference between (a) and (b) can be practically neglected, because the locutions "it is necessary that $A \vee \neg A$" and 'the formula $A \vee \neg A$ is necessary" can be regarded as equivalent. The situation changes in the case of first-order modal logic. Consider the formula (the symbol $\Diamond$ means "it is possible that"):

(*) $\Diamond \exists x P x \Longrightarrow \exists x \Diamond P x$.

For instance, we can argue that it is possible that the son of Sigismund Augustus (the last Polish king from the Jagiellonian dynasty) exists, but the sentence "there is an *x* such that he could be the son of Sigismund August" appears problematic. In other words, although it is true in the real world that possibly someone was the son of Sigismund Augustus, it is dubious whether we can derive from this premise the conclusion that there is (in the real world) a possible son of Sigismund Augustus.

This (*) is called the Barcan formula and is somehow controversial among logicians and philosophers. It is regarded as an illustration of certain difficulties (or, at least, areas lacking clarity) stemming from the interplay of modalities (in this case possibility, but a similar problem arises for necessity as well) *de dicto* (the antecedent of (*)), modalities *de re* (the consequent of (*)), and the existential quantifier. More specifically, the question arises whether the concept of existence can be applied only to realia (real, actual beings) or also extended to possibilia, considered as a special category of things (see Williamson 2013: 30–44 for discussion). If someone rejects (*), he or she denies that the transition from *de dicto* to *de re* modalities is logically legitimate. Since my subsequent considerations on modalities are restricted to propositional calculus, the Barcan formula does not matter very much. Consequently, I assume that ontological and logical modalities obey the same formal principles. Thus, my task is more modest than that formulated in Williamson (2013: 44) in the following words: "for quantified modal logic in particular one of its main roles is to supply a core to theories of modal metaphysics" (I would say modal ontology). Following this account, I assume that logical and ontological modalities are formally parallel. Additional explanations concerning this assumption will be formulated following presentation of the formal machinery.

How can a minimal core of modal logic be displayed? Since I will use monadic modal operators of the type ●A, where the symbol ● refers to a modality (for instance, the formula ◊A is an instance of ●A, where A represents an arbitrary expression of propositional calculus without modalities within it), the best strategy is to use a diagram (**D1**) (see Woleński 2008).

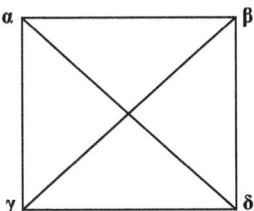

(**D1**) is the logical square of modalities, well-known from its role in the theory of categorical sentences dominant in traditional (Aristotelian) logic. However, it can also (as acknowledged by Aristotle himself) be interpreted by modal sentences. I consider modal rules for modalities generated by (**D1**) as constituting basic modal logic (**BML**).

Interpreting α as □A (it is necessary that A), β as – □¬A, γ as ◊A, and δ as ◊¬A, we have the following facts (theorems of **BML**):

(1) ¬(α ∧ β) (α and β are contrary);
(2) α ⟹ γ (α entails γ; γ is subordinated to α);
(3) β ⟹ δ (β entails δ; δ is subordinated to β);
(4) α ⟺ ¬δ (α and δ are contradictory);
(5) β ⟺ ¬γ (β and γ are contradictory);
(7) γ ∨ δ (γ and δ are complementary);
(8) □A ⟺ ¬◊¬A (□ is definable as ¬◊¬A);
(9) ◊A ⟺ ¬□¬A (◊ is definable as ¬□¬)
(10) β ⟺ □¬A (β is definable as □¬A);

Due to (8)–(10), negation placed before □ or ◊ is always eliminable. Thus, necessity and impossibility are contrary, necessity entails possibility, impossibility entails possibility-not, necessity and possibility-not are contradictory, impossibility and possibility-not are contradictory, possibility and possibility-not are complementary, necessity is equivalent to non-possibility-not, possibility is equivalent to non-necessity-not, and impossibility is equivalent to necessity-not (also necessity is equivalent to impossibility-not).

(**D1**) can be generalized to (**D2**) (the logical hexagon):

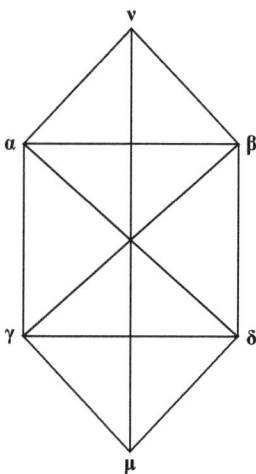

The points ν and μ mean $\alpha \vee \beta$ (A is necessary or A is impossible; it is not equivalent to the statement that A is necessary or impossible, that is, A is necessary or $\neg A$ is necessary; it is not the excluded middle) and $\gamma \wedge \delta$ (A is possible and $\neg A$ is possible; it is not equivalent to the statement that $A \wedge \neg A$ is possible, because contradictions are impossible). We have two new theorems, which, in fact, can be justified by (**D1**) and propositional calculus (I omit others, in particular, $\alpha \Longrightarrow \nu$ or $\mu \Longrightarrow \gamma$).

(11) $\neg(\nu \Longleftrightarrow \mu)$ (ν and μ are contradictory);
(12) $\alpha \vee \beta \vee \mu$ (α, β, μ are mutually exclusive and jointly exhaustive).

Perhaps it is important to note that point μ can be also understood as "A is contingent." Consequently, we have two notions of contingency, one displayed by "non-necessity" (one-sided possibility or simple possibility) and the other as defined by the conjunction "A is possible and $\neg A$ is possible" (double possibility)."

Finally, we have the diagram (**D3**) (a logical octagon):

Reflections on Existential Ontology

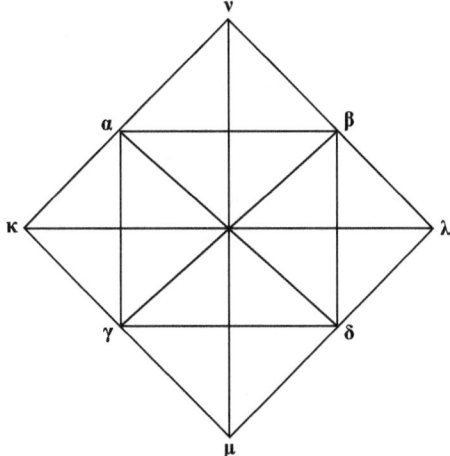

Point κ refers to A, point λ to $\neg A$. The intended meaning of the former is "A is true"; that of the latter is "A is false," if modalities are understood as logical, and "A is actual (real)" in the case of ontological modalities. We stipulate:

(13) $\alpha \Longrightarrow \kappa$;
(14) $\beta \Longrightarrow \lambda$;
(15) $\kappa \Longrightarrow \gamma$;
(16) $\lambda \Longrightarrow \delta$.

At this point we must return to the assumed parallelism between both kinds of modalities. How should "A is necessary (possible, etc.)" be understood if modalities are ontological? The official interpretation of the expression ●A says that the letter A represents sentences, that is, linguistic items. Clearly, this is not plausible for ontological modalities. Instead, we should say that what is asserted (a fact, a state of affairs) by A is necessary (possible, etc.). Another and perhaps more plausible device consists of nominalizing sentences. Consider the sentence "Warsaw is the capital of Poland." Convert it into "that Warsaw is the capital of Poland." In general, we apply the notation "[A] is necessary, actual, etc." where brackets [] indicate that a sentence A is nominalized. This operation enables us to consider the symbol [A] as a nominal expression which refers to its denotatum understood as a reification (objectivization) of a fact (state of affairs). Thus, the distinction *de dicto* versus *de re* appears as well on the level of modal propositional calculus.

The formulas (13)–(16) suggest the following: necessity entails truth (actuality, reality), impossibility entails falsehood (non-actuality, non-reality), truth (actuality, reality) entails possibility (logical and ontological), and falsehood (non-actuality, non-reality) entails non-necessity (logical and ontological, possibility-not). Reversed, the connections do not obtain in most cases, but there are exceptions. It is not without reason that we stipulate (13)–(16). (**D1**) and (**D2**) appear as fully legitimate for logic and, provided that the related parallelism is assumed, for ontological modalities as well. First of all, (**D3**) does not work for modalities other than logical and ontological. Let us take deontic modalities. Now the symbol $\Box$ refers to obligation, the symbol $\Box\neg$ stands for prohibition, the symbol $\Diamond$ expresses permission, and the symbol $\Diamond\neg$ functions as permission-not. Accordingly, obligation and prohibition are contrary, obligation entails permission, prohibition entails permission-not, obligation and permission-not are contradictory, prohibition and permission are contradictory, permission and permission-not are complementary, obligation is equivalent to non-permission-not, permission is equivalent to non-obligation-not, and prohibition is equivalent to obligation-not (also, obligation is equivalent to prohibition-not). Furthermore, the formula "$\Diamond A \land \Diamond \neg A$" can be read as "$A$ is indifferent, that is, neither obligatory nor prohibited." All of the formulas (13)–(16) fail in deontic logic; in particular, being obligatory does not entail being actual, since something that is obligatory can be non-actual (formula (13), reversed, expresses Hume's famous dictum, namely, that is-assertions do not entail ought-assertions). This is why (**D3**) transcends **BML**. Consideration of truth as a modality leads to an interesting schema, that is, (13) in version (13a), "if A is true, then A' is plausible." However, its converse, that is, (13b), "if A, then it is true that A'," raises some doubts. It is true that the conjunction of (13a) and (13b) gives the T-scheme "A is true if and only if A"; if the distinction between language and metalanguage is absent, the unrestricted T-scheme produces semantic paradoxes. Moreover, the T-scheme cuts (**D3**) to the triangle $\alpha\nu\beta$ in the logic of truth. In this case, ν expresses the principle of the excluded middle. Accepting (13a) without (13b) opens doors for many-valued logic or so-called truth-value gaps (see Woleński 2019: 92–103 for a more detailed outline). However, the suggested reading of κ and λ is still plausible without the T-scheme, because truth is not reducible to necessity (truth and necessary truth are distinguished). Moreover, we can stipulate that the disjunction $\kappa \lor \lambda$ expresses the excluded middle. In such a case, (**D3**) is an extension of classical propositional calculus. In any case, differences between various modalities are not trivial.

However, some ontologists observe that (**D3**) gives rise to some doubts. Let us take (16), which states that falsehood implies non-necessity (possibility-not). Prima facie, if something expressed by A is ontologically false, it does not obtain in the real world (whatever that means), but this statement is somehow stronger than the statement that the fact (recall the suggested ontological reading of A) in question is not necessary. Perhaps this problem stems from understanding (I would say *confusing*) being false as equivalent to not existing in reality (this idea is motivated by the classical account of transcendentalia, that is, overcategorical concepts). However, if we remember that ontological falsehood is equivalent to non-actuality (non-reality), acceptance of (16) is easier. The crucial intuition suggests that we can speak about ontological items as non-actual and contingent (non-actual possibilia) as well as about beings which are actual and contingent (actual possibilia). Some authors (see Perzanowski 1989) propose the formula $\Diamond A \implies \Box A$ (the Leibniz axiom) as the characteristic rule (assumption) for strongly rationalistic modal logic.[4] Ontologically speaking, this implies that nothing is accidental. Moreover, we have $A \implies \Box A$; every truth (actuality) is necessary (in Leibniz's formulation *unumquodque, quando est, oportet esse* (whatever is, if it is at all, is necessary)). Hence, what is non-necessary is also non-actual, and conversely, no existing item is accidental. I do not agree with this approach to logical as well as ontological modalities (see the following for further remarks) and prefer **BML**, extended by principles derived from (**D3**) as the formal machinery for investigations concerning relations between modal logic and ontology.[5]

Ingarden distinguished existential moments and moments of being. Here is his original formulation (Ingarden 2013: 99, 104, 108–9):

> The being-real, being-ideal, being-possible, and the like are modes of being of this something. Non-being, on the other hand is, is no mode of being, but rather the outright *privation* of all being . . . Every object appears to be able to exist in only *one* mode of being, in the sense that anything at all that can be distinguished in it (hence, in particular, all of its properties exist in *the same* mode of being as the object itself). As we shall presently see, the situation is different with regard to the existential *moments* . . . We can . . . say that no existential moment suffices by itself for the existence of entity in some particular mode of being . . . It appears possible in the case of existential moments that within the framework of one and the same individual object, not all of the object's moments have to subsist in the same existential moment, but can, depending on their form and matter, occur in different existential moments . . . I shall initially distinguish four different pairs of opposite existential moments:

1. autonomy—heteronomy;
2. originality—derivativeness;
3. self-sufficiency—non-self-sufficiency;
4. independence—dependence.

Ingarden did not offer a definition (or anything similar) of modes of being or existential moments. Some hints for his understanding of these concepts can be derived from given examples and comments. For instance, he describes absolute being by citing autonomy, originality, self-sufficiency, and independence as constituting a complete and unique collection of existential moments. On the other hand, we have eight kinds of relative beings, characterized, for instance, (i) by autonomy, derivativeness, self-sufficiency, and independence; and (ii) by autonomy, derivativeness, self-sufficiency, and dependence. Absoluteness and relativity of being are modes of being. The former is defined by the fixed and stable list of existential moments, whereas the latter, taking into account (i) and (ii), differs with respect to independence and dependence.

Some modes of beings listed by Ingarden (being possible, being real) are present in (**D3**) (I will consider this diagram); others (e.g., ideality, absoluteness, relativity) are not. In what follows, I will consider the former only. There are at least two problems for analysis. First, we should decide whether all categories present in (**D3**) could have been accepted by Ingarden as modes of being. I see no problem with necessity, actuality, possibility, and accidentality—if the last is accepted, so is non-necessity. On the other hand, impossibility and non-actuality seem problematic, and, due to Ingarden's explicit statement that non-being is not a mode of being, I surmise that Ingarden was guided by the intuition that being exists by necessity and, if so, impossibility (I will treat non-actuality as follows) cannot be one of its modes. However, we can change our manner of speaking by using the phrase "modal predications," applied to ontological items under consideration. If the expression "impossibility as a mode of being" appears puzzling, the following way out might be proposed. Let us agree that necessity, actuality, possibility, and accidentality are modes of being in the strict sense. Let us say that impossibility is needed as a modal predication expressing the negation of possibility—for obvious reasons we cannot exclude negations if their positive counterparts are admitted. I see no obstacle to saying "squaring the circle is impossible" when referring to the denotatum of "squaring the circle"— this sentence is even true. It seems that Ingarden was not consequent, because he considered possible, not actual, ontological models.

Second, Ingarden explicitly separated possibility and actuality (a fortiori, necessity as well).[6] This view is at odds with (**D3**). Let symbols **NEC, ACT, POS,** and **ACC** refer to sets of items—necessary, actual, possible, and accidental, respectively. Here the inclusions are summarized (I omit impossibility, non-actuality, and necessity; due to (**D3**) the related inclusions are easily obtainable and analogous to the following list):

(17)

    (a) **NEC** ⊆ **ACT**;
    (b) **ACT** ⊆ **POS**;
    (c) **NEC** ⊆ **POS**;
    (d) **ACC** ⊆ **POS**.

Moreover, non-empty can be (though are not necessarily) the intersections (I mention the cases more important from the ontological point of view) **NEC** ∩ **ACT** and **ACT** ∩ **ACC**. Thus, we can say that ontological inventories of the world consist of necessary items (without accidental objects, per Leibniz), necessary and accidental items (Thomism), or accidental items (without necessary objects, i.e., ontological naturalism). Which model is satisfied in reality depends on metaphysical considerations and cannot be justified by logic as such. In particular, the formula $x \in$ **NEC** $\vee$ $x \in$ **NEC** ∩ **ACT** $\vee$ $x \in$ **ACT** ∩ **ACC** is not a theorem of the (**D3**) theory (logic) of modality. Thus, this theory entails that possibility is not separated from actuality. Ingarden's view requires a deep modification of logic of modalities. It is unclear how such reform would be accomplished. Incidentally, a similar problem occurs in normative discourse, because permission appears to be separated from obligation. On the other hand, since (**D2**), not (**D3**), generates deontic logic, the situation is simpler than in the case of (**D3**) theory and its explanation, since it indicates that permission, which can be interpreted either as λ or as μ, suffices to clarify the problem. In the case of ontological possibility, although its combination with actuality complicates the issue, logic suggests which modalities are separated and which are not. For instance, we have that **NEC** ∩ **ACC** = ∅, that is, no object can be simultaneously necessary and contingent.

My subsequent analysis concerns originality and derivativeness. Ingarden's text runs as follows (Ingarden 2013: 116, 46):[7]

(A) An entity is existentially original if, in accordance with its essence, it cannot be produced by any other entity. In contrast, an entity is existentially derivative if it can be so produced. If an original entity exists at all, that is only because it is incapable of not existing at all in virtue of its essence . . . If . . . an entity is existentially derivative, then it is also inherent in *its* essence that it can or does exist in virtue of having be produced by some other object. This represents the absolute, unconditional existential derivativeness of an entity. It is to be distinguished from *contingent, empirical* derivativeness. The negation of derivativeness can signify either the relative non-derivativeness of an object with respect to some other *specific* object X, or originality. The latter does not necessarily follow from the former.

(B) Existential originality and existential derivativeness are mutually exclusive and exhaust all possible cases.

Every object is then *either* original *or* derivative.

(C) If it were ascertainable about a particular object X that it exists and is absolutely derivative, then there also exist some original objects which are the source of existence of object X.

(D) Nothing is contingent . . . not even that every derivative entity exists "contingently," namely that it does not have the indispensable source of its being.

Since I consider originality and derivativeness to possess modal factors, I will apply (**D3**) in my subsequent analysis.

I begin with passage (D). Perzanowski considers that this fragment justifies his Leibnizian interpretation of Ingarden's formal ontological system. We can convert Ingarden's original formulation into: (i) if something exists accidentally, then it is not accidental that the item in question exists accidentally. Assume that being accidental means being accidental and contingent (= not necessary and not impossible). Define $\blacklozenge A$ as $\lozenge A \land \lozenge \neg A$. Thus (E) can be formalized by

(18) $\blacklozenge A \implies \square \blacklozenge A$.

However, the Leibniz axiom is not the formula $\lozenge A \implies \square A$, unless we assume that everything is necessary. On the other hand, this is a very strong claim (see earlier). Another approach is to accept that accidentality is the same as contingency (= not necessity, possibility-not). Then we could apply the characteristic axiom of system S5,

(19) $\lozenge A \implies \square \lozenge A$,

as formalized (E). Since I am not sure whether Ingarden would agree with this proposal, the issue must be left open. In accordance with my intuitions, I will use **BML** extended by (**D3**).

Fragment (A) provides a definition of existential originality (in what follows, I will omit the adjective *existential*). In order to extract the logical content, I ignore the reference to the concept of essence. My proposal consists in interpreting the passage in question as involving necessity in understanding the ontological status of original items. Denoting the predicate "produced" by the symbol ▶ (the formula $y \blacktriangleright x$ means "x is produced by y"), we have (using quantifiers in (20), (21), and further formulas does not mean that I am relinquishing propositional modal logic in favor of first-order; all dependencies encoded by (**D3**) remain; no new ones have been added.)

(20) $x \in \mathbf{Or} =^{df} \Box \neg \exists y(x \blacktriangleright y) \; (\Longleftrightarrow x \in \mathbf{Or} =^{df} \neg \Diamond \exists y(x \blacktriangleright y)).$

Thus, originality of an item (object, entity) x means that there is, by necessity, no entity y which produces x (or that such an object is impossible). Eventually, remembering that Ingarden rejected the idea of *causa sui* being for any item, we can add that $x \neq y$. Dually, we define **DE** (derivativeness) as

(22) $x \in \mathbf{DE} =^{df} \Box \exists y(x \blacktriangleright y) \; (\Longleftrightarrow x \in \mathbf{Or} =^{df} \neg \Diamond \neg \exists y(x \blacktriangleright y)).$

Furthermore, the fragment (B) can be formalized by (**V**, the universe of all objects)

(23)

(a) $\mathbf{OR} \cap \mathbf{DE} = \emptyset, \neg(x \in \mathbf{OR} \wedge \neg(x \in \mathbf{DE});$
(b) $\mathbf{OR} \cup \mathbf{DE} = \mathbf{V}, x \in \mathbf{OR} \vee x \in \mathbf{DE}).$

These last two formulas reproduce the thesis that the division of one item into original and derivative is mutually exclusive (no item is original and derivative) and exhaustive (every item is original or derivative). The nature of the objects which populate universe **V** is not an ontological problem, because it pertains to metaphysics.

A more complicated interpretative issue concerns (C). This passage is stylized as a rule of inference using the following form:

(24) $\exists x(x \in \mathbf{OR} \wedge x = a)) \vdash \exists y(y \in \mathbf{De} \wedge y \blacktriangleright a).$

If we apply (22) to the premise of (24), the result is that object a is necessarily produced by an object y. On the other hand, the conclusion of (24) says that there is a necessary item which produced a. Assuming that the symbol ▶ is a kind of implication, (24) reminds us of the rule

(25) $\Box(A \Longrightarrow B), A \vdash \Box B,$

which provokes controversy (see Forbes 1985: 6 for criticism and Perzanowski 1989: 302 for a defense). Although it is only an analogy, it shows that the interplay of modalities and modes of existence in Ingarden's formal ontology leads to difficulties. In order to simplify the issue, one can adopt the ontological axiom (a counterpart of (25)):

(26) $\exists x(x \in \mathbf{DE} \land x = a) \Longrightarrow \exists y(y \in \mathbf{OR} \land y \blacktriangleright a).$

Expressed in words: if a is a derivative object, it is produced by some original objects.

Now I will examine Ingarden's ontological theses with the help of (**D3**).[8] If we agree that modal concepts are, at least implicitly, present in definitions of **OR** and **DE**, we can propose the following interpretations (**NOR**: non-original, **NDE**: non-derivative):

(27)

    (a) $\alpha - x \in \mathbf{OR}, \Box \neg \exists y(x \blacktriangleright y);$
    (b) $\beta - x \in \mathbf{DE}, \Box \exists y(x \blacktriangleright y);$
    (c) $\gamma - x \in \mathbf{NDE}, \Diamond \neg \exists y(x \blacktriangleright y);$
    (d) $\delta - x \in \mathbf{NOR}, \Diamond \exists y(x \blacktriangleright y);$

If this reconstruction is correct, the ontological theorem (23) partially fails; (23a) is justified, but (23b) must be rejected on the basis of (**D3**), because **OR** and **DE** are contraries, but not contradictories. The interpretation via (**D3**) (in fact, the usual logical square is sufficient) suggests the following case (omitted by Ingarden), namely

(28) $\mu \Longleftrightarrow (\gamma \land \delta), \mathbf{NDE} \cap \mathbf{NOR}, \Diamond \neg \exists x(x \blacktriangleright y) \land x \in \mathbf{NOR}, \Diamond \exists x(x \blacktriangleright y).$

For Ingarden, $\alpha \lor \beta$ is an ontological theorem. This view excludes $\gamma \land \delta$ as an ontological possibility. However, if **OR** and **DE** are contraries, but not contradictories, **NDE** and **NOR** appear to be complementary. In other words, they are mutually compatible, and **NDE** ∩ **NOR** is a consistent category, which approximately constitutes the region (class) of accidental items in the classical sense.

The full ontological panorama related to (**D2**) and Ingarden's theorems interpreted as including modal content is captured by (see (12)):

(29) **OR ∪ DER ∪ NDER ∩ NOR**, $\forall x(x \in \mathbf{OR} \lor x \in \mathbf{DER} \lor x \in \mathbf{NDER} \cap \mathbf{NOR})$.[9]

Introducing (**D3**) and actuality (**ACT**) requires defining this last category. Clearly, since (23b) fails we cannot say

(30) **ACT = OR ∪ DE**,

which implies

(31)

(a) **OR ⊆ ACT**;
(b) **DE ⊆ ACT**.

Although (31a) is plausible (necessity implies actuality), (31b) is not, because (according to (**D3**)) **DE ⊆ NACT**, due to the fact that $\beta \Longrightarrow \lambda$. The latter, along with (31b), leads to the statement that something can be simultaneously actual and non-actual, that is, to an explicit contradiction. If we wish to retain (31b), something must be changed in the definition of modes of existence. As a first step, I propose the elimination of modalities from (27) as well as the modification of occurrences of quantifiers. As a result we have:

(32)

(a) $\alpha - x \in \mathbf{OR}, \forall y \neg (x \blacktriangleright y)$;
(b) $\beta - x \in \mathbf{DE}, \forall y (x \blacktriangleright y)$;
(c) $\gamma - x \in \mathbf{NDE}, \exists y \neg (x \blacktriangleright y)$;
(d) $\delta - x \in \mathbf{NOR}, \exists y (x \blacktriangleright y)$;

Formula (32b) codes an impossible situation, namely, that there are items which are produced by all other entities.[10]

However, citing this definition as an expression of properties of derivative items is highly counterintuitive. Hence, for the sake of a more adequate symbol, I propose to replace **DE** with **ARO** (anti-original—it is a much better fit to state that α and β are contrary under the proposed reading). This leads to the following definition:

(33) **DE = NAOR ∩ NOR**, $x \in \mathbf{DE} \Longleftrightarrow x \in \mathbf{NAOR} \land x \in \mathbf{NOR}$.

The intuition behind (33) is that derivative items are accidental (a derivative entity is produced by some object(s), but there are objects which are neutral with respect to being producers of *a*). Both (30) and (31) can be accepted. Through nominalization, [*A*] ∈ **DE** if and only if [*A*] ∈ **DE** and [¬*A*] ∈ **DE**.

To say that derivative items are accidental requires introducing modalities to (32). This can be achieved by stipulating that if *x* ∈ **OR**, then *x* is necessary. Other cases are easily obtainable using **BML**. Modalized (33) reproduces the view that every item is necessary (i.e., not created by any other object) or derivative (i.e., produced by something else); this statement yields a justification for (24) and (26). However, there is also another possibility. Let us define actuality (*a* is an individual constant (proper name) referring to a concrete item) as:

(34) $a \in \mathbf{ACT} \iff \exists x(x = a)$.

All definitions captured by (32) are retained. In order to obtain all dependencies of (**D3**)-logic, we should add the axiom (I omit **AOR**):

(35) $a \in \mathbf{OR} \implies \exists x(x = a)$.[11]

Now we have:

(36)
(a) **OR** ⊆ **ACT**;
(b) **DE** ⊆ **ACT**.

Does **ACT** = **OR** ∪ **DE**? The answer is negative because this equality has no justification in (**D3**)-logic. On the other hand, we have

(37)

(a) **ACT** ⊆ **NAOR**;
(b) **NACT** ⊆ **NOR**.

These settings justify the thesis

(38) $\exists x(x \in \mathbf{ACT}) \land \neg \exists y(x \blacktriangleright y) \land (x \notin \mathbf{OR})$.

If we accept that **OR** = **NEC**, we admit, by virtue of (38), actual non-necessary objects. It seems that we have two kinds of originality, namely, strong (**SOR**) and weak (**WOR**). Consequently, we define (the definition (27d) now concerns derivativeness, that is *x* ∈ **DE** if and only if $\exists y(x \blacktriangleright y)$):

(39)

(a) $x \in \mathbf{SOR} \iff \Box \neg \exists x(x \blacktriangleright y)$;

(b) $x \in \mathbf{WOR} \iff \neg \exists x(x \blacktriangleright y)$;

A similar distinction (strong vs. weak) concerns derivative objects. We define:

(40)

(a) $x \in \mathbf{SDE} \iff \Box \exists x(x \blacktriangleright y)$;
(b) $x \in \mathbf{WDE} \iff \exists x(x \blacktriangleright y)$.
(c) $x \in \mathbf{DE} \iff x \in \mathbf{SDE} \vee x \in \mathbf{WDE}$.

Finally, we have:

(41) $x \in \mathbf{ACT} \iff x \in \mathbf{SOR} \vee x \in \mathbf{WOR} \vee x \in \mathbf{DE}$.

Weakly original objects are contingent as non-necessary and non-anti-original. The same concerns derivative items. One can distinguish strongly contingent (derivative and contingent) and weakly contingent (weakly original and contingent).

Modal factors in originality and derivativeness are external, that is, they require the addition of some modal stipulations, such as **OR** = **NEC**. Thus, in order to apply modal logic to ontology, we need to combine these concepts in some way. Ingarden offered very valuable hints for doing so, but his analysis contains gaps and inaccuracies. One controversial issue concerns the definition of the ontological universe. Although it is tempting to define the ontological universe using **V** = **ACT** (Ingarden seems to accept this identity), I abstain from this step for reasons (see earlier) concerning the existential import of the word *something*. Another solution states that actuality is always relativized to a given possible world and that the real world is one possible universe. In any case, we always have the thesis that if something is actual, it is also possible. Thus, Meinongian or paraconsistent ontology is rather inconsistent with the outlined solution. We have also a serious problem with strongly derivative items, because saying that $\Box \exists x(x \blacktriangleright y)$ raises the question of whether the necessity of the producing relation necessitates its members (both or perhaps x). Formal ontology cannot decide whether the metaphysical inventory of the world consists of necessary items, contingent items, or both; or, eventually, looking at the issue from another perspective, of strongly original, weakly original, strongly derivative, weakly derivative, or "all that jazz." How can we interpret the category denoted by **WOR**? Democritean atoms, ultimate elementary particles, Russellian individuals, and the entire natural universe appear as possible candidates to serve as instances of weakly original objects, but this is only a preliminary suggestion. One problem seems to be solved by the foregoing analysis. According to Ingarden, (24) (or (26)) holds true in all ontological models; that is, contingent items are derivative and cannot exist without their (necessary) producers. However, if we admit weak originalities, ontological models populated by such items and weak derivatives are perfectly possible. Thus, (24) fails independently of logical doubts concerning its legitimacy as a rule of inference; the same concerns (26). This justifies the thesis that creationist ontologies do not exhaust all possibilities.

Notes

1. In what follows, I neglect, apart from parenthetical (mostly comparative) remarks, deontic, epistemic, erotetic, etc. modalities and concentrate on alethic modals and their ontological counterparts.
2. Since Ingarden contrasts ontology (roughly speaking, investigations of possible models of being) and metaphysics (roughly speaking, looking for an ontological model present in the real world), I use the word "ontology" in the question concerning the relationship between modal logic and ontology.
3. One word on references to Ingarden is in order. This chapter analyses some themes from his magnificent *Controversy over the Existence of the World*, a book identified by Father Bocheński as the greatest work of Western metaphysics since Aristotle. The book was published in Polish in 1946 (v. 1) and 1948 (v. 2); the English translation (by A. Szylewicz) appears as Ingarden 2013–16 (further references are to this edition, more precisely to v. 1, and are indicated as Ingarden 2013). In the last years of his life, Ingarden became interested in modal logic. When I told him that I had obtained Becker (1952), Ingarden asked me to lend him this book. I know nothing about his reaction to Becker's work. In general, Ingarden did not regard logic as a guide for philosophy. For him, philosophy had to be presuppositionless with respect to logic. My standpoint is precisely contrary.
4. Due to some technical features (details omitted) of the logic with Leibniz's axiom, it does not result in the reduction of necessity to possibility and truth.
5. Perzanowski interpreted Ingarden's ontology as strongly rationalistic. Of course, this is possible, provided that the Leibniz axiom is adopted. Clearly, the scope of logic to some extent is a matter of convention and this allows a flexible use of the term *logic*. Briefly, my view is that **BML** is, doubtless, a (modal) logic, but at least some of its extensions are rather formal theories of modalities, because they are not universally valid. This qualification concerns the (**D3**)-theory of modality and the account with the Leibniz axiom. I consider the former more intuitive than the latter. On the other hand, if we wish we can speak about (**D3**)-logic or Leibniz-style modal logic.

6 Ingarden analyzed this problem with respect to so-called empirical possibility in his writings. In his seminars in the early 1960s (in which I participated), he extended this treatment to logical and ontological possibility as well.
7 In Woleński 1986 I used the terms "primitivity" and "secondarity." Here I follow Szylewicz's translation. In the original Polish, Ingarden's terms are *bytowa pierwotność* and *bytowa pochodność*.
8 This approach is preliminary and will be modified by the end of this chapter.
9 In Ingarden's original scheme, the gap between **OR** and **DE** cannot be filled by the items he called relatively derivative (see Ingarden 2013: 144–5), because this concept operates on a different level of analysis.
10 It seems that not even the model (a kind of metaphysical holism) in which every entity is related to any other entity fits (27b).
11 (36a) does not follow from (32a), nor does (32b) entail (36b).

References

Becker, O. (1952), *Untersuchungen über den Modalkalkül* (Investigations into Modal Calculus), Meisenheim: Anton Hain.
Forbes, G. (1985), *The Metaphysics of Modality*, Oxford: Clarendon Press.
Ingarden, R. (2013–16), *Controversy over the Existence of the World*, vol. 1 (2013), vol. 2 (2016), Frankfurt am Main: Peter Lang.
Perzanowski, J. (1989), "Logiki modalne i filozofia" (Modal Logic and Philosophy), in *Jak filozofować* (How to philosophize), ed. J. Perzanowski, 252–345, Warsaw: Państwowe Wydawnictwo Naukowe.
Williamson, T. (2013), *Modal Logic as Metaphysics*, Oxford: Oxford University Press.
Woleński, J. (1986), "Remarks on Primitivity and Secondarity as Moments of Existence," *Reports on Philosophy* X: 81–7.
Woleński, J. (1990), "Momenty bytowe i modalności" (Modes of being and modalities), *Studia Filozoficzne* (Philosophical Studies) 2–3: 111–21; reprinted in Woleński, J. (1996), *W stronę logiki* (Towards logic), 72–83, Kraków: Aureus.
Woleński, J. (2008), "Applications of Squares of Oppositions and Their Generalizations in Philosophical Analysis," *Logica Universalis* 2(1): 13–29; reprinted in Woleński, J. (2011), *Essays on Logic and Its Applications in Philosophy*, 255–69, Frankfurt am Main: Peter Lang.
Woleński, J. (2019), *Semantics and Truth*, Cham: Springer Nature.
Żegleń, U. (1990), *Modalność w logice i w filozofii. Postawy ontyczne* (Modality in logic and philosophy. Ontic foundations), Warsaw: Polskie Towarzystwo Semiotyczne.

… 3

Questions Concerning Reality
Ingarden's Erotetical Path Toward Realism

Giuditta Corbella

In *Essentiale Fragen* (Ingarden 1925; from now on *EF*, ang. On Essential Questions), Roman Ingarden reflects on the nature of questions, the features of essential questions, and on essence itself. Though these topics were often considered to be separate, both Ingarden's theory of questions and his ontology are present in this text, which has to be interpreted as a systematic whole. To achieve this, the ontological claims contained in the erotetic analysis must be underlined. Hence, in the following pages I will read Ingarden's 1925 theory of question in the light of his anti-psycologistic and realist convictions and I will claim that the investigation of questions offers an unusual argument in favor of realism.[1]

In 1925, Ingarden published the text *Essentiale Fragen: ein Beitrag zu dem Wesensproblem* (On Essential Questions: A Contribution to the Essence Problem) in the *Jahrbuch für Philosophie und phänomenologische Forschung*. Ingarden's work was originally written in Polish and presented to the University of Lvov two years earlier—1923—as a "habilitation" thesis (Ingarden 1972a). Unfortunately, there was no possibility to publish it in the original language; that is why Ingarden turned to Husserl and his *Jahrbuch*.

Ingarden speaks about the purpose of *Essentiale Fragen* in two places: in the preface to *Essentiale Fragen* and in the preface to the *Controversy over the Existence of the World*. In the preface to *Essentiale Fragen*, Ingarden states that the work is intended to provide a solid foundation for the phenomenological method and the phenomenological interpretation of essence (*EF*: 125). From this point of view, the text is directed against the non-phenomenological public, which denies the possibility of any *Wesensschau* by refusing the existence of essence. In response, the investigation of essential questions aims to demonstrate the necessity of admitting essences and ideas.[2] Within this project, erotetic analysis must be interpreted as a strategic choice. The motives which lead Ingarden to use erotetics as the framework of eidetic analysis are understood by Ryle (1973: 72) as follows: "[Ingarden] takes as his theme 'Essential Questions' rather than 'Essential Judgements' in order to make no *petitio principii*, and, in particular, to prove that even the ignorance which asks questions postulates that there *are* Essences."

Elsewhere, in the preface to the *Controversy over the Existence of the World*, Ingarden (2013: 19–24) integrates *Essentiale Fragen* into his lifelong philosophical project. As he states in this brief intellectual autobiography, Ingarden had begun to argue against any idealist or anti-realist conception in 1918. Around 1923—the publication year of the Polish version of *Essentiale Fragen*—a methodological turn occurs: Ingarden realizes that the solution to the controversy over an external, independent reality has to be established on an ontological basis rather than on an epistemological one. Hence, to prepare the ground for his *opus magnum metaphysicum*—the *Controversy*—he begins to "carry out a series of preliminary [ontological] investigations, proceeding both in a positive and negative direction" (Ingarden 2013: 19). As stated in the *Controversy*, *Essentiale Fragen* stands among the first group of writings and contributes positively to the metaphysical goal. The reflections contained therein investigate the difference between an individual object, the realm of ideas, and the individual essence of the object. In the same preface, Ingarden alerts his reader to the fact that all his works written after 1923 deal with the idealism-realism controversy despite their apparent distance from it.

Ingarden's (1972b) well-known book *The Literary Work of Art* belongs to the same group of writings, that is, the ontological reflections contributing positively to Ingarden's realist philosophy. The parallels between *On Essential Questions* and *The Literary Work of Art* can aid an understanding of Ingarden's strategy: in the latter work, he strategically provides a description of the ontological structure of purely intentional objects in order to highlight the difference between purely intentional and real objects, thus showing that the real world cannot be purely intentional. Likewise, in *On Essential Questions* Ingarden points out how ideal beings are different from real individual objects, since the structure of any idea contains variables and constants, while any real object is fully determined and lacks variables.[3]

With his *Ideenlehre* Ingarden seeks to (a) admit the existence of essence, ideas, and essentialities, thus demonstrating the legitimacy of the phenomenological method, and (b) underline the ontological peculiarities of ideas to point out the difference between real and ideal beings, thus allowing a better understanding of the multiple realms of being.

To this first *eidetic-ontological purpose*—characterized differently in the two prefaces—I would like to add a second *erotetic-ontological purpose* which is the focus of the following reflections. Chapter 1 of *Essentiale Fragen* shows that the cognitional act of questioning possesses, thanks to its structure, an anti-psychologistic and anti-conventionalist potential since it transcends itself and points directly to an external reality.[4]

Before embarking on an analytical description of the book's content, it is useful to recall the structure of *Essentiale Fragen*. The text has six chapters: in the first, Ingarden sets out a general conception of the nature of questions; Chapters 2 to 5 elaborate on the different types of essential questions as well as the notions of idea, essence, and essentialities; finally, Chapter 6 employs the results of previous analyses to argue against "epistemological conventionalism," that is, any philosophy stating that the cognized object depends on the cognitional act.

This chapter aims to consider the first and the last sections as interconnected, by showing how, even in the first erotetic part, Ingarden offers several statements that are comprehensible only in the light of his stand against conventionalism.

Status quaestionis

The genesis of Ingarden's text played a pivotal role not just in its development but also in the history of its reception. The two versions of the text—the German and the Polish—are different and were meant for two different philosophical environments. The early Polish reception of the text tended to be centered on the erotetic dimension. Ingarden himself endorsed this kind of reading of the Polish text, regarding himself as the pioneer of erotetics in Poland. What is more, Ingarden accused Ajdukiewicz of drawing inspiration from his theory of questions without making any reference to it (Ajdukiewicz 1928; Witwicki 1927). Polish scholars often studied *Essentiale Fragen* through the lens of erotetics as a specific field of inquiry, sometimes disregarding the text as "instrumental" (Śpiewak 2002: 81) because of its ontological aim.[5] Some recent contributions may lead to the impression that Ingarden's text coincides wholly with its erotetic part, despite the fact that this makes up only the first chapter. Conversely, phenomenological scholars emphasized the eidetic analysis contained in Chapters 2 to 5. Several phenomenologically oriented interpreters have moved on very quickly toward purely ontological investigation, on the basis of the methodological claim made by Ingarden: "We mean to clarify and legitimate certain *logical* problems regarding essential *questions* by clarifying certain *ontological* states of affairs which represent the objects of the true *answers* to those questions" (*EF*: 146).

Generally speaking, there is a twofold rejection to interpreting the erotetical and the eidetic-ontological as two parts of a whole and to foreseeing the possibility of mutual enrichment. Ingarden's erotetics has been interpreted either as an isolated and complete theory or as a very peculiar approach to the *vexata quaestio* of the nature of essence. It has to be underlined that in both cases the text has been taken in high regard, as can be seen in the letters from Ajdukiewicz (1928), Szuman (1936a,b), and Husserl (1994: 222-5), as well as in the reviews by Ryle (1927, 1973) and Ewing (1926).

It must be said, in order to clarify this complex reception, that Ingarden himself translated *Essentiale Fragen* from Polish into German. He did not merely translate it properly—not too literally nor too creatively—but he actually changed and modified the text in several ways.

Ingarden's Theory of Erotetic

I will now proceed to a more detailed analysis of §2 of *Essentiale Fragen*. At the beginning of the text, Ingarden complains about the vagueness of philosophical questions and expresses his desire to display the conditions that the structure of every question must fulfill in order to receive a proper answer: a well-posed question is univocal in each one of its parts.

To understand what the content of the question is, Ingarden reshapes the different elements of the judgmental structure in order for them to be suitable for the analysis of interrogative sentences. Following Pfänder's scholastic terminology, Ingarden affirms that every judgment possesses an *objectum formale* and an *objectum materiale* (OF and OM for brevity). The former indicates the intentional state of affairs and exists only as long as the question exists, while the latter indicates the objective state of affairs that exists independently of the cognizing subject and the cognitional act. These two features are also found in interrogative sentences which possess an OF in the proper sense and also an OM, although only in an improper sense. As a matter of fact, if questions possessed no OM at all, then it would be impossible to distinguish between correct and incorrect questions; yet, at the same time, if questions possessed OMs in the proper sense, then problems, as merely intentional correlates of the content of questions, could exist independently from the interrogative sentence. Hence, it would be impossible to have wrong answers.

Despite the identical definition, the OF of questions has two peculiarities: (1) it contains known as well as unknown elements and (2) is undetermined with respect to its existential character.

As far as the former feature is concerned, it must be noted that the presence of one or more unknown elements does not represent a defect for the interrogative sentence. The only defective aspect would be for it to have an insufficiently located unknown:

> A question whose object is fully determined by positive moments with respect to *each one* of its aspects [. . .] is absolutely impossible. It would no longer be a question. There is an error in the question only if [. . .] the unknown is not univocally located in the object of the question, when it is not clear what is determined and what is undetermined. On the other hand, a question whose object consists of nothing but "unknowns" is equally impossible. (*EF*: 130)

Finally, the function of the answer is to eliminate this unknown element that appertains to the matter of the OF.

The second feature of the OF of questions is its indeterminacy (ger. *Unbestimmtheit*). As Ingarden says, while "the formal object of every judgment is univocally determined with regard to the existential character of what constitutes its matter, [. . .] the matter of the formal object of a question has no such self-determined character of the mode of existence" (*EF*: 131).

The existential character (ger. *Seinscharakter*)[6] of judgments is the intentional correlate of the assertoric function of the copula, and its peculiar form is determined by the mode of the predicative or connective function of the copula. Thus, the judgment is regarded as categorical, problematical, or apodictical. In the interrogative sentences, indeterminacy has two different variations depending on which function of the copula is emphasized. In the case of the *Hinbeziehungsfunktion* (connective function), as in material questions such as "What state is sulphur in at 1000°?," the indeterminacy concerns the connection between subject and predicate. In cases in which the copula assumes a *Behauptungsfunktion* (assertoric function), as in existential questions such as "Is God omniscient?," and there is no unknown element in the matter of the OF, the indeterminacy concerns the whole, although, even in the latter case, the indeterminacy also encompasses the relationship between the subject and its predicate.

I will now focus on Ingarden's reflections on the second feature of questions, that is, its indeterminacy. The passages that I take into account are contained only in the German text, while §2 of the Polish version is slightly reduced.

The first distinction that Ingarden makes is that between indecision (ger. *Unentschlossenheit/Schwanken*) as a mental state (ger. *psychischer Zustand*) that affects the questioner and indeterminacy (ger. *Unbestimmtheit*) as a feature of the cognitional act expressed in the interrogative sentence.

Indeterminacy as a feature of the intentional correlate of the act underlines that "the question knocks at reality (ger. *pocht an die Wirklichkeit*)" (*EF*: 132). It not only addresses and demands reality but, in doing so, the question is a way in which we try to overcome an undecided status and to "transcend the sphere of our subjectivity" (*EF*: 132). This brief description of the questioning act contains a first profession of realism, since reality is identified as the point of arrival of the subjective dynamics, and as implied by the question as embryonic act of knowledge.

The notion of transcendence plays a pivotal role in Ingarden's thought. This concept is explored in several texts (Ingarden 1975, 1992, 2013) and is one of the main vectors on which Ingarden builds his criticism of Husserl.[7] In *Essentiale Fragen*, two different concepts of transcendence are introduced. In Chapter 1, Ingarden affirms that "by questioning, we seek to transcend [*transzendieren*] the sphere of our subjectivity" (*EF*: 132), while in Chapter 6 he maintains that "between the cognitional act and the objects that exist autonomously from the cognizing subject there is a relation of 'real transcendence' [*realer Transzendenz*]" (*EF*: 287). The historical influence of the latter concept—real transcendence—is pointed out in the footnote quoting Hedwig Conrad-Martius's (1920) *Zur Ontologie und Erscheinungslehre der realen Aussenwelt* (On the ontology and theory of phenomena of the real outside world).[8]

In the sixth *Osloer Vorlesung* (Oslo Lecture) Ingarden divides the different concepts of transcendence into three main groups: epistemological, ontic-ontological, and ontic-metaphysical transcendence. The last is left out of the inquiry, while the epistemological concept of transcendence deals with the inadequacy of human perception with respect to the perceived object and is concerned with the "possible or actual cognition of the cognitional object" (Ingarden 1992: 177). The ontic-ontological notion of transcendence is introduced—by Husserl and by Ingarden—to clarify the relationship between the consciousness of something and the realm of psychological processes. Husserl (1983: 70) defines this connection positively by saying that, as Ingarden (1992: 177) quotes: "a material physical thing [. . .] is by essential necessity not a mental process but a being of a wholly different mode of being." A material thing constitutes no real component of consciousness, but rather transcends it. No higher structure unifies both entities, that is, thing and mental process; thus, the thing is simultaneously transcendent—since it is not a component nor a part of the cognitional act—and inseparable—as *cogitatum*—from consciousness.

Unfortunately, the use of the verb "to transcend" present in §2 of *Essentiale Fragen* does not fit in this extended semantics of "transcendence." It differs from all these concepts since it is not static but dynamic and does not express the idea of an object which transcends the subject (ger. *transzendent gegenüber*), or vice versa, but rather the idea of a consciousness which transcends itself (ger. *transzendiert*) toward reality.

Transcending our subjectivity is necessary since the subject does not have enough knowledge to provide an answer to his question, to eliminate the unknown, and to overcome his undecided status. Questions entail one's ignorance but by dealing with such lack of knowledge, they seek to address reality. The questioning act implies that one's actual knowledge does not provide a solution since one has insufficient means but also that one has enough means to search for a solution, that is, to address reality. In the case of an unlocated unknown, what is missing is precisely this resolute "knocking at reality." If it wants to receive a proper answer, the undecided questioning mind must express itself with resoluteness and pose a univocal question that aims for a particular goal. To achieve this, the blind spots in the OF must be precisely located and circumscribed.

After some reflection, Ingarden provides a more extended definition of the act of questioning: "Questioning is an act essentially directed to someone else and that, through and across this other subject, knocks at reality taking advantage of the other's knowledge" (*EF*: 132).

Ingarden adds that even in the most intimate questioning there are two different subjects. One can actually distinguish inside oneself the "I" that poses the question from the "I" to which the question is posed. Despite the necessity of another subject, the question engages in a dialogue with reality itself, and not with these other subjectivities *through and across* whom the "knocking" takes place. They are not the real interlocutors.

At the end of the section analyzed earlier, Ingarden sums up several reasons due to which the OF of a question is undetermined with respect to its existential character. First, the act of questioning "only 'knocks' at reality" (*EF*: 132). Consequently, it "posits nothing and does not attempt to posit anything" (*EF*:

132): a question is a non-positing act and when we question we do not state anything. Third, the act of questioning "is loaded with a moment of waiting and connected with a suspension of judgment" (*EF*: 132); when someone formulates a question, he is not returning from a previous judgment or presupposition, but is rather waiting to receive the pieces of information needed in order to posit something, to provide a positing judgment. Finally, the act of questioning "emerges from the depths of indecision and ignorance" (*EF*: 132), otherwise there would be no unknown element. That is why the formal object of a question, that is, what we ask about, bears the character of indeterminacy with respect to its mode of being.

This is how Ingarden explains his theory of question before tackling the problem of specific essential questions. In these first chapters, Ingarden introduces several historical references to phenomenological texts such as the *Logic* of Pfänder (1921), which provides the terminological basis for Ingarden's analysis, and Husserl's *Logical Investigations*, as well as his *Ideas*. Entering into the long and complicated story of Ingarden's criticism of Husserl exceeds the framework of this chapter. My aim here is rather to focus on Ingarden's reference to Husserl and elaborate on the parallel between indeterminacy and neutralization that Ingarden draws when he writes: "One could be tempted to speak here [*viz.*, in the discussion about indeterminacy] of modification of neutrality of the mode of being—see E. Husserl, *Ideas*, §§109–111. However, the mode of being here seems not to be neutralized but rather still undetermined" (*EF*: 132). Ingarden comments on this possible comparison by saying that the suspension of any existential judgment belonging to the OF of every interrogative sentence is not neutralization, since its purpose is to give rise to an existential resolution given in the answer to that question. The common aspect shared between the two processes is their non-positing nature. However, the difference is that the question is meant to make a positing judgment possible, it indirectly provides it and does not come back from a previous positing judgment or natural presupposition. Further difference concerning the interrogative sentence can be seen if one expands the exegetical basis and looks at the Husserlian erotetic theory as a whole. In the last chapter of *Logical Investigations*, Husserl argues against Bolzano's tenet, according to which questions are a special kind of proposition and are hence truth-evaluable (Bolzano 1985: 114). In opposition, Husserl sticks to the Aristotle's position in *De Interpretatione* 4, according to which not every sentence is a statement-making sentence, and non-declarative sentences—prayers, questions, commands—do not have a truth-value. This crucial historic-philosophical debate is not addressed directly by Ingarden who, however, unfolds the peculiar structure of questions and compares them to judgments. Taking into account §§67–70 of the *Logical Investigations*, §§77–79 of *Experience and Judgement* and §§109–111 *Ideas I*, two differences may be underlined: on the one hand, the lack of interest regarding Husserl's critique of Bolzano on interrogative sentences and their hypothetical propositional content[9] and, on the other hand, Ingarden's belief in a priority of the posed question over the interior question.

Ontological Erotetics and Metaphysical Commitment

I maintain that in §2 of *Essentiale Fragen*, Ingarden makes several trans-logical or ontological statements while building his general theory of questions. I would like to point out the increasing level of this ontological commitment.

Ingarden discovers a reference to reality within the logical structure of questions "knocking" at it. What is more, he separates the psychical state of indecision from the indeterminacy that affects interrogative sentences *as such* and that is linked to questioning as an act of pure consciousness. Because of this, Ingarden's erotetics possesses an anti-psychologistic potential.

To understand the structure of questions, Brożek (2011: 392–5) creates a triadic scheme which may be employed to understand the Ingarden paragraph dealt with here. There are three dimensions implied in any inquiry: the volitional component, the positive cognitive component, and the negative cognitive component. Ingarden mentions all of them: the positive component coincides with the known elements in the matter of the OF, the negative component matches with the unknown of the OF and, finally, indecision as feature of the mental state of questioning conveys the volitional component.

Ingarden mostly stresses the cognitive component of the inquiry. He writes that indecision "does not create by itself the essence of the question, nor does it represent the moment which makes the question a question" (*EF*: 131). What is more, Ingarden constructs a strong and complex connection between the OF and indecision; as a matter of fact, drawing on Husserl's phenomenology, he understands that the indeterminacy of the former and the presence of the latter as mental state, despite their coexistence, may be phenomenologically separated. It is thanks to the analysis of the existential character that the tensional component, which bridges the gap between questions and answers and normally appertains to the volitional state, penetrates not just the psyche of the cognizing subject but also the question itself as logical construct.

The third trans-logical commitment coincides with the introduction of the other subject—the knowledgeable one—who attests to the impossibility of resolving the entire act of questioning within the questioner. This introduction ensures that Ingarden's erotetic theory differs from Husserl's reflection on questions, since the latter reduces both the *Anfrage* and the *Sich-an-sich-selbst-wenden* to an uninteresting communicative aspect of the act of questioning: "communication with others continues to be left out of consideration here; but also we can leave out of account turning—toward—oneself, which would make oneself an end of communication like another person" (Husserl 1973: 308–9).

The logical structure of questions entails a three-level ontological commitment: it knocks at the reality, from this reality it longs to be determined, and it is directed toward another subject, different from the cognizing one. However, it should be noted that Ingarden's erotetics does not seek to have a metaphysical impact on philosophy; this can be deduced from its length as well as from its methodology. There are no statements regarding the existence and the mode of being of any external reality or the mentioned subject. That we should not overestimate Ingarden's attempt is also made clear by the differences between Chapter 1 and the arguments contained in Chapter 6. As mentioned earlier, the hypothesis of this chapter is that Chapters 1 and 6 are interconnected. To demonstrate this, I must briefly summarize the analysis contained in Chapter 6 and point out the common aspects and the differences between the two chapters.

The last part of Ingarden's study engages in a dialogue with "epistemological conventionalism," that is, any theory maintaining that there is a dependent relationship between the object and the cognitional act; namely that the former is not as it is in itself but rather is as the latter builds it. The final section of *Essentiale Fragen* blends into the overall project of the text and presents the following argument: epistemological conventionalism can assume the form of eidetic skepticism. This latter theory is firmly promoted by "philosophizing mathematicians" and states that any essential judgment is the result of a scientific process which aims to create a conventional definition. The so-called nature of the object would therefore be determined by our social conventions. The issue becomes particularly critical when these reflections exceed the boundaries of mathematical objects and "similar considerations are made also with respect to the real objects and the whole problem assumes a more wide-reaching influence" (*EF*: 254).

To eradicate the motivations beyond skepticism, Ingarden's last chapter widens the text's horizon and investigates not only the nature of the essence but whether the object is in general dependent on the subject or, as Ingarden puts it in Chapter 5, "if—in what sense and to what extent—the cognizing subject can arbitrarily alter the cognitional object" (*EF*: 307). The possible answers are offered immediately: either there are at least some objects, or there are no objects at all but only fictions. If objects exist, then they cannot be properly created from the cognitional act that meets them. The skeptical hypothesis according to which real objects would be no more than mere fictions must be eliminated, since even in the case of pure fictions (centaurs, ice palaces, etc.), the subject does not properly create an object but rather combines preexistent elements in a new whole-complex. What the cognizing subject is able to alter is the quasi-relative property ("X is bigger than Y"). However, even in this latter case, the subject does not arbitrarily invent these properties, which are already given *potentialiter* as soon as a class of objects is given; the subject is responsible only for the selection and the actualization of this pre-given quasi-property.

Ingarden applies these two options—either there are at least some objects, or there are no objects at all but only fictions—to the eidetic issue and states that "the cognizing subject would be free to form the 'nature' of objects [their essence], only [A] if the object at stake was a fiction or [B] if the nature of an existentially autonomous object was a quasi-relative property" (*EF*: 294–5). The [A] reduction of every object to a mere fiction is, according to Ingarden, an overly radical choice even for an eidetic skeptic, while [B] the latter option requires a more extended counterargument. The aforementioned "philosophizing mathematicians" maintain that objects are mere "bundles of properties" and that "essence" is the name for an arbitrary selection of various properties that we identify in different bundles. Ingarden replies that "such a 'nature' [as a quasi-relative property] cannot in general arise [*entstehen*] nor exist [*existieren*]. A quasi-relative property can namely exist only if there are objects in our sense, with their own absolute qualities and natures. Since all this is denied by the aforementioned theory, consequently also the existence of a quasi-relative property is impossible" (*EF*: 300).[10]

As can be observed, even when the line of reasoning seems weaker when compared with the "labyrinthine argumentation" (Mitscherling 1997: 1) of the *Controversy*, the demonstration scheme of Chapter 6 is rigid, and the distinction between possible scenarios is drawn with extreme precision. All of this seems to be lacking in Chapter 1, where Ingarden not only avoids making any metaphysical commitment but also does not ask any precise question regarding the hypothetical existence of the treated object. What Chapters 1 and 6 have in common is their anti-skeptical goal: the erotetic part achieves this with its three-level ontological commitment, while Chapter 6 accomplishes this goal by trying to understand if and how objects depend on the cognizing subject. There is, however, a methodological difference: while Chapter 6 draws a direct argument against epistemological conventionalism as a form of antirealism, in Chapter 1 one finds an exclusively erotetic analysis which simultaneously reveals an ontologically realistic background.

Nevertheless, the strictly erotetic part of *Essentiale Fragen* is the attempt to find a reference to some external being within the logical structure of questions, thus being connected to the anti-psychologistic section of Chapter 6, as well as to the eidetic-realist arguments contained in the other chapters. The nature of an object is not created by the subject and is autonomous. Hence, we need to admit the existence of ideas, essences, and essentialities. The idea is distinct from the real object, and it is structurally affected by a level of indeterminacy that does not pertain to the latter:

> While the latter [...] cannot be undetermined or ambiguously specified in any respect relevant to them, special sorts of constituents occur in an idea's content that we call "variables." For example, every individual person has at any stage of her or his life a specific skin complexion, no matter how much it may change during the course of that life. The content of the idea "any person," in contrast, has only the variable "having some skin complexion." (Ingarden 2013: 68–9)

Another kind of indeterminacy is that which affects the question, which, precisely because of its relationship with the real object, points toward reality. These two kinds of indeterminacy together argue in favor of the realistic perspective that Ingarden intends to defend.

Even if it does not present a demonstration of the existence of independent reality, the erotetic analysis unveils Ingarden's realistic attitude and is fully comprehensible only in the light of his realistic convictions. Paradoxically, the ontological scope of Ingarden's research turns the hierarchical order of judgments and questions upside down: the interrogative sentence stands higher than the declarative statement. Due to its imperfection—namely its hybrid nature where known and unknown are both present and well-located—the act of questioning does not only address reality but achieves this in a more perceivable way than the assertive judgment. Thus, questions entail an intensification of the directional component of the act of consciousness. The questioner is not only saying something about reality; he rather interrogates reality about itself, demanding it to give him a proper answer.

Far from being the main path to a realistic solution, Ingarden's erotetic inquiry has to be understood as a tool by which to unravel the enigma that tormented him ever since the publication of Husserl's *Ideas I* and that witnesses the pervasiveness of the ontological-metaphysical purpose that helps Ingarden to make every philosophical theme—be it erotetics or aesthetics—a suitable field for ontological reflections.

Abbreviation

EF Ingarden, R. (1925), "Essentiale Fragen. Ein Beitrag zu dem Wesensproblem" (On Essential Questions: A Contribution to the Essence Problem), *Jahrbuch für Philosophie und phänomenologische Forschung* 7: 125–304.

Notes

1 Although unusual, the erotetic path towards realism is not totally alien to phenomenological philosophy *latu sensu*. See for example the interesting reflections on the concept of the problem and the act of questioning elaborated by Nicolai Hartmann (1931; 1957: 278–322).
2 The construction of an *Ideenlehre* is based on Héring (1921) notions of essence (ger. *Wesen*), idea (ger. *Idee*), and essentiality (ger. *Wesenheit*), see De Santis (2014: 7–136). The Göttingen Circle regarded Héring text as one of the most fundamental achievements of the phenomenological movement and as the basis for other phenomenological analysis. See, for example, Conrad-Martius (1957: 48).
3 The complex mechanism of variables and constants within the content of ideas is clarified in Ingarden (*EF*: 173–84; 2013: 68–73; 1972b: 261–70). Ingarden (1965: 231–64) provides a systematic explanation of this theme and distinguishes the variables of the idea from the spots of indeterminacy entailed in every purely international object and from the alterability that affects the individual existentially autonomous object.
4 It can be said that Ingarden's use of erotetics is similar to his use of aesthetics, since both fields of research aim to understand if and to what extent an external independent reality can be admitted, although the latter develops this much more extensively. As Mitscherling (1997: 1) states: "We are not in a position accurately to interpret and evaluate Ingarden's studies in aesthetics until we place them within the framework provided by his realist ontological position as a whole, and [. . .] conversely, we cannot fully appreciate the force of Ingarden's arguments in

his 'non-aesthetic' epistemological and ontological investigations [. . .] without understanding how Ingarden intended his studies in aesthetics to provide those investigations, and his own position with regard to the idealism/realism debate, with a solid foundation."

5 Śpiewak (2002) compares Ingarden's and Ajdukiewicz's theory of question and argues that Ingarden's erotetics did not receive the proper reception because of its ontological nature, that is, of its concentration on essential questions. Brożek (2011) integrates *EF* into her history of Polish erotetics in which Ingarden ranks among the first theorists of the logic of questions. Nevertheless, no reference is made to the ontological sections and the eidetic analysis therein attempted. Sobota (2013) deserves a special place inside the present survey, since he roots Ingarden's attempts not in the Polish interest for erotetics but rather in the phenomenological theory of questions elaborated by Husserl as well as by Daubert and Heidegger. A paper by Riska (1976) offers a systematic insight into Ingarden's logic and theory of language. The author affirms that the "analyses [contained in *EF*] are of great importance for the logic of questions," even if—unfortunately—"the essay is dominantly of ontological-epistemological nature" (212).

6 For the German phenomenological lexicon, I follow the English translation of the *Streit*, see Ingarden (2013).

7 A detailed commentary on Ingarden's notion of transcendence is provided in Chrudzimski (1999).

8 For an introduction to Conrad-Martius's text, see Hart and Parker (2020: 9–17).

9 For an introduction to this debate, see Künne (2003).

10 Ingarden (1965: 164–74) presents a similar argument. Regarding Ingarden's hostility toward every interpretation of the object as a mere bundle of properties, see Piwowarczyk (2020).

References

Ajdukiewicz, K. (1928), "Letter to Roman Ingarden, 03.01.1928." Available online: http://ingarden.archive.uj.edu.pl/archiwum/list-od-kazimierza-ajdukiewicza-z-03-01-1928 (accessed April 15, 2022).

Bolzano, B. (1985), *Wissenschaftselhre, Bd. 1* (Science Teaching, Vol. 1), Stuttgart-Bad Cannstatt: frommann-holzboog [Bernard Bolzano-Gesamtausgabe, 11].

Brożek, A. (2011), *Theory of Questions: Erotetics through the Prism of Its Philosophical Background and Practical Applications*, New York: Rodopi.

Chrudzimski, A. (1999), *Die Erkenntnistheorie von Roman Ingarden* (Roman Ingarden's epistemology), Dordrecht: Springer.

Conrad-Martius, H. (1920), "Zur Ontologie und Erscheinungslehre der realen Außenwelt" (On the ontology and theory of phenomena of the real external world), *Jahrbuch für Philosophie und phänomenologische Forschung* 3: 345–542.

Conrad-Martius, H. (1957), *Das Sein* (The existence), München: Kösel.

De Santis, D. ed. (2014), *Di idee ed essenze. Un dibattito su fenomenologia e ontologia (1921–1930)* (About ideas and essences. A debate on phenomenology and ontology (1921–1930)), Milano: Mimesis.

Ewing, A. C. (1926), "Roman Ingarden, Essentiale Fragen" [Review], *Mind* 35: 250.

Hart, J. C. and R. K. B. Parker, eds. (2020), *Hedwig Conrad-Martius' Ontological Phenomenology*, Dordrecht: Springer.

Hartmann, N. (1931), *Zum Problem der Realitätsgegebenheit* (On the Problem of the Givenness of Reality), Berlin: Pan Verlag.

Hartmann, N. (1957), *Kleinere Schriften*, Bd. 2 *Abhandlungen zur Philosophie-Geschichte* (Smaller Writings, Vol. 2 Essays on the History of Philosophy), Berlin, Boston: De Gruyter, 278–322.

Héring, J. (1921), "Bemerkungen über das Wesen, die Wesenheit und die Idee," (Remarks Concerning Essence, Ideal Quality, and Idea), *Jahrbuch für Philosophie und phänomenologische Forschung* 4: 497–543.

Husserl, E. (1973), *Experience and Judgement: Investigations in a Genealogy of Logic*, trans. K. Ameriks and J. S. Churchill, London: Routledge.

Husserl, E. (1983), *Ideas Pertaining to a Pure Phenomenology and to a Phenomenological Philosophy*, vol. 1, trans. F. Kersten, Den Haag: Nijhoff.

Husserl, E. (1994), *Briefwechsel*, (Correspondence), ed. K. Schuhmann, Dordrecht: Springer [Husserliana, Dokumente, 3].

Ingarden, R. (1925), "Essentiale Fragen. Ein Beitrag zu dem Wesensproblem" (On Essential Questions: A Contribution to the Essence Problem), *Jahrbuch für Philosophie und phänomenologische Forschung* 7: 125–304.

Ingarden, R. (1965), *Der Streit um die Existenz der Welt, Bd. 2.I* (The Controversy over the Existence of the World, Vol. 2.I), Tübingen: Niemeyer.

Ingarden, R. (1972a), "O pytaniach esencjalnych (1923)" (On Essential Questions) in R. Ingarden, *Z teorii języka i filozoficznych podstaw logiki* (From the theory of language and the philosophical foundations of logic), 328–482, Warszawa: PWN.

Ingarden, R. (1972b), *Das literarische Kunstwerk. Mit einem Anhang von den Funktionen der Sprache im Theaterschauspiel* (The literary work of art. With an appendix on the functions of language in theatrical play), Tübingen: Niemeyer.

Ingarden, R. (1975), *On the Motives Which Led Edmund Husserl to Transcendental Idealism*, trans. A. Hannibalsson, The Hague: Nijhoff [Phaenomenologica, 64].

Ingarden, R. (1992), *Einführung in Edmund Husserls Phänomenologie. Osloer Vorlesungen (1967)* (Introduction to Edmund Husserl's Phenomenology. Oslo Lectures (1967)), Tübingen: Niemeyer [Roman Ingarden Gesammelte Werke, 4].

Ingarden, R. (2013), *Controversy over the Existence of the World*, vol. I, trans. A. Szylewicz, Frankfurt am Main: Peter Lang.

Künne, W. (2003), "Are Questions Propositions?," *Revue internationale de philosophie* 224 (2): 45–56.

Mitscherling, J. (1997), *Roman Ingarden's Ontology and Aesthetics*, Ottawa: University of Ottawa Press.

Pfänder, A. (1921), "Logik" (Logic), *Jahrbuch für Philosophie und phänomenologische Forschung* 4: 139–494.

Piwowarczyk, M. (2020), "Roman Ingarden's Early Theory of the Object," W. Płotka and P. Eldridge (eds.), *Early Phenomenology in Central and Eastern Europe*, Dordrecht: Springer, 111–126.

Riska, A. (1976), "Language and Logic in the Work of Roman Ingarden," *Analecta Husserliana* 4: 187–218.

Ryle, G. (1927), "Roman Ingarden, Essentiale Fragen" (Roman Ingarden, On Essential Questions), [Review], *Mind* 36: 366–70.

Ryle, G. (1973), "Roman Ingarden, Essentiale Fragen" (Roman Ingarden, On Essential Questions), [Review], *Journal of the British Society for Phenomenology* 4(1): 72–5.

Sobota, D. (2013), "Fenomenologia Pytania. Daubert, Heidegger i Ingarden" (The phenomenology of the question. Daubert, Heidegger, and Ingarden), *Kwartalnik Filozoficzny* 41(1): 15–43.

Szuman, S. (1936a), "Letter to Roman Ingarden, 03.12.1936." Available online: http://ingarden.archive.uj.edu.pl/archiwum/list-od-stefana-szumana-z-03-12-1936 (accessed April 15, 2022).

Szuman, S. (1936b), "Postcard to Roman Ingarden, 10.11.1936." Available online: http://ingarden.archive.uj.edu.pl/archiwum/kartka-pocztowa-od-stefana-szumana-z-10-11-1936 (accessed April 15, 2022).

Śpiewak, R. (2002), "Kazimierza Ajdukiewicza i Romana Ingardena teorie pytań" (Kazimierz Ajdukiewicz's and Roman Ingarden's theories of questions), *Studia Philosophiae Christianae* 38(1): 69–82.

Witwicki, W. (1927), "Letter to Roman Ingarden, 27.03.1927." Available online: http://ingarden.archive.uj.edu.pl/archiwum/list-od-wladyslawa-witwickiego-z-27-03-1927 (accessed April 15, 2022).

4

Sounds and/or Tones? Scruton, Ingarden (. . . and Levinson) on Musical Aesthetics and Ontology

Edward M. Świderski

Does an ontology of music bring anything of substance to musical aesthetics? Does an adequate description of musical experience—arguably the main concern of musical aesthetics—require an account of what musical "works"[1] are? The point of such questions is to inquire into the distinctive intentionality of musical experience. Though perhaps too schematic, the following alternative comes to mind: (i) Is musical experience directed to sounds pressed into service to, among other things, encode "objective," extra-experiential musical organization ("works")?; or (ii) Is reference to musical organization shorthand for a subjective capacity—a specific intentionality—to discern *tonal patterns* within successions of sounds that sounds as such do not display? Overall, among philosophers of music the first alternative has predominated: to understand the distinctive character of musical experience we need to attend to its "objects" and their properties—be they real things or ideal things, or things within yet another category—and inquire how they shape that experience, what the conditions are for the experience to be judged adequate to the "objects." According to this line of thinking, ontology has the upper hand. There are dissenters, however, who believe that aesthetics—musical experience—should have pride of place to the detriment of ontology that they see as of minimal relevance for understanding our musical practices. A somewhat distant cousin of this dissent are historicist arguments to the effect that the Western concept of the musical work did not crystallize before the end of the eighteenth century as the "fine arts" achieved autonomy.[2] Here, too, ontology loses salience to the advantage of socioculturally mediated "experience" relative to established practices. However, the disquiet I want to examine here about whether musical aesthetics requires ontology stems not from historical considerations about the emergence of the work concept and the like but from the "phenomenology" of musical experience, broadly understood, as suggested by (ii) earlier. The aim is to inquire into the nature of music and by extension its manifestations, including so-called works, the leading questions being (i) whether that phenomenology sustains a distinction between sounds and tones?, and (ii) how would that distinction, if valid, impact the ontology-aesthetics issue?

One prominent philosopher of music who consistently defended the position that musical ontology is at best a peripheral concern without greater significance for musical aesthetics was Roger Scruton. Over the course of many publications, Scruton insisted that musical experience is not of sounds but of *tones*. Tones, he claimed, are nowhere else than *in* hearing enlivened by imagination in the absence of which we would be deaf to pitch, timbre, harmony, rhythm, and melodic line, the salient constituents of musical experience. Our capacity for musical experience is testimony to our ability to engage in a kind of projective experience largely indifferent to conceptual concerns—such as knowing what sounds are, how they occur, what causes them, and so on—without thereby being devoid of meaning. Are we not alive to and avidly follow the "rise and fall" of melodic line, often describing it in just such terms, all the while aware that we are not experiencing some "thing" literally moving from place to place along a trajectory within a kind of auditory analogue of worldly spacetime and causality? Scruton liked to speak in this connection of the experienced "virtual causality" of the musical line but was quick to add that such descriptions, indeed the very hearing itself, are not to be understood literally, as about facts of some kind. With Scruton, then, we have a philosopher of music who steadfastly adhered to the view that musical experience is to be understood from within, so to speak, rather than by reference to something without, in the world, from which it would draw its content and raison d'être as meaningful experience. The business of a philosophy of music consists in aesthetics, not ontology.[3]

Scruton's musical aesthetics has been characterized as phenomenological in the following sense.

> Scruton does not claim to *explain why* we understand music as we do but aims only to *describe what form* that understanding takes. (The question "*How* do we do that?" is here typically interpreted as "*What is it like* to do that?") This is in keeping with Scruton's broadly phenomenological approach... which conceives of the philosopher's task as making perspicuous the structures of experience and its intentional objects, rather than investigating their causal history. (Denham 1999: 417)

Although I suspect that Scruton bristled on learning that he had been inducted into the phenomenological camp,[4] there is a point to the inclusion that bears on the nature of tones. If we grant that his is, or closely approximates, a phenomenological account of musical experience as of tones, not sounds, is he then within his rights to set aside musical ontology as superfluous? Perhaps not. Roman Ingarden, a staunch advocate of phenomenology, would have largely seconded, I believe, many of Scruton's claims on behalf of a musical aesthetics based on tonal experience. However, Ingarden did, where Scruton did not, advance the cause of musical ontology so as to anchor tonal experience in an "objective" basis.[5] A tentative, initial statement of their differences could be the following. Scruton favored an internalist, intransitive, and anti-realist perspective on the nature of musical experience, a perspective he felt sure the nature of tones virtually dictated. This is of a piece with his insistence that musical hearing and description are by nature metaphorical.[6] Ingarden, by contrast, tended to an "externalist" perspective on musical experience. For him, musical experience is quintessentially of higher-order tonal organization, namely, created musical works.[7] Therefore, as musical experience is "of" something, a musical aesthetic cannot be complete in the absence of an account of the "objective" character of these structured tonal formations. In contrast to Scruton, then, Ingarden comes across as "realist" with respect to the sought-for "objectivity."[8]

One difficulty for Ingarden, however, has been that few, if any, Anglo-American philosophers subscribe to his account of that objectivity. The work for Ingarden is not something physical ("real"), nor something mental ("psychic"), nor finally an ideal something or other in the manner of, say, the types, norm-kinds, and the like to which contemporary musical ontologists have appealed. Instead, Ingarden assigned musical works, like artworks generally, to a realm of "purely intentional objects." Scruton, for one, could make little sense of this and characterized Ingarden's conception as a "metaphysical fantasy." True, Scruton concedes, "[t]here is nothing in the material world of sound that *is* the work of music. But this should not prompt those metaphysical fantasies that lead philosophers to situate the work in another world, or another dimension, or another level of being" (Scruton 1997: 108).[9]

Now, there are philosophers of music who, far from discounting musical aesthetics, nevertheless resist the sounds-tones duality and swear by musical ontology. They provide a valuable foil, then, in the attempt to gain a clear understanding of the ins and outs, the strengths and weaknesses, of views put forward by the likes of Scruton and Ingarden. An exemplary representative here is Jerrold Levinson.[10] It is fortunate for my purposes that Levinson produced a critical review of Scruton's central work in musical aesthetics in which he explains—to his satisfaction at least—in what Scruton's errors consist (Levinson 2000b). Levinson's main objection, we shall see, is that Scruton has fallen victim to a "phenomenological-idealist" perspective, a criticism which is nominally applicable, with certain caveats, to Ingarden as well.

I will consider the following points:

1. Levinson disputes Scruton's obsession with tones, regarding them instead as properties of sounds that are public objects, in the world. The challenge Levinson lays at Scruton's feet is to account for the "public" character of musical experience, a challenge that, on his reading of Scruton's "phenomenology," he is unable to meet. It is a weighty charge given how much effort Scruton expended in characterizing—and often criticizing—the extant musical *culture*![11]
2. Levinson is silent, however, on what is plausibly Scruton's nod to phenomenology, namely, that there is evidence for a so-called acousmatic experience. We have the ability, as Scruton and those he cites are certain, to attend to "pure" sounds separable from their worldly causes, thanks to which they can acquire properties—musical properties—that no succession of "mere" worldly sounds has. But would this alone be reason enough to claim that musical experience is confined to the inner life of the subject sensitive to tones? Levinson, in any case, read Scruton to be saying as much, which is why he charged him with phenomenological idealism.
3. We do not find in Ingarden any mention of acousmatic experience.[12] Instead, his presses into service[13] a phenomenology of tonal *qualities* which is reminiscent of Husserl's conception of *Spezie* and ideation, although another interpretation—a Gestalist view—is plausible as well. On either interpretation, when attending to an actual musical occurrence, that is, a performance of a musical work, we are said (to be able) to experience beyond what we hear *in concreto* to corresponding "pure" ("ideal") tone qualities. We hear the latter not as discrete units but as concatenated in "higher-order tone formations"—musical *Gestalten*. Ingarden toyed with fixing work identity by adverting to such qualitative structures that "transcend" yet inform all those occasions when we experience the "same" work. However, for any of this to happen, he places a necessary condition on the experiencing subject, namely, that he/

she be in the appropriate, that is, aesthetic, attitude. In the essay on the musical work, it remains unclear whether Ingarden meant that the auditor should adopt this attitude in advance, or whether he believes that it, so to say, "assails" the auditor in a sudden awakening of attention, a musical frisson, as some say.[14] Am I "struck by" and drawn to identify patterns of tonal qualities that transcend the concrete auditory events?[15] This idea does bear a degree of resemblance to Scruton's claim that we experience tones only because, and when, we fix on sounds without regard for their physical causes. He like Ingarden underscores how significant the change of attitude, the shift of attention, is for the very possibility of attending to music, although, unlike Ingarden, Scruton does not say that the acousmatic experience is "aesthetic apprehension." Be that as it may, does not Ingarden, by insisting on the centrality of the "aesthetic apprehension" of tonal formations, in fact, attribute pride of place to musical experience, notwithstanding his initial aim to clarify the ontology of the musical work? And if so, does he not fall victim as well to Levinson's objection to Scruton that insistence on (subjective) musical experience of tones purportedly distinct from sounds is unable to account for the public character of music?

We need to examine each of the foregoing points in more detail.

Ad.1. Levinson wrote of Scruton that he is a "tone-intoxicated man" whose philosophy of music is veritably "tone drunk" (Levinson 2000b). So inebriated was Scruton, it seems, that he failed to comprehend that although sounds do count as music, thanks to distinctive sorts of perceptual experiences, neither sounds nor the music they convey are *experiences*. That we hear *tonal properties of sounds* when we listen to music does not alter the fact that music is an objective public, cultural phenomenon, not sets of experiences.

Levinson characterizes Scruton-style "phenomenology" as heir to the Collingwoodian tradition of believing that artworks abide in the mind only and are but contingently related to artifacts of some sort. According to this way of thinking, although our access to a musical work may be *via* some organized noises "out there," the work itself, its intrinsic status as an aesthetic object, does not involve a constitutive connection to a mind-external artifact. Earlier, I noted that Levinson is silent about Scruton's fascination with acousmatic experience, thanks to which we are said to experience "pure sounds" separated from their worldly causes, an experience providing access to the perception of the "virtual causality" of tonal movement within a "musical field of force."[16] However, Levinson does offer an indirect, implicit criticism of the supposed import of acousmatic experience for musical aesthetics. For Scruton, that experience delivers tones free of timbre, that is, free of instrumental sounds, since instruments are among the worldly causes of sounds from which acousmatic experience allegedly frees us. In response, Levinson writes "*pace* Scruton, we do not normally hear musical tones in abstraction from how they are produced, oblivious to the human actions that generate them, not if we are interested in the full expressiveness that the music built upon such tones conveys" (Levinson 2000b: 613).[17] Although Scruton did not respond directly to the charges Levinson levels against him, he does have an answer of sorts to Levinson's objection:

> timbre, and tone-colour generally, presents no parallel system of musical organization, on a par with rhythm, melody, and harmony. Those last three weave the musical surface together and create the tonal space in which its movement is heard. Nothing will be lost if . . . we set timbre to one side . . . . (Scruton 1997: 77–8)

> In describing the timbre of a tone, we are not situating it in musical space; nor are we identifying anything essential to it as a musical individual. (Scruton 1997: 77–8)

For Scruton, then, there is no doubting the "phenomenological" basis of musical experience, namely, sounds heard free of their causes and imbued with meaning without purchase in the ambient world.

Ad. 2. Levinson's objection that Scruton's aesthetics rests on a subjective-idealist phenomenology in the Collingwoodian vein runs into trouble perhaps, at least if we take Scruton's statements of his own motives into account. For one thing, he took a dim view of Husserlian phenomenology, going so far as to say that Husserl's style of philosophizing is "proof of how philosophy should not be done (Scruton 2012: 8)."[18] Notwithstanding the severity of that remark, he did align himself with the "Brentano-Husserl concept of intentionality" according to which "intentionality is not an *addition* to a mental state, but a part of its structure" (Scruton 1997: 166). So understood, intentional consciousness does not consist of an "inner realm," the dwelling of a Cartesian subject. To back up his cause, Scruton invokes, on the one hand, Wittgenstein's arguments against the very idea of a "private language" as well as, on the other, Hegel's doctrine that "our inner life is realized in, and constituted by, its *Entäusserung* in social life" (Scruton 1997: 166). By appealing to these distinct philosophical paradigms Scruton hoped to sustain his conviction that we (are able to) perceive the physical events that are sounds in a way that invites and justifies the distinction between sounds and the music we hear in them. The task he set himself was to show how this "way of perceiving," however subjective it may seem at first to be, is after all "publicly recognizable, publicly teachable, part of a way of life and a culture" (Scruton 2012: 9)

Of the cluster of concepts Scruton mobilized to account for musical experience, namely, acousmatic experience, double intentionality ("hearing in"), imagination, sounds/tones, metaphorical hearing and description, cultural context, double intentionality is central. While hearing sounds (detached from their physical causes), we come to hear pitches, rhythm, tempi, and harmonies—the properties of tones—across the virtual causality of a musical line. One kind of hearing here, another there—double intentionality, each "prong" with a distinct import.[19] In the case of the sounds as such, our hearing is belief-laden, so to speak; we know and affirm that we are hearing sounds. With respect to tones "heard in" the sounds, the focus is of another kind, assimilable, Scruton's claims, to "entertaining" something non-assertively.

Consider an analogous case: Would it not be a pity to suppress the fun of seeing the elephant in the cloud? Would you not impoverish your experience by insisting that all you "see" is the cloud in the sky? Why deny the powers of imagination and how it may inform perception? Similarly, it would be a pity and would entirely miss the point if you chose to "understand" your musical experiences as being about no more than successions of sounds taken as mere acoustic phenomena (or even more implausibly: the effects of sound waves at frequencies to which the ear is sensitive but below or above the threshold of musical perception). Importantly, however, it's not all up to us: we learned standard and extended uses of the term "elephant" in commerce with others, thanks to which not only our standard linguistic practices, but also, allowing for the liberty shared imaginings enable, our common experience is enriched. So, is there any principled obstacle in getting your friend to see the elephant in the cloud?

Scruton's point is the same in the case of musical experience: though imagination is mandatory if there is to be musical experience at all, it draws on a store of public, cultural values about music that we share and communicate. Recall the task he set himself: to show how the musical experience is publicly recognizable, teachable, part of a way of life, a culture. He settled therefore on a "third person" account of consciousness and concludes "it is surely obvious that what we hear *in* sound depends upon the state of the musical culture, and this culture is a dynamic and developing thing" (Scruton 2012: 8)—which amounts to Scruton's answer to Levinson's charge that a "tone-intoxicated" philosophy of music fails to account for music's public character.

All these considerations underpin Scruton's firm position stated earlier: attempts to account for the numerical identity and individuation of musical works—that is, musical ontology—are largely "irrelevant."

> "[M]usical works are the intentional objects of musical perceptions, not the material objects of hearing. We hear sounds; but we also hear music *in* those sounds." In short: "Questions of ontology [. . .] are not questions of musical aesthetics." (Scruton 2012: 7)

Ad. 3. Earlier, I suggested that Scruton and Ingarden agree *de facto* on assigning pride of place to musical experience, notwithstanding Ingarden's declared purpose to provide an ontology of musical works. But just how far does this agreement reach? At the verbal level at least, Scruton would have largely seconded the following sentence by Ingarden: "it is extremely important to establish that the musical work as an object of aesthetic perception refers to no . . . real facts." Ingarden emphasizes the point: as an object of aesthetic apprehension, the musical work "is . . . no real event and no real object" (Ingarden 1989: 35). He precedes these remarks by noting that we hear all manner of sounds—he cites bird calls, dogs barking, car horns—as real events in the natural world. By contrast, "aesthetic apprehension" generally takes us out of the world of ordinary things, including mere sounds, such that experience of musical works, as the quoted sentences state, cannot be of something real (worldly). To this extent at least, Scruton's "hearing tones in sounds" appears to be largely of a piece with Ingarden's conviction that when we deal with musical works, we are no longer within the realm of worldly things.

But there is more. The importance Ingarden attributed to aesthetic experience stems in large measure from the significance he attaches to performance. Across the sections of his essay on the musical work, particularly in the last section ("The problem of the identity of the musical work"), Ingarden increasingly focuses his attention on performances, that is, how a work comes to be understood in the light of shifting performance practice and reception, such that by the end of his discussion strict work identity appears questionable. The work itself turns out to be no more than a kind of asymptote, an ideal, toward which past and present performance practices strive, with each successive phase typically modifying the perception and understanding of the work beyond narrow readings of scores, extant recordings, current critical evaluation, and the like.

In the essay, Ingarden was already working with the conception he deployed to great effect in the magisterial study devoted to the ontology of the literary work, namely, that an artwork is essentially a schematic, partly indeterminate construct that invites completion ("concretization"), now one way, now another, depending on how its determinate features and their interplay are perceived and balanced. In this respect, however, the musical work presents a challenge that the literary work, among others, does not. The latter, being at base a linguistic phenomenon of higher order, that is, a complex text, is, multi-stratified, with each stratum bringing specific qualities and demands to the readerly reception of the work (assuming, of course, a reader's fidelity to the text). By contrast, the musical work, Ingarden concludes, knows none of this complexity, it consists of but one stratum, that of tone formations as specified by a score, the rest being up to performance, more exactly, performance practices that, as they change over time, impact, and modify the aesthetic perception and understanding of the work. In this regard as well, Ingarden and Scruton have a point in common: although tones are not worldly sounds, and the works the former constitute are not "real" but "intentional" objects, performance practices are collective, cultural institutions that both rely on and shape public perception and understanding of the schematic musical work. Ingarden draws his argument to a close writing of a synthetic aesthetic object, "the intentional correlate of the opinion not of a single listener, but of a whole community of listeners," including performers of course, many of whom appreciate that access to music presupposes and depends on "aesthetic apprehension." Several points in this summary exposition deserve closer consideration.

First, the matter of work identity vis-à-vis performances and how in this regard Ingarden and Scruton do diverge. To ground the "same again" experience in our commerce with performances of musical works Ingarden affirms:

> When we hear [in a purely aesthetic attitude] a certain individual performance but attend to the work itself, we abstract, so to say, from the [individual] tones and tone formations which we are just then hearing [. . .]; we extract only the pure qualities of the tone formations from the individual concretum we are just then hearing. (Ingarden 1989: 36)

There are two possible ways to interpret this passage. One is to understand the pure tonal qualities and the operations—abstraction and extraction—to attain them along the lines of Husserl's conception of *Species* and ideation respectively, as put forward initially in his *Logical Investigations*. That Ingarden subscribed to this conception is clear: in his *Essentiale Fragen* (1925) (On Essential Questions) he enlists it to develop his conception of Ideas, the "contents" of which consist of "pure ideal qualities" (Ingarden's preferred terminology). The downside of this interpretation is that pure tonal qualities would thereby acquire the status of universals, that is, abstract objects outside the causal order. However, the tenor of Ingarden's essay on the musical work speaks against such a "Platonist" interpretation, a familiar difficulty of which is to account for the cultural, that is, created, status of musical works that Ingarden certainly recognized.[20] The second interpretation is more benign than the first, in that pure tonal qualities could be understood instead as perceptual (i.e., auditory) Gestalts, a term Ingarden does employ. Ingarden was no stranger to Gestalt theory,[21] often referring to how interconnected qualities give rise to a higher-order individual or "holistic" quality. This is how he characterizes "higher order tonal formations" immediately following the passage quoted earlier: "In the reciprocal qualitative modifications of the tone formations . . . and in the final quality of wholeness, unique in its kind, that results from this reciprocal qualitative modification, lies the sole basis of the individuality of a musical work" (Ingarden 1989: 37). All the same, doubts may linger as to how to understand this passage, whether it is to be read in terms of Gestalt psychology absent ontological overtones or as a piece of *a priori* essence-analysis of the kind Ingarden advocated in *Essentiale Fragen* (and earlier as well as later). In the end, Ingarden's talk of pure tonal qualities, what they are, how they are accessed, and what they are meant to accomplish in regard to the self-identity of the musical work remains underdeveloped and ambiguous.

Scruton puts forward a view about the identity of musical works that resonates favorably with Ingarden *in case* Ingarden's take on "pure tonal qualities" is read in the second, Gestaltist way:

> the identity of musical works is determined not by nature but by convention. The most convenient way of identifying them is as temporally ordered patterns of pitched sound. Whether we call such patterns "types" or "kinds," or whether we identify them as abstract individuals . . . is a matter of indifference . . . What matters is that such patterns can be "realized" in performance [. . .] [I]t is enough to recognize that a performance aims to present the particular pattern as an object of intrinsic interest (Scruton 1997: 441).

We can safely assume that Ingarden would raise doubts about Scruton's lack of concern about the category to which musical works belong, but *if* his conception of the pure tonal qualities is read in Gestalist terms, Scruton's "patterns of pitched sounds" come out very much like Ingarden's higher-order tone formations in-the-hearing, in which case worries about work identity indeed do recede. On this reading, Ingarden's "abstraction" and "extraction" of pure tone qualities highlight performance and its aesthetic significance for musical understanding.

Ingarden does differ from Scruton in one aspect (and in this he would agree with Levinson, see earlier): the aesthetic contribution of performance to the appreciation of a musical passage does include the quality of the instrumental sounds—the timbre of the instrument—for which the passage is scored. But the salient point concerns the role of performance, and on this Scruton and Ingarden largely agree. Scruton writes:

> [T]he aim of the performance is not merely to produce a particular pattern of pitches, but to present those pitches as music, *and therefore to make whatever additions and adjustments are required by a musical understanding* [italics added—EMS]. Performance is the art of translating instructions [codified in the score—EMS] to produce certain *sounds* into an organization of *tones*. (Scruton 1997: 441; italics added by the author)

In this assertion, Scruton addresses what Ingarden considers to be the aesthetic issue of importance, namely, how performance "concretizes" the musical potential of music. I noted earlier that over the course of his essay Ingarden focuses increasingly on how musical practices impact the perception and appreciation of music, such that finally no definite line, no fast and firm arbiter of work identity, ontologically speaking, in relation to performances, can or need be laid down. The phrase I highlighted in Scruton's passage concerning "additions and adjustments" as required for "musical understanding" conveys as well, I submit, the significance Ingarden attributes to aesthetically meaningful performance ("concretization"). He says of the musical work that we must not regard it merely a schematic trunk encoded in a score and whose indeterminacies need to be completed, now this way, now that with an eye (sic! . . . an ear) to coherence and harmony, but rather as "the formation determined by the score, but with its full content, that is, together with the possibilities for filling out its places of indeterminacy . . . taken in their potentiality" (Ingarden 1989: 114–15). This talk of possibility and potentiality together with full content is not easy to grasp. From the context of the passage, it appears that Ingarden is wobbling between a strict sense of work identity—he writes of a "philosophical" concept involving "an unchanging object and a constant stock of possibilities" (Ingarden 1989: 114–15)—and another one corresponding to how a work is actually experienced in changing circumstances of reproduction, reception, namely, as "an object enduring in historical time that slowly, yet inevitably changes" (Ingarden 1989: 114–15). Where the former "philosophical" conception can be called strongly structural, that is, ontological, the latter is relative to aesthetic experience in the same sense in which Scruton writes about the "*intrinsic interest*" we invest in tonal patterns, even going so far as to add more features than the pattern as such specifies for the sake of musical understanding, that is, aesthetic satisfaction. This suggests a plausible way to disambiguate Ingarden's talk of "possibilities" and "potentiality" in the quoted passage: the "structural" possibilities to fill out what the score leaves indeterminate are subordinated to purely aesthetic potentiality resonating with how a work is understood at a given time relative to extant musical practices and the range of values a community happens to ascribe to music. Earlier, I drew attention to Ingarden's view that a musical work is communally experienced as an intersubjective aesthetic object that undergoes change "when the givens of musical experience change, for example, as a consequence of a change of taste" (Ingarden 1989: 119). And this leads Ingarden to opine that there is a sense in which, in view of changing performance practices and shifting intersubjective conceptions of a work as aesthetic object, the work *as such* may be thought of as a transcendent "ideal" (Ingarden 1989: 110) never ultimately exhausted in its aesthetic potential.[22]

Conclusion

At the outset, I raised the question, does a musical aesthetic require a musical ontology, that is, a statement concerning the nature, properties, and mode of existence of musical works? I situated the space of the discussion that followed in the distinction—argued for explicitly by Scruton, less explicitly by Ingarden—between sounds and tones, and called on phenomenology, broadly speaking, to adjudicate whether the distinction holds water and how it impacts the initial question. I brought in Levinson as a foil in that he roundly rejects the distinction, charging those who advance it with succumbing to idealism—music is not simply musical experience—and ignoring the public, objective status of music (and musical works). Over the course of the discussion, it has become quite clear that the onus falls on having to demonstrate that there is an "acousmatic" experience (Scruton) that provides access to the realm of tonality and/or "aesthetic apprehension" of pure tones (Ingarden), where in both cases the claim is that what we experience musically is no "real" object but something "imaginary" (Scruton) and/or an "ideal," an asymptote read out of performance practices (Ingarden). Scruton discounts ontology altogether as a misguided search for the strict numerical identity of a chimera, and Ingarden, notwithstanding his probing, finally relinquishes strict identity in favor of a historical account of work identity, a kind of ongoing communal cultural plebiscite over the course of shifts—Scruton's "adjustments and additions"—in musical practice and the influence these exert on aesthetic understanding. The answer to the initial question, therefore, is that, if we agree that musical experience is directed to tonality, not sounds, then musical ontology, to the extent that it has anything to contribute to musical understanding conveyed in practice, is but a distant cousin to aesthetics.

Notes

1. Although the "works" here will be those familiar from the canon of Western "artmusic," does that thereby exclude the simple ditty, humming under one's nose, maybe even running through a tune in one's head—are these not musical experiences as well?
2. Cf. Goehr (1992) and Kristeller (1951).
3. For the purposes of this chapter, I have consulted several of Scruton's publications. In chronological order: *Art and Imagination* (1974) (2015); *The Aesthetic Understanding* (1983) (hereafter *AU*); *The Aesthetics of Music* (1997); *Understanding Music. Philosophy and Interpretation* (2009); "In Search of the Aesthetic" (2007); "Working Towards Art" and "A Guarded Response" (2012).
4. His source of inspiration regarding the nature of the aesthetic is mainly Kant. Scruton's final statement to this effect is his "In Search of the Aesthetic" (2007).
5. The reference is to "The musical work" (1989).
6. I choose not to dwell in detail on Scruton's thesis—controversial as it has been—that not only the (linguistic) description of musical experience but the experience as such is metaphorical. Malcolm Budd, Nick Zangwill, Paul Boghossian, among others, have queried the plausibility and cogency of this view.
7. Ingarden did not examine musical experience per se, that is, he did not ask "what is music"; he fixed attention on the musical work. Scruton considered musical awareness to be a mode of consciousness sensitive to tonality, the most salient manifestation of which is in musical works.
8. I acknowledge that talk of "realism" in this context could be confusing; this is not epistemological realism tied to a truth-functional semantics. From the perspective adopted here, it must be said that Ingarden sometimes muddies the water when he writes, for example, "sounds *or* tones," as if it were simply up to us to prefer what to hear when listening to music. For example: "Every individual musical work is a formation consisting of various phases, in which *tonal or sonic qualities* . . . constitute the fundamental moments of the work" (Ingarden 1989: 47; italics added—EMS). Moreover, to clarify the matter in general, we would have to examine

the several meanings of "transcendence" Ingarden distinguishes, that is, the different ways in which objects ("things") and mere intentional objects "transcend" perceptual and other acts (e.g., by not being "proper parts" of the intentional act). (Cf Ingarden's Oslo lectures: Ingarden 1992/2012, lecture six in particular.) When Scruton, for example, tells us that our musical hearing is "metaphorical," involving imagination only, is he putting in doubt any "transcendence?" In Ingarden's case, the issue is further complicated by his conception of "aesthetic apprehension," the aesthetic attitude, about which more below.

9   Peter Kivy, in his review of the first English translation of Ingarden's essay, found it hard to understand what Ingarden had in mind by his claim that musical works are "intentional objects." Kivy charges Ingarden with ambiguity and vacillation on the key point of a musical work's identity over and against performances thereof. Cf. Kivy (1987).

10 The reference is to Levinson's early work, *Music, Art, and Metaphysics. Essays in Philosophical Aesthetics* (1990).

11 Never was the cultural dimension of music—in an axiological sense—absent in Scruton's analyses and reflections. The last chapter of *The Aesthetics of Music*, simply entitled "Culture," is representative of his vision.

12 Once again because he did not examine musical experience per se. See note 7.

13 He nowhere says so; this is my conclusion.

14 I borrow the expression "musical frisson" from Jerrold Levinson (2000a). Ingarden first elaborated his concept of aesthetic experience and its objects in the initial 1937 Polish text of *On the cognition of the literary work of art*, expanded later in the first German edition of 1962. Ingarden wrote of the "originary emotion" (ger. *Ursprungsemotion*), an experience which, according to him, entirely modifies a subject's ordinary experience, virtually transporting her into an aesthetic "attitude." There is not sufficient textual evidence in the 1928 essay on the musical work to affirm that he was already thinking of musical experience in such heady terms.

15 Ingarden is content to speak of a quality triggering this emotion, but he is non-committal as to whether the quality belongs to the category of expressive or simply descriptive properties.

16 Scruton's extended treatment of the acousmatic experience—a notion taken over from Pierre Schaeffer—is in his (1997), especially Chapter 2, "Tone," pp. 19-79. He later condensed the presentation in the early chapters of (2009), "Introduction" and "Sounds."

17 Andy Hamilton (2007), Chapter 4, while conceding Scruton's point about acousmatic experience, nevertheless insists that the timbral dimension is essential to it.

18 As an example of Husserl's style Scruton cites, *The Phenomenology of Internal Time Consciousness*. Scruton declared his dislike of phenomenology as earliy as in his

1974 dissertation (1974), first in the Introduction and later in Part II in the sections devoted to the imagination. The general tenor of his criticisms is that Husserl was perhaps on to something, but his phrasing it makes his views largely unintelligible. Much more to Scruton's liking was Sartre's *L'imaginaire*.

19 "Double intentionality arises when a mental state involves both belief and imagination: the first focused on realities, the second on what can be imagined in those realities. And because they belong to different orders of mental organization, beliefs and imaginings can co-exist, with a common focus, so that the one informs and controls the other; that, in short, is the origin of the 'double intentionality' that governs our experience of art" (Scruton 2009: 45).

20 This is perhaps not quite so clear. For one thing, Ingarden spoke almost mystically about the reasons why we create cultural entities such as artworks: we do so to bring "down to earth," so to speak, values that we do not create but sense their transcendent presence. He tells us that we live in "two worlds," that of nature and culture, which is properly human. However, the human world, culture, is pervaded by a sense of "higher powers" that we invoke when we speak of the True, the Good, the Beautiful, and, Ingarden adds, Justice. In addition, Ingarden discerns "metaphysical qualities" in great works of literature and comes to the conclusion that the ultimate foundation of the literary work consists in transcendent ideal concepts (Ingarden 1973: §66; 1983).

21 Later, in his study of the literary work of art, Ingarden has recourse to the Gestalt concept to clarify "word sounds," basically "tokens-of-a-type" that crystalize over time in a cultural setting (Ingarden 1973: 34–5). Are his "pure tonal qualities"—the "same tones" on different occasions of hearing a given musical passage—analogues of word sounds?

22 This surely can apply only to so-called masterworks of the musical canon, the paradigmatic examples of the musical art. Scruton's—and, for instance, Adorno's—lamentations concerning the steady decline in musical sensitivity and taste show the degree to which Ingarden was indeed idealizing the aesthetics of music, in a sense that is certainly Romantic.

References

Denham, A. E. (2009), "The Future of Tonality," *British Journal of Aesthetics* 49(4): 427–50.
Goehr, L. (1992), *The Imaginary Museum of Musical Works*, Oxford: Oxford University Press.
Hamilton, A. (2007), *Aesthetics and Music*, London: Continuum.
Ingarden, R. (1973), *The Literary Work of Art*, Evanston: Northwestern University Press.

Ingarden, R. (1983) "Man and Nature," trans. A. Szylewicz, in R. Ingarden, *Man and Value*, 17–21, München: Philosophia Verlag.
Ingarden, R. (1989), "The Musical Work," in R. Ingarden, *Ontology of the Work of Art*, trans. R. Meyer and J. T. Goldwait, 3–136, Athens: Ohio University Press.
Ingarden, R. (1992), *Einführung in die Phänomenologie Edmund Husserls* (Introduction to Edmund Husserl's phenomenology), Gesammelte Werke, Bd. 4, Tübingen: Max Niemeyer Verlag.
Kivy, P. (1987), "Review of *The Work of Music and the Problem of Its Identity* by Roman Ingarden," *Journal of Aesthetics and Art Criticism* 45(4): 413–15.
Kristeller, P. (1951), "The Modern System of the Arts," *Journal of the History of Ideas* 12: 496–527 and 13: 17–46.
Levinson, J. (1990), *Music, Art, and Metaphysics*, Ithaca and Cornell: Cornell University Press.
Levinson, J. (2000a), "Musical Frissons," *Revue française d'études américaines*, No. 86, *Aspects de l'esthétique* américaine: 64–76.
Levinson, J. (2000b), "Review of the *Aesthetics of Music* by Roger Scruton," *Philosophical Review* 109(4): 608–14.
Scruton, R. (1974), *Art and Imagination. A Study in the Philosophy of Mind*, London: Methuen.
Scruton, R. (1983), *The Aesthetic Understanding*, London: St Augustine's Press.
Scruton, R. (1997), *The Aesthetics of Music*, Oxford: Oxford University Press.
Scruton, R. (2007), "In Search of the Aesthetic," *The British Journal of Aesthetics* 47(3): 232–50.
Scruton, R. (2009), *Understanding Music: Philosophy and Interpretation*, London: Continuum.
Scruton, R. (2012), "Working toward Art" and "A Guarded Response," in *Scruton's Aesthetics*, ed. A. Hamilton and N. Zangwil, London: Palgrave-Macmillan.
Świderski, E. M. (2020), "Ingarden and the Quandary of Musical Ontology," in *Roman Ingarden and His Times*, ed. D. Czakon, N. A. Michna, and L. Sosnowski, 239–54, Kraków: Księgarnia Akademicka.

Part II

Aesthetics

5

Lipps, Stein, and Ingarden on Empathy and the Coexperiencing of Value in the Aesthetic Experience

Jeff Mitscherling

Introduction

Roman Ingarden describes the aesthetic experience, which he refers to as a "relatively complicated process" (Ingarden 1973b: 181), as developing through a series of increasingly complex emotional and cognitive states and activities and culminating in the appearance of an aesthetic object that possesses significant aesthetic properties, that is, aesthetic values. While Ingarden's lengthy description of this process of the aesthetic experience in his *Cognition of the Literary Work of Art* is extraordinarily rich in insights, it must be acknowledged that it is also extraordinarily difficult to comprehend as a whole. In this chapter, I examine features of his account that, despite its rigor and detail, still remain somewhat nebulous. I'll be focusing on his remarks concerning empathy, emotional coexperiencing, and the aesthetic encounter with value, examining what some of Ingarden's predecessors and contemporaries had been saying about these and similar concepts. Particularly important in this regard are Theodor Lipps and Edith Stein. Stein's criticisms of Lipps's account of empathy provided the starting point for the development of the view she presents in *The Problem of Empathy*, and it was in response to Lipps that she formulated the most distinctive features of her position. As we shall see, Ingarden too adopted significant features of Lipps's account in his own description of what he called the "emotional coexperiencing of psychological occurrences of portrayed persons" (1973b: 237) in our cognition of the literary work of art.

Theodor Lipps on Imitation, Projection, and Empathy

In a passage about two-thirds of the way through §24 of *Cognition of the Literary Work of Art*, "The Aesthetic Experience and the Aesthetic Object," Ingarden is discussing the fifth of seven "most important traits of the structure of the aesthetic experience" (Ingarden 1973b: 187), namely, the "forming of the apprehended qualities in categorial structures" (Ingarden 1973b: 202). "Here," Ingarden writes, "in the process of imputing a new subject of attributes to the given qualities, takes place what Theodor Lipps probably has in mind when he speaks of 'empathy' [*Einfühlung*] and of 'aesthetic reality' [*aesthetische Wirklichkeit*] as a correlate of empathy" (Ingarden 1973b: 203). In his footnote to this sentence Ingarden observes that "Lipps means by 'empathy' very diverse phenomena and subjective activities, which he does not distinguish from one another. It is not possible to sort this out here. I should like, however, to emphasize that, when I speak of 'empathy' here, I mean only one kind of the facts which Lipps covers with this expression" (Ingarden 1973b: 203n.31). We should make two observations here. First, Ingarden is critical of Lipps's failure to make distinctions among "very diverse phenomena" and subjective activities in his description of empathy; and second, Ingarden does appear to be admitting into his own account "one kind of the facts" described by Lipps. When we turn to descriptions offered by Lipps, we can easily identify at least some of the "facts" that Ingarden finds admissible.

In the description of empathy in his 1903 book *Leitfaden der Psychologie* (*Introduction to Psychology*), Lipps offers the following brief descriptions of parts of the *operation*[1] of empathy:

> In truth there is only *one* possibility of explanation: My understanding of the life-expressions [e.g. expressions of joy, happiness, sorrow, etc.] of another has its ground in, on the one hand, the instinctive drive [*im instinktiven Triebe*] to imitation and, on the other hand, the instinctive drive to express my own psychic experiences in a particular manner.
>
> In every case, however, I experience the affect or its drive to consummation as directly bound to or belonging to the perceived gesture. That is, it is *felt into* the gesture [*Er ist in die Gebärde* eingefühlt]. If the drive to consummate the affect accords to my own nature, then the empathy is positive or sympathetic [*sympathische*]. If my own nature is opposed to it, then it is negative or antipathetic [*antipathische*] empathy. (Lipps 1903: 193; my translation)

Using a few terms drawn from some of his other accounts, we can attempt the reassembly of this portion of Lipps's view of empathy as follows: the behavior that we observe of another, be this the ongoing behavior of a living person or the "captured" behavior represented in, say, a painting may be expressive, and this instance of expression may be emotionally significant or "suggestive"—it may, that is, be a "life-expression" of joy, sorrow, or whatever. This expression "infuses" into me (as Hume might say)[2] a corresponding affect, a positive or negative response that I'm capable of experiencing by virtue of an innate impulse to imitate the emotionally significant suggestion, which I am then driven by another innate impulse to express outwardly not in my own physical or gestural behavior, but in my projection of the emotionally significant content (of the "internalized" response) into the gestural behavior of the other person that initiated this process. And this entire process of inward and outward "movements" is referred to as "empathy," which is "positive empathy" if this process accords to my nature and "negative empathy" if it is opposed to my nature. If this is a case of positive empathy—if, that is, it is fully in accord with my own nature—I will lose myself in that experience of the emotional significance to such an extent that the distinction between myself and the other will vanish, and a "oneness" with the other will be experienced.

This quick look at Lipps's position suffices to direct us to two of its most distinctive features, namely, the concept of *projection* and what Stein will refer to as "the expression of experiences." To repeat: if another's gesture (or gestural behavior) appears to us as emotionally significant, a natural instinct drives us (first) to imitate that gesture and thereby experience that emotion for ourselves, and then (second) to project outward onto the behavior of the other the emotion that we are feeling—that is, to "feel [the emotion] into" the other's gesture or behavior. What I'm feeling when I do this is not the other's feeling but *my own* feeling projected into the other, with whom, if this projection is consummated, I subsequently identify myself in what Lipps calls *complete* empathy, which is essentially the disappearance of the self: the self and the other become one in the experience of the emotion.

While he may strongly disagree with Lipps's view of "complete empathy," Ingarden does find at least some features of his account attractive. In fact, the following passage from Lipps's 1905 paper "Empathy and Aesthetic Pleasure" largely reads as if Ingarden himself had been the author. Here's the first sentence:

> Whoever speaks of empathy and wishes to take part in the controversy about it ought first of all to know what it means to be giving something aesthetic attention, to know how to distinguish aesthetic experience from the experiencing of those things that occur in the real world, to know that one must not designate this

experiencing with any term that reminds us of the experience which practical life and the context of reality force upon us. (Lipps 1905: 411–12)

The necessity of separating aesthetic attention from everyday attention, and the aesthetic experience from our practical life and reality, had been common to aesthetic theory since at least the early days of the romantic period in English literature when Coleridge wrote of the "willing suspension of disbelief [in the non-reality of the represented world]."[3] In *The Literary Work of Art* Ingarden calls this the "disposition of reality acceptance" that arises from the adoption of an "aesthetic attitude." He writes: "It is precisely this disposition for a reality acceptance that never reaches serious consummation, that is always held back at the last moment, as it were, that forms the special nature of the aesthetic attitude and carries with it that unique stimulation we get from dealing with works of art in general and with literary works in particular" (Ingarden 1973a: 342). Ingarden would also agree with much of what Lipps says later in this same passage, although he would probably want to challenge Lipps on a couple of points. Here's the remainder of the passage in Lipps:

> In attending to something aesthetically, I remove it into an ideal realm, or I turn it into a self-contained ideal world. Even the aesthetic inspection of reality, of the real landscape, for example, makes a picture or an image of it. It releases it from the actual, from the context of reality and makes it into an ideal object. I must ignore the fact that it belongs to the humdrum context of reality, which I also inhabit, and that I may be helped or harmed by it. It is quite otherwise for what is represented in the work of art. This inherently and without any effort of mine belongs to an ideal sphere, precisely because it is something represented. It is inherently a picture, an image . . . the work of art leads me and forces me, the observer, to step out of and beyond myself, and the more it deserves the name of a work of art the more forcibly it does so, immersing me and confining me wholly in an ideal world. To the degree that it does this, the art work leads me and compels me to observe this world, the world of representation, to glimpse in its depths what usually escapes me in the observation of reality. The work of art not only reveals all this but illuminates it brilliantly. (Lipps 1905: 412)

An obvious problem arises with Lipps's use of the term "ideal," which, for Ingarden, is correctly to be applied only to that which neither comes into being nor ceases to be and therefore simply doesn't apply to the world representationally brought into being in a work of art.[4] The second point of disagreement concerns the extent to which I, "the observer," really do "step out of and beyond myself," and whether I am in fact immersed in and wholly confined to the world represented in the work of art. Ingarden doesn't go as far as Lipps in this regard. In fact, Ingarden seems almost to be pointing to an inconsistency in Lipps's account. Recall the passage from *The Literary Work of Art* cited earlier: in order for our aesthetic experience to unfold and realize its "special nature," our disposition for reality acceptance—that is, our suspension of disbelief—must never reach "serious consummation," but must be "always held back at the last moment, as it were." Only by drawing the line between the represented world of the work of art and the real, everyday world that we inhabit is it possible for us fully to take advantage of the unique opportunity that we're being presented in this encounter. This is the aesthetic principle that Edward Bullough named "psychical distance" in a famous paper in the *British Journal of Psychology* in 1912, in which he writes:

> Distance . . . is obtained by separating the object and its appeal from one's own self, by putting it out of gear with practical needs and ends. . . . But it does not mean that the relation between the self and the object is broken to the extent of becoming "impersonal" . . . On the contrary, it describes a *personal* relation, often highly emotionally colored, but *of a peculiar character*. Its peculiarity lies in that the personal character of the relation has been, so to speak, filtered. It has been cleared of the practical, concrete nature of its appeal . . . One of the best-known examples is to be found in our attitude towards the events and characters of the drama. (Bullough 1912: 91).[5]

Ingarden would entirely agree with Bullough that it is only by virtue of establishing and maintaining psychical distance between ourselves (the observers or readers) and the persons inhabiting the world represented on stage (or on screen or in the text) that a personal and emotionally significant relation is possible. As we'll see in a moment, by replacing the observer encountering a representation with a person encountering another person, Stein brought to our attention the necessity of the other not only for the creation of intersubjectivity but also for our own achievement of self-knowledge.

Edith Stein on Empathy and the Recognition of Value

In her *Life in a Jewish Family* (posthumously subtitled *An Unfinished Autobiographical Account*), Stein recounts that she had started her university studies in Göttingen in the summer semester of 1913 and had immediately applied for acceptance in Husserl's lecture course on "Nature and Spirit."[6] After speaking with her personally, Husserl happily allowed her to take the course—it was standard practice at the time that a student apply to the professor personally for admission—and it was toward the end of that same semester that she approached Husserl regarding his possible supervision of her doctoral dissertation. He was surprised at this because, as Stein explains, "He was accustomed to having people study under him for years before they dared to attempt an independent thesis" (Stein 1986: 268). After a bit of discussion, Husserl agreed to supervise her dissertation. And as Stein recounts:

> Now the question needed to be settled: what did I want to work on? I had no difficulty in this. In his course on nature and spirit, Husserl had said that an objective outer world could only be experienced intersubjectively, i.e., through a plurality of perceiving individuals who relate in a mutual exchange of information. Accordingly, an experience of other individuals is a prerequisite. Husserl named this experience *Einfühlung*, in connection to the works of Theodor Lipps, but he didn't speak about what it consists of. Here was a lacuna to be filled; therefore, I wished to examine what empathy might be. The Master found this suggestion not bad at all. However, almost immediately, I was given another bitter pill to swallow: he required that, as format for the dissertation, I use that of analytical dialogue with Theodor Lipps. He liked to have students clarify, in their assignments, the relation of phenomenology to the other significant directions current in philosophy. This was not *his* forte. He was too occupied with his own thoughts to take time for comparative study of others. And whenever he demanded that of us, he found us as unwilling. He used to say, with a smile: "I educate my students to be systematic philosophers and then I'm surprised that they dislike any tasks that have to do with the history of philosophy."
>
> At first he was inexorable. Though it went against the grain, I had to make a thorough study of the long list of works by Theodor Lipps (Stein 1986: 269, with minor revisions to J. Koeppel's translation from the German).

Unlike the other authors whose positions she examined (with the possible exceptions of Lipps and Scheler), Stein's approach in her PhD dissertation was entirely in line with the phenomenologists' imperative to go "back to the things themselves."[7] The "thing itself" in this case was the experience of empathy— her *personal experience* of empathy—and to examine this clearly she had first to clear away the conceptual prejudices of previous "investigations," and most importantly those pursued in, or based upon, the studies of the new, empirically oriented psychology. Lipps himself had treated empathy as an act of cognition— he presented his treatment of empathy in the final chapter of the "Cognition" section of his *Introduction to Psychology*—and Stein's criticisms of Lipps are accordingly restricted largely to its cognitional aspects, which she deals with in the first of the three chapters of *On the Problem of Empathy*. However, as she explains in *Life in a Jewish Family*: "In the first section [of the dissertation], based on some indications from Husserl's lectures, I had examined the act of 'empathy' as a particular act of cognition. After that, however, I went on to something which was personally close to my heart and which continually occupied me anew in all later works: the constitution of the human person" (Stein 1986: 397).[8] The commentators have tended to concentrate on this portion of Stein's treatment of the cognitional aspects of empathy, yet the material presented in the two chapters that follow strikes me as far more significant. It's here, after all, that she addresses, as she puts it, "The question of how the objects in the usual theories, such as the psycho-physical individual, personality, etc., arise within consciousness" (Stein 1964: 35).

In the first chapter of *On the Problem of Empathy*, while Stein tells us that her description of empathy agrees in many respects with that offered by Lipps, she proceeds to offer numerous criticisms of his position, including the following: (i) she rejects Lipps's claim that empathy originates in (or even involves) an innate impulse to imitate the gestural behavior of another; (ii) she dismisses Lipps's argument that our own "I" disappears in the act of empathy into a unity, or "oneness," with the "foreign 'I'"—that is, in the act of empathy there occurs "the full experiencing of foreign experience"; and (iii) she rejects the further claim [following from (ii)] that the experience of our act of empathy has the same object as that of the experience of the person with whom we empathize; for Stein, the object of our act of empathy is the other's experience, not the object of the other's experience: empathy is an act "in which foreign experience is grasped" (Stein 1964: 6). These three central criticisms of Lipps's account, along with many others, are further developed in the context of the second and third chapters of her book. At the opening of the second chapter, Stein's frustration with the authors of the existing literature on empathy becomes obvious. She remarks that "the investigations of empathy so far could not be satisfactory because . . . these thinkers have overlooked [the] basic questions" regarding "how the objects in the usual theories, such as the psycho-physical individual, personality, etc., arise within consciousness." Here, again targeting Lipps in particular, she adds:

> This is very clear in Lipps who has certainly achieved the most toward our goal. He seems to be bound by the phenomenon of the expression of experiences. . . . With a few words he lays aside the profusion of questions present in the treatment of this problem. For instance, he says about the conveyor of these phenomena of

expression, "We believe a conscious life to be bound to certain bodies by virtue of an 'inexplicable adjustment of our mind' or a 'natural instinct.'"

This is nothing more than the proclamation of wonder, declaring the bankruptcy of scientific investigation. And if science is not permitted to do this, then especially not philosophy. (Stein 1964: 35)

In her second and third chapters, Stein confronts these "basic questions" head-on. Her discussions of (i) the constitution of the "I" (or ego) and its "selfness" and (ii) the constitution of the world in which the "I" encounters the other are the most suggestive features of her account with regard to the aesthetic experience, so we'll focus on them in what follows. We have to begin, however, with a word of caution. As she wrote to Ingarden (in a letter from Freiburg dated April 27, 1917) (Stein 1993: 15; German text 1991: 52–3):

> I, too, am aware that the concept of the psyche is not yet clearly developed [in *On the Problem of Empathy*]. That will be possible only when the concept of the intellect has been completely clarified. There, too, a whole lot is missing (although the Fourth Part [i.e., "Empathy as the Comprehension of Mental Persons"] is the only thing I produced *con amore*)
>
> Moreover if the psyche [concept] has not been clearly explained in my work so far, it is by no means clearer in Scheler's. (Stein 1993: 15; German text Stein 1991: 52–3)

While her treatment of it remains incomplete, what she does tell us about the psyche is provocative with regard to empathy and the aesthetic experience. The selfness of the I—its experienced individuality or identity—is, she writes, "first brought into relief in contrast with another when another is given" (Stein 1964: 36), and every I is characterized by an "inviolable unity" characterizing the stream of consciousness qualifying the ongoing experience of the I. Were I to "lose myself" in the experience of empathy—that is, were I to become "one" with another as Lipps suggested—both "my" stream of consciousness and the experience of my own identity would be disrupted to such an extent that no experience could be possible at all.

Now, while we all exist as psychophysical individuals, each with our own unifying self-identical stream of consciousness, our day-to-day experience proceeds in a social world we share with others, the world of practices and institutions embodying the cultural values of our society. This social-cultural world embodies basic values that have been intersubjectively established, shaped, and molded over time. These include those values that are operative in our conscious choices and decisions, and also those values that lie so deep in our institutions and behavior that they rarely attract our attention. These values necessarily inform our own behavior as well as our understanding of the behavior of others, our grasping of the meanings of their actions, their intentions, and their motivations. Our effort to understand our fellow inhabitants of this social world is Stein's general topic in the third chapter of her book, "Empathy as the Comprehension of Mental Persons," and her basic claim is that it is through empathy that we are able to perceive the operative *values* informing the behavior of the other, so it is empathy that ultimately underlies our recognition of the mental life of the other. As she explains:

> I can be skeptical myself and still understand that another sacrifices all his earthly goods to his faith. I see him behave in this way and empathize a value experiencing as the motive for his conduct. The correlate of this is not accessible to me, causing me to ascribe to him a personal level I do not myself possess. In this way I empathically gain the type of *homo religiosus* by nature foreign to me, and I understand it even though what newly confronts me here will always remain unfulfilled. (Stein 1964: 104–5)

The correlate of the other's act of "sacrificing" all of his stuff is the value that here functions as the principle in accordance with which the other acts as he does. I do not possess this value, it is not accessible to me; it subsists at a level of the person that I do not encounter within myself. So I simply "ascribe" that level to the other, and in so doing, I gain indirect access to a level of personhood that I would not otherwise enjoy, and I am thereby enabled to "understand" it, although it is "by [my] nature" foreign to me. To recall my previous brief description of Stein's concept of empathy, we can see that when she writes that she empathizes "a value experiencing as motive for ... conduct," she is remaining consistent with her view that through empathy, we experience not the *object* of another's experience but, rather, that experience as a whole: the object of *our* experience is the experience of the other, not the *object of* the experience of the other.

Before leaving Stein, and looking ahead to the more focused treatment of the aesthetic experience, I'll quote one more very brief passage from another of her works that will prove helpful: in *Philosophy of Psychology and the Humanities*, speaking of objective (material) and subjective (personal) values, Stein remarks:

> personal values, like all values in general (the existential values excepted) have substance independently of the existence of their carrier. They can be experienced in fictive carriers just as well as in real carriers, and either way they deploy their full efficacy in the experiencing individual. Those values correspond

to attitudes whose contents have an invigorating power intrinsic to them. The beauty of a figure that I behold ignites in me the enthusiasm that spurs me to artistic creation. The hero of an epic poem fills me with admiration, and out of that admiration the urge wells up to emulate him. In both cases the experienced values are not only motives that prescribe the direction of my deed, but at the same time they furnish the propellant power that it requires. (Stein 2000: 216)

For Stein, intersubjectively established values are constitutive not only of our social life world but also of artworks, both in their creation and in their reception by an audience. Art is clearly a cultural institution that embodies our values, so we should certainly suspect that we'll see our values represented in that art, and even as motivating the behavior of the characters that we may find represented in a work of art. When we read a novel or watch a film, we may understand the behavior of the "fictive" characters represented in the work as being motivated by, or being consistent with, the same "real," independently existing values that we find operative in our real world. I am granted access to these values through the representation of a fictional character in a film or a novel, and I feel motivated by the "invigorating power" of these values to behave accordingly.

Ingarden's Move from Empathy to Emotional Coexperience

Ingarden's detailed studies of the ontology of artworks and of our cognition of them present analyses of: (1) the elements of which the various strata of these works are constituted; (2) the manner in which they're constituted individually and, most importantly; (3) the manner in which all of the strata belonging to a particular work of art may be woven together in such a way as to yield what Ingarden called a "polyphonic harmony." Ingarden's preferred illustration of this stratified structure was the literary work of art, so we'll concentrate on that in what follows.

The literary work has four strata: (1) the stratum of word sounds and the phonetic formations of a higher order built upon these sounds; (2) the stratum of meaning units of different orders; (3) the stratum of represented objects; and (4) the stratum of schematized aspects. Each of these strata is, in its own way, "schematic"; that is, each stratum presents us with features that we must in some way complete or "flesh out" in the course of our active engagement with the text, in which we "concretize" the work of art as an aesthetic object. We can speak of this concretization with regard either to the countless individual elements belonging to the work or to the work as a whole. That is, we can speak, for example, not only of concretizing the figures of Huck, Jim, and Miss Watson but also of concretizing *The Adventures of Huckleberry Finn*. (In both cases, we speak of the product of the act of concretization as the "aesthetic object.") The essentially schematic character of the work of art constitutes both an essential structural moment of the work and the framework within which all cognition of the work proceeds. In all works of art, certain features are given only schematically and remain to be "filled out"—actualized or concretized—by the person who apprehends the work. This feature of the literary work of art appears most prominently in the last two of the strata listed earlier. The represented objects belonging to a literary work of art are, quite simply, the various entities that we encounter throughout our reading of the work—basically, the characters and their actions, the events, along with their causes and results, and so on. When we read J. R. R. Tolkien's *Lord of the Rings*, for example, we encounter hobbits and elves, wizards and dwarves, forests and mountains, and trolls and dragons, all of which inhabit or belong to the realm of Middle Earth. All of these are, in Ingarden's language, "represented objects": they are one and all entities that are represented in the work of art, as are all the actions they perform, the events in which they participate, and the innumerable situations in which they find themselves. Chief among the schematically presented features of the literary work of art are what Ingarden referred to as spots ("gaps" or "places") of indeterminacy and schematized aspects, both of which are present in all literary works of art. We can illustrate this by looking at the schematic character of the literary work. For example, in "building" a particular character, Mark Twain presented first one feature of that character—say, Huck Finn's mischievousness—and subsequently other features—such as Huck's generosity, humility, and honesty. At any given point in the novel, it's the reader's task to concretize the character with regard to the various aspects that have been given. The precise manner in which this concretization is to proceed, however, remains largely undetermined, or underdetermined, by the text, for the character is only schematically represented. The situation is identical in the case of "spots of indeterminacy." An author can never provide all the physical details of a person's appearance, for example, or all the details of a particular setting—how long were Huck's arms, and exactly how wide was the raft?—and the reader is thereby forced to "fill in" and "determine" these gaps during the course of the reading. If the author continues to provide further details regarding particular places of indeterminacy, the reader will alter the manner in which he or she concretizes both the individual features of the work and the work as a whole. As Ingarden explained:

several of its strata, especially the stratum of portrayed objectivities and the stratum of aspects, contain "places of indeterminacy." These are partially removed in the concretizations. The concretization of the literary work is thus still schematic, but less so than the work itself... The places of indeterminacy are removed in the individual concretizations in such a way that a more or less close determination takes their place and, so to speak, "fills them out." This "filling-out" is, however, not sufficiently determined by the determinate features of the object and can thus vary with different concretizations. (Ingarden1973b: 13–14)

While Ingarden offers no in-depth analysis of everything that's involved in the process, he is clear that the manner in which we concretize any given literary work of art is determined to a greater or lesser extent by the social and personal values that inform all of our behavior—that is, those same intersubjectively shared values that Stein, following Dilthey as well as Husserl, identified as essential to our lifeworld existence. The world represented in art, in other words, embodies the same values as does the rest of our lifeworld. This observation is far more significant than it might first appear to be. As he explained in *The Controversy over the Existence of the World*, shortly after he had begun that work in 1935, a whole new set of problems had suddenly arisen from his concern with "the possibility of an intersubjectively secured cognition of a text fixed in literary form, which appeared to me as the problem of the possibility of intersubjectively secured science *in general [überhaupt]*" (Ingarden 2013: 23; German text 1964: ix). So he temporarily ceased work on *Controversy* and turned to the investigation of *The Cognition of the Literary Work of Art*, during the course of which he came to feel that he had finally established to his satisfaction that the literary work of art subsists independently of the acts of consciousness both of its author and of its readers, and that it persists in such a way as to be intersubjectively accessible to any number of aesthetically engaged subjects. In short, before he felt ready to attack the problem of the existence of the real world, he knew he had first to deal with issues arising from our immersion in the social world and community.

As we have seen, in the description of aesthetic experience that he presents in *The Cognition of the Literary Work of Art*, Ingarden combines, with some revisions, a number of features of the accounts of Lipps and Stein. In the passage I cited much earlier—and to which I may now finally return—he borrows more from Stein than might initially be evident, so we should bear in mind Stein's claim that "personal values, like all values in general (the existential values excepted) have substance independently of the existence of their carrier. They can be experienced in fictive carriers just as well as in real carriers." As Ingarden writes:

> Here, in the process of imputing a new subject of attributes to the given qualities, takes place what Theodor Lipps probably has in mind when he speaks of "empathy" [*Einfühlung*] and of "aesthetic reality" [*aesthetische Wirklichkeit*] as a correlate of empathy. This is especially evident when we impute a psychological or psychophysical subject to the qualities given us. We then "empathize" into those qualities not only this subject but also his definite psychological states and acts, precisely those acts and states whose "external expression" . . . appears among the qualities we are given. We are struck by the phenomenon of this expression; when it is apprehended in emotional sympathy, it leads to "empathizing," e.g. the joy or joyful admiration of the person we have imagined, into the perceived phenomenon and transforms it thoroughly. (Ingarden 1973b: 203)

Ingarden is here developing further the account, left incomplete by Stein, of how values—which are substantial and "exist" independently of any real or fictional carriers—come to be presented to us in our aesthetic experience of works of art. This happens, initially, when we creatively recognize a character in the work as a psychophysical subject just like ourselves, a subject who is feeling the same emotions and exhibiting the same behavior that we might feel or exhibit were we in the same situation as that depicted in the work. In order for that to happen, of course, the world represented in the work of art must be one in which we too can meaningfully navigate, and whose 'represented' inhabitants behave in a way that is believable and realistic. Ingarden continues:

> But as soon as the act of empathy is performed, there takes place that strange direct intercourse or companionship with the imagined person and his condition. Feelings arise in us which are very similar to the feelings we would have if we were close to such a person and his states in reality. These acts of emotional coexperiencing are the first form of the emotional response of the aesthetically experiencing subject to the constituted aesthetic object.

Some thirty-four pages later, Ingarden returns to this point:

> It was once very common to speak of "empathy," and perhaps this could be applied in the cognition of persons portrayed in literature, if there is actually such a thing as empathy. Basically, it is here more a matter of feeling along with the people portrayed for us, hence of a certain sympathy with them. In any case, it is no purely intellectual or mental act and also no mere mental image, but an experience in which the element of feeling, as well as the element of an emotional coexperiencing of psychological occurrences along with the portrayed persons, plays an essential role. (Ingarden 1973b: 237)

Despite the seeming inconsistency, Ingarden is not contradicting himself here. He's merely pointing out that previous thinkers, such as Lipps, had taken the initial "act of empathy" performed early in the aesthetic experience to extend throughout the entirety of that experience. This led thinkers, most obviously Lipps, to collect all of those "very diverse phenomena and subjective activities" arising throughout the course of the aesthetic experience and refer to them jointly as "empathy." It was his recognition of the separate identities of these "subjective activities" that enabled Ingarden to elaborate his analyses of the phases of the aesthetic experience as he did. But as his analyses demonstrate, not all of the "activities" comprising the aesthetic experience lend themselves to straightforward analysis, and the case is the same with Stein's description of the "levels" [*Schichte*] of the experience of empathy. It is misleading to describe the empathic experience according to Stein and the aesthetic experience according to Ingarden as proceeding in a series of discrete and independent steps, or stages. Each of these authors points out that the experience they're describing proceeds in a nonlinear manner, the various "stages" (*Schichte*) of which are overlapping and recurring. What's most important for our purpose is that we recognize that both authors stress the immediacy of the encounter with value and that the experience of this encounter does not proceed as an act, or series of acts, of cognition that lends itself to definitive analysis. Simply stated, the encounter with value is intuitive in character and, in the case of the aesthetic experience, the concretizations of the aesthetic object originate in and revolve around this encounter. Ingarden repeatedly explains that while the literary work of art is an intersubjective object, the same cannot be said of its concretizations, for "purely subjective, individual factors" influence their formation: "These factors are quite variable, are independent of the work of art being read and of one another, and cannot be predicted in their conjunctions. Thus the differences among individual concretizations of the same work are quite multifarious and, in general, unpredictable" (Ingarden 1973b: 413). Despite this subjectivity and unpredictability, however, Ingarden nevertheless continues to maintain that a "science of literary aesthetic objects" is possible and that his own analyses have provided precisely the sort of foundation that this science requires.

Ingarden's analyses, however, extend far beyond the field of aesthetics. The final footnote of *Cognition* offers a provocative statement that holds good not just for Ingarden's work in aesthetics but for his philosophy as a whole:

> If we take "science" [*Wissenschaft*] in the narrow sense of the word, then, of course, literary scholarship can never be "science" in that sense; nor does it

aspire to be. There is no longer ground for argument here. There is simply no justification for holding the narrow sense of "science" to be the only possible or admissible one. (Ingarden 1973b: 414n.54; German text 1968: 433n.54. This footnote is not included in the Polish text, Ingarden 1957.)

A number of contemporary scientists, in fields as diverse as physics and neuropsychology, have remarked on the fact that contemporary science remains wedded to the metaphysical and epistemological presuppositions of early modern philosophy.[9] Some of these scientists have called on philosophers to offer a new foundation for scientific research that might be of more use in addressing developments in the sciences over the last century. I believe that Ingarden's groundbreaking work in ontology and metaphysics points us in the direction that we might follow in order to do just that. Ingarden's distinction between the literary work of art and its concretizations rests upon the recognition of the intentional being of the literary work of art. I am convinced that his discovery of the power inherent in such intentional being—a power that Ingarden continued to investigate in *Controversy over the Existence of the World*—supplies us with an extremely promising line of further research that might well give rise to a broader concept of science and a metaphysical foundation that may better serve our colleagues in the sciences.[10]

Notes

Earlier drafts of the sections of this chapter dealing with Lipps and Stein, entitled "Empathy and the Aesthetic Experience in Early Phenomenology," were delivered at meetings of the Boston Phenomenology Circle (on April 6, 2019) and the North American Society for Early Phenomenology at St. John's, Newfoundland (on May 30, 2019). I remain grateful to the organizers of these meetings, Zachary Joachim and Vicente Muñoz-Reja at Boston, and Kimberly Baltzer-Jaray and Charlene Elsby at St. John's, for providing me such exceptional opportunities to present and discuss this material.

1 We should note that Lipps treated empathy as an activity of cognition, as did his predecessor Robert Vischer, who "used the term to describe the viewer's active perceptual engagement with a work of art.... Physical, emotional, and psychological, the process of *Einfühlung* placed the spectator at the center of aesthetic discourse" (Juliet 2006: 139). For the slightly earlier Rudolf Hermann Lotze, however, empathy was decidedly passive. In his *Mikrokosmos* (1858), Lotze had coined the German term *Einfühlung* as a translation of the ancient Greek ἐμπάθεια, which meant "physical affection," or "passion."

2. As Dan Zahavi observes in a footnote on the history of the concepts of sympathy and empathy: "Incidentally, Lipps might have been influenced by Hume's account since it was Lipps who translated Hume's *A Treatise of Human Nature* into German." See Zahavi (2014): 103n2. Zahavi is perhaps being overly cautious here. We might want to make a stronger statement, as do Christiane Montag, Jürgen Gallinat, and Andreas Heinz, who write that, "From translating Hume's *A Treatise of Human Nature* into German, Lipps had learned the concept of 'sympathy' as a process that allows the contents of 'the minds of men' to become 'mirrors to one another'" (Montag, Gallinat and Heinz 2008: 1261). Montag and her colleagues here cite p. 365 of the *Treatise*, where we read the following: "In general we may remark, that the minds of men are mirrors to one another, not only because they reflect each other's emotions, but also because those rays of passions, sentiments and opinions may often be reverberated, and may decay away by insensible degrees." Even more informative passages are to be found earlier in the *Treatise*. For example, Book II, Part I, Section XI: "Of the love of fame," where Hume describes how "affection is infus'd by sympathy" (Hume 1888: 317).
3. I discuss this point at more length in Mitscherling (2020). In that paper I also deal at greater length with Stein, emphasizing the similarity between features of Ingarden's analyses and her own, especially regarding community and coexperiencing.
4. While this might appear to be merely a matter of word choice, it in fact points to the metaphysical issue regarding the separate, independent existence of value, which Ingarden revisited throughout the course of his career. Ingarden discusses this along with a variety of other matters pertaining to numerous sorts of value in the essays collected in *Man and Value* (Ingarden 1983).
5. See Susanne K. Langer's discussion of the principle in *Feeling and Form* (1953: 318–19); also see Mitscherling (1988).
6. Stein describes her first meetings with Adolf Reinach and Husserl in *Life in a Jewish Family*, 247–52.
7. Stein (1891–1942) wrote her dissertation between February and October 1916, while employed as a substitute teacher (Latin, German, history, and geography) at a secondary school in Breslau. (This, the *Victoriaschule*, was the school that Stein had attended several years before.) Stein sent the complete dissertation to Husserl in Freiburg "Shortly after Easter" 1916. Over that Easter vacation, as she tells us in *Life in a Jewish Family* (397–8), she had dictated her thesis to her cousins, Adelheid Burchard and Grete Pick, and "Shortly after Easter, the *opus*, thus constructed, was on its way to Freiburg by parcel post. I asked Husserl to examine it in the course of the summer. In July [1916], during the long vacation, I would come there myself in order to take the orals for the doctorate." Stein defended and received her doctorate in August 1916 at the University of Freiburg. Chapters 2, 3 and 4 of the dissertation were published at Stein's own expense in 1917 (*Zum Problem der Einfühlung*, Halle: Buchdruckerei des Waisenhauses).

8   The passage (at Stein 1986: 397) continues: "In connection with my original work, research along this line was necessary to show how the comprehension of mental associations differs from the simple perception of psychic conditions. Max Scheler's lectures and writings, as well as the works of Wilhelm Dilthey, were of the utmost importance to me in connection with these questions."
9   See, for example, Stapp (2007).
10 I have discussed this elsewhere; see, for example, Mitscherling (2010) and (2014).

References

Bullough, E. (1912), "'Psychical Distance' as a Factor in Art and an Aesthetic Principle," *British Journal of Psychology* 5: 87–117.

Hume, D. ([1888] 1968), *A Treatise of Human Nature*, Oxford: Clarendon Press.

Ingarden, R. (1957), "O poznawaniu dzieła literackiego," (The Cognition of the Literary Work of Art), in *Dzieła filozoficzne, Studia z estetyki*, vol. 1, 1–251, Warsaw: PWN.

Ingarden, R. (1964), *Der Streit um die Existenz der Welt* (Controversy over the Existence of the World), vol. 1, Tübingen: Max Niemeyer.

Ingarden, R. (1968), *Vom Erkennen des literarischen Kunstwerks* (On the Cognition of the Literary Work of Art), Tübingen: Max Niemeyer.

Ingarden, R. (1973a), *The Literary Work of Art*, trans. G. G. Grabowicz, Evanston: Northwestern University Press.

Ingarden, R. (1973b), *The Cognition of the Literary Work of Art*, trans. R. A. Crowley and K. R. Olson, Evanston: Northwestern University Press.

Ingarden, R. (1983), *Man and Value*, trans. A. Szylewicz, München: Philosophia Verlag.

Ingarden, R. (2013), *Controversy over the Existence of the World, Volume 1*, trans. A. Szylewicz, Frankfurt: Peter Lang GmbH.

Langer, S. K. (1953), *Feeling and Form*, New York: Charles Scribner's Sons.

Lipps, T. (1903), *Leitfaden der Psychologie* (Introduction to Psychology), Leipzig: Verlag von Wilhelm Engelmann, https:// archive.org/details/leitfadenderpsy00lippgoog (accessed April 16, 2022).

Lipps, T. (1905), "Empathy and Aesthetic Pleasure," trans. K. Aschenbrenner, in Aschenbrenner, K. and A. Isenberg, eds. (1965), *Aesthetic Theories: Studies in the Philosophy of Art*, Englewood Cliffs: Prentice-Hall.

Mitscherling, J. (1988), "The Aesthetic Experience and the 'Truth' of Art," *British Journal of Aesthetics* 28: 28–39.

Mitscherling, J. (2010), *Aesthetic Genesis: The Origin of Consciousness in the Intentional Being of Nature*, Lanham: University Press of America.

Mitscherling, J. (2014), "Consciousness, Intentionality, and Causality," in *Substantiality and Causality*, ed. M. Szatkowski and M. Rosiak, 129–49, Boston, Berlin, and Munich: de Gruyter.

Mitscherling, J. (2020), "Empathy and Emotional Coexperiencing in the Aesthetic Experience," *Horizon* 9(2): 495–512.

Montag, C., J. Gallinat, and A. Heinz (2008), "Theodor Lipps and the Concept of Empathy: 1851–1914," *American Journal of Psychiatry* 165: 1261.

Stapp, H. P. (2007), *Mindful Universe: Quantum Mechanics and the Participating Observer*, New York: Springer.

Stein, E. (1964), *On the Problem of Empathy*, trans. Waltraut Stein, The Hague: Martinus Nijhoff.

Stein, E. (1986), *Life in a Jewish Family*, ed. L. Gelber and R. Leuven OCD, trans. J. Koeppel, OCD, Washington, DC: ICS Publications; vol. 1 of *The Collected Works of Edith Stein*.

Stein, E. (1991), *Briefe an Roman Ingarden, 1917–1938* (Letters to Roman Ingarden, 1917–1938), Freiburg, Basel, and Vienna: Herder; vol. 14 of *Edith Steins Werke* (*The Collected Works of Edith Stein*), ed. L. Gelber and M. Linssen OCD.

Stein, E. (1993), *Self-Portrait in Letters: 1916–1942*, trans. J. Koeppel, OCD, Washington, DC: ICS Publications; vol. 5 of *The Collected Works of Edith Stein*, eds. L. Gelber and R. Leuven, OCD, Washington, DC: ICS Publications.

Stein, E. (2000), *Philosophy of Psychology and the Humanities*, ed. M. Sawicki, trans. M. C. Baseheart and M. Sawicki, Washington, DC: ICS Publications.

Zahavi, D. (2014), *Self & Other: Exploring Subjectivity, Empathy, and Shame*, New York: Oxford University Press.

6

8-Bit Mystique

An Ingardenian Aesthetic Analysis of the Appeal of Retro Computer Games

Matthew E. Gladden

Introduction

Judged by contemporary artistic standards, the kinds of computer games produced in the 1980s—a period that roughly corresponds to what is now described as the "8-bit era"[1] of gaming—are, in many objective senses, undeniably "crude." In retrospect, their low-resolution 2D graphics appear terribly poor; their storylines seem simplistic or nonsensical; their artificial-sounding music possesses limited expressivity; and the architecture of their gameworlds is repetitive and contrived. In the decades following the 8-bit era, advances in computing technologies and the maturation of the game industry transformed the nature of the typical computer game as a work of art: today's most sophisticated games incorporate deep, engaging literary plots involving complex moral dilemmas, difficult strategic choices, and meaningful character development; architecturally diverse environments; lavish musical scores; and hyperrealistic 3D visuals, meticulously crafted sound effects, and richly interactive gameplay dynamics that immerse players in an engaging fictional world.

Given the apparent superiority of contemporary games as artistic products, it might not be unreasonable to expect 8-bit games to have faded from critical and popular consciousness, remembered today as little more than necessary (but flawed) precursors to the "true" works of art that are today's best computer games. And, indeed, the even simpler "pre-8-bit" games of the 1970s have largely faded into such oblivion: they are studied as historical artifacts but rarely played or enjoyed today for their own sake. The journey of the 8-bit games from the

1980s, however, has followed a different course: in recent years, not only have many games from the 1980s been re-released for contemporary devices, but a whole "retro" gaming movement has emerged, in which game designers create new "8-bit-style" games whose look, feel, and gameplay experience lovingly imitate or evoke those of 1980s games.[2]

This revival of the 8-bit aesthetic has become so widespread that scholarly efforts have been made to explain its causes. One frequently offered explanation is that of the "nostalgia theory," according to which the resurgent popularity of 8-bit (or 8-bit-style) games is a result of the now-middle-aged generation of gamers who were children in the 1980s returning to the games of their youth as a means of recapturing some of the joy and innocence of their childhood. In that account, the renewed popularity of 8-bit games has nothing to do with the games' inherent artistic properties; rather, the games generate a positive emotional response in today's older gamers simply because they are associated with pleasant childhood memories.[3]

In this text, however, we argue that while nostalgia may play a role in the allure that 8-bit or 8-bit-style games hold for many players, Ingarden's phenomenological aesthetics suggests that nostalgia is by no means the only (or perhaps even the most important) explanation for such games' ongoing appeal. In constructing such an analysis of the unique aesthetic value of such games—of their particular charm or "mystique"[4]—we draw primarily on Ingarden's phenomenological aesthetic account of the mental process of the concretization of a work of art. We then demonstrate how the "life cycle" manifested by many 8-bit games over the last four decades reflects—from an Ingardenian perspective—the typical life cycle of true works of art and not that of kitsch. In formulating such an analysis, it will be helpful to first explore the most notable artistic characteristics of 8-bit and 8-bit-style games.

The Nature of the 8-bit Game and 8-bit-Style Retro Game

The Apparent Artistic "Crudeness" of the 8-bit Game

On the surface, the typical 8-bit game might appear to be a singularly crude artistic product. For example, such games' visual elements are rudimentary and lack any "realism": because of the games' low resolution and restricted color palette, an entire human being might be represented onscreen by a single letter or by a blocky shape that only vaguely suggests a head, arms, and legs.

Likewise, the objects depicted in such a game often display a rigid uniformity, with a typical "forest" comprising dozens of identical trees all arranged in a perfect grid; instead of presenting distinct persons, a game may be populated by characters that are represented by visually identical sprites and behave in identical ways. Such characters generally lack any visible facial expressions, and the sound of their voices is never heard; all conversations are presented through bits of onscreen text. The broader architecture of such games' worlds is simplistic—with the environment often neatly reduced to a series of identically sized rectangular screens—while the games' 2D perspective eliminates any sense of depth, compressing a game's action into a single plane. Moreover, the grid-like division of the screen into square tiles of equal size often yields an implausible space, with an individual person, a tree, a dragon, a house, and even an entire town all appearing onscreen next to one another, with each represented by an icon of the same size. Such games' storylines are often minimally developed, with their perfunctory plots sometimes rendered more confusing by poor translation of onscreen text from Japanese into English. The audio hardware of historical 8-bit game systems was also generally incapable of playing back recorded music or replicating the sound of real musical instruments; instead, games generated what was (at best) a thoughtfully composed series of obviously electronic beeps and tones. At the time of their original release in the 1980s, such historical 8-bit games were considered technological marvels; however, when compared to many contemporary computer games, 8-bit games might appear to be almost laughably primitive artistic products.

The Underlying Reality of the 8-bit Game as a Sophisticated Organic Whole

While a typical 8-bit game might thus seem to be a "rudimentary" artistic creation by today's popular standards, from an Ingardenian perspective, it is actually an incredibly sophisticated work of art that integrates into a single organic whole a literary work of art (the game's characters, plot, and themes); one or more musical works of art (the tunes that form its soundtrack); digital "paintings" in the form of the game's sprites, backgrounds, and other visual art; architectural works of art (the carefully designed buildings, landscapes, levels, and other spatial structures that a player explores); and even forms of artistic "dance" (the intricate choreography of real-time jumping, dodging, attacking, or otherwise interacting with the environment that must be mastered in many 8-bit action games).

In this sense, an 8-bit game resembles an opera, ballet, or theatrical play that combines in a single organic whole many qualitatively diverse schematic constructs that are presented simultaneously through elements ranging from the production's set design and lighting schemes to its spoken text, live music, and performers' gestures and facial expressions.[5] Such multimediality contributes to an 8-bit game's ontological richness, as reflected in the game's qualitatively diverse layers and the ways in which they are "anatomically" and "physiologically" interconnected to create a single organism-like whole.[6] While for Ingarden a literary work possesses at least (1988: 53–4) four distinct layers, a representational painting three (1966a: 9–23, 31–69), an architectural work two (1966b: 129–41), and a work of instrumental music one (1966c: 252–6), an 8-bit action RPG combines all of those layers (and more) into a single organic whole.

Moreover, such a game possesses a degree of interactivity that is absent in works like conventional paintings or films: the way in which it reveals itself is largely driven by (and a tailored response to) actions undertaken by a player in real time; the player is not simply a "passive" recipient[7] of the work but its active coauthor. Likewise, its (simple) AI gives the game a degree of organism-like "agency" that is lacking in most traditional forms of art; the game dynamically determines what contents to present (and in what order), often seeking to counteract strategic or tactical decisions made by a player.

The 8-bit-Style Game as a Unique Opportunity for Concretization

Ingarden's Account of Concretization

We would argue that perhaps the most significant and recognizable artistic characteristic of an 8-bit-style game—as viewed from an Ingardenian perspective—is the nature and extent of its *indeterminacy*. For Ingarden, a work of art as fixed by the author, artist, or composer who fashioned it is an incomplete "schematic construct": it possesses great potential but is, in itself, unrealized. It is a sort of scaffolding or skeleton that provides a framework upon which a recipient's experience of the work can be built—but which also contains countless "gaps" or loci of ambiguity and indeterminacy that must be filled in by the recipient through some combination of imagination and judgment. The process whereby an individual human consciousness fills in those gaps to give rise to a unique apprehending of a work of art is known as "concretization":

through concretization, the contents of a work's regions of indeterminacy become determined; from among its many possible expressions and interpretations, one actual expression and interpretation is realized.[8]

For a "conventional" work of art (e.g., a particular painting or novel), each of the millions of people who experiences that work (e.g., by viewing the painting or reading the novel) begins with more or less the same schematic scaffolding as a starting point: in that sense, everyone who views Cezanne's *Annecy Lake* or reads Grahame's *The Wind in the Willows* essentially encounters "the same" work of art. And yet, everyone who views the painting or reads the novel also enjoys a radically different experience, because every mind will necessarily "fill in" the work's countless gaps in differing ways, as influenced by a recipient's unique intellectual capacities, personality, character, and life experiences.

The Indeterminacy of the Retro Game's Constituent Literary Work of Art

There are numerous ways in which 8-bit-style games are inherently more indeterminate than today's more technologically "advanced" computer games. When historical 8-bit games were originally created, such indeterminacy was unavoidable, due to game systems' technical limitations. Today, 8-bit-style or retro games are purposefully designed in a way that mimics or recreates such indeterminacy, because of the enjoyable experience that it gives rise to within many players' minds—despite the fact that it is no longer technologically necessary.

For example, the low resolutions of 8-bit game systems' graphics and the properties of the CRT televisions common in the 1980s made it impossible to display text onscreen using tiny letters: instead, text had to be presented using relatively large typefaces, which meant that the amount of text that could fit onscreen at any given time was fairly small (see Figure 6.1). This limitation—along with the fact that 8-bit-style pixel fonts are relatively difficult and wearying to read—made it impractical to employ lengthy passages of text as a way of conveying information to players.

As a result of these practical technical constraints, when conveying information via onscreen text, 8-bit games tend to employ the smallest possible number of words. Instead of using several paragraphs to recount some character's backstory or explain the quest that a player is being charged with carrying out, a game designer might distill that literary content down to just one or two vague and cryptic sentences that compel players to mentally construct

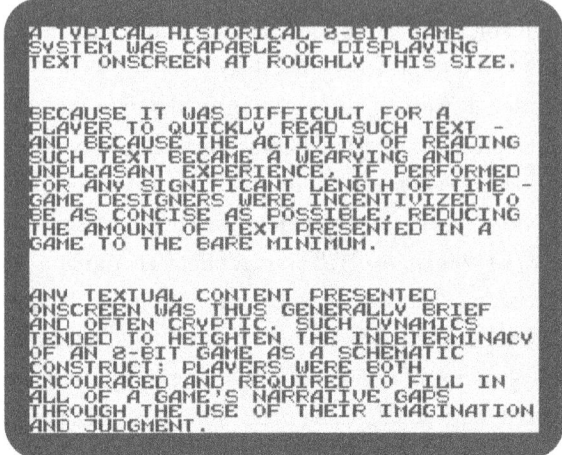

Figure 6.1 Technical limitations of historical 8-bit game systems' graphics (as reflected in this simulated screenshot) made it difficult for players to absorb large quantities of information through passages of text. © Matthew E. Gladden.

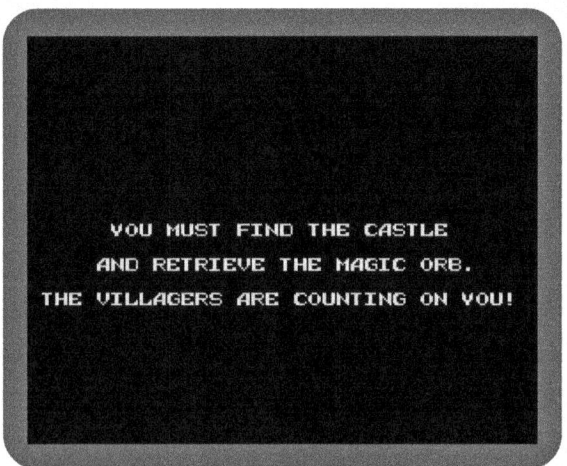

Figure 6.2 8-bit and 8-bit-style games often present critical information using brief text that possesses a high degree of indeterminacy (as reflected in this simulated screenshot). © Matthew E. Gladden.

most of the plot's details for themselves. For example, Figure 6.2 illustrates how a player character might be given a lengthy and challenging quest by means of two simple sentences: "YOU MUST FIND THE CASTLE AND RETRIEVE THE MAGIC ORB. THE VILLAGERS ARE COUNTING ON YOU!"

A player presented with such instructions might naturally wonder, "Who (or what) is giving me this task? What is that entity's relationship to me? What castle am I looking for? Why is its location a mystery? Who took the magic orb? What are its powers? Why is the orb so significant? Why am I the only one who can retrieve it? Where do I look for the castle? What will happen to the villagers if I fail?" Because of its technical constraints, it is infeasible for an 8-bit game to immediately answer those questions by displaying lengthy blocks of text (as a novel might do) or playing a voiceover narration (as a film might do). Instead, each player is left to formulate some tentative answers to these questions through the use of his or her imagination and judgment. Whatever answers a given player develops have not (yet) been provided by the game's schema itself but are a product of that player's unique concretization of the game's highly indeterminate structure—and because the game offers so little data for the player to draw on when filling in the gaps, the concretization will necessarily draw heavily on the player's own life experiences, expectations, biases, preferences, values, and worldview. In this way, the game becomes more deeply customized, personalized, and adapted to the particular player's own psyche.

From an Ingardenian aesthetic perspective, an 8-bit-style game's cryptic and indeterminate manner of conveying information through brief texts is neither inherently "better" or "worse" than that of a contemporary game employing lengthy texts or audible narration; however, it is qualitatively *different*, and it can appeal to players who value a different type of aesthetic experience (e.g., those who enjoy being called upon to deeply personalize a work of art through their imagination).[9] Such dynamics likely play a role in the fact that 8-bit-style games remain popular among many players, despite the development of contemporary game technologies that are objectively far more powerful and "advanced."[10]

The Indeterminacy of the Retro Game's Visual Depiction of Objects

On the whole (and by necessity), 8-bit and 8-bit-style games are also quite indeterminate with regard to how they visually represent the appearance and behaviors of the player character (PC), non-player characters (NPCs), and other objects within the gameworld. However, even among such games, differing degrees of visual indeterminacy exist. Figure 6.3 depicts various representative formats available to the designers of 8-bit-style games, ranging from (a) a *maximally indeterminate* format, in which an object is represented by a one-color 8 × 8-pixel text character, to (h) a *moderately indeterminate* format, in which an object is represented by a four-color 16 × 16-pixel sprite.

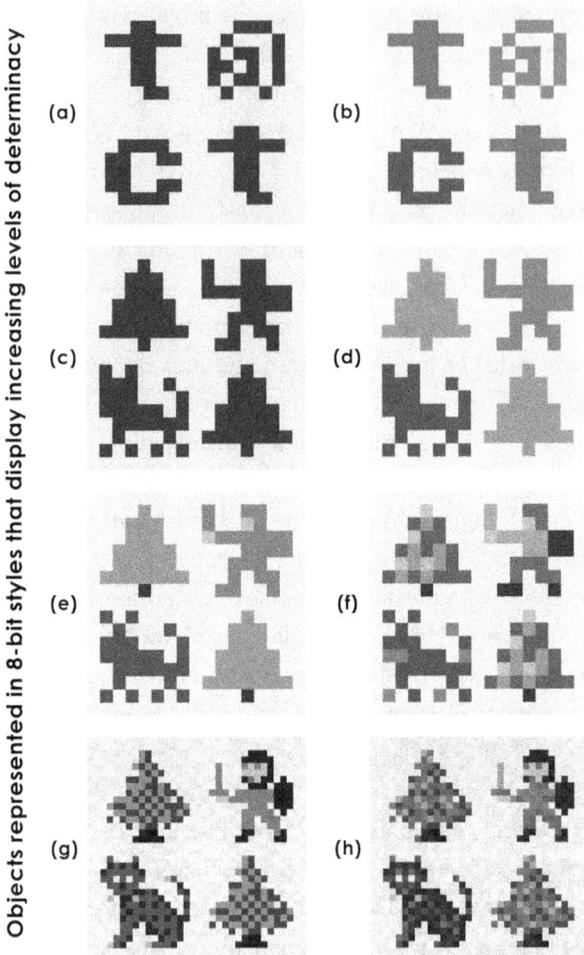

Figure 6.3 When representing objects visually, 8-bit-style games employ formats ranging from (a) the maximally indeterminate, which requires more extensive acts of concretization in a player's mind, to (h) the moderately indeterminate, which possesses fewer visual "gaps" that must (or can) be concretized. © Matthew E. Gladden.

The more determinate formats—(e) through (h)—relieve a player of much of the "work" of having to imagine what objects look like; they also allow a game to *surprise* a player by presenting objects whose appearance is bizarre, incongruent, mysterious, or unexpected. On the other hand, the least determinate format—(a)—gives a player almost total freedom to imagine what the tree, cat, or player character represented by a textual symbol "really" looks like; it does not impose any particular visualization on the player. At the same time, though, a game employing that maximally indeterminate format is unable to "surprise" the player by presenting objects that possess a bizarre, jarring, or unexpected appearance, since every object is represented by a letter or symbol whose appearance is wholly unremarkable and perfectly familiar to the player; a player who imagines what the cat or tree "looks like" cannot be *surprised* by his or her own internal visualization in the way that he or she could be surprised by strange images suddenly appearing onscreen.

From an Ingardenian aesthetic perspective, none of the 8-bit-style visual formats presented in Figure 6.3 is inherently "better" or "worse" than another (or "better" or "worse" than the formats of contemporary games that employ high-resolution, photorealistic 3D graphics to depict objects). Each format appeals to a different subset of players who prefer a particular degree of indeterminacy or particular kind of gameplay experiences (e.g., being surprised and intrigued by a game's visual depictions of objects versus being able to let one's imagination run free).

The Retro Game and the Life Cycle of a Work of Art

Ingarden's Efforts to Connect Aesthetics and Theoretical Biology

Ingarden's account of the "life cycle" of a work of art can shed light on the changing popularity of 8-bit games over the last four decades. Ingarden most explicitly explores the organism-like life cycle of a (literary) work of art in *Das literarische Kunstwerk* (*The Literary Work of Art*) (1931: e.g., 364–5). Because he explicitly states that a literary work of art only possesses "life" in a figurative sense,[11] one might be inclined to suppose that (1) the organism-like quality of a work of art is not an essential part of its nature and (2) constructing an Ingardenian account of the literary work of art can be done without studying insights from the field of biology. However, we would argue that both presumptions are misguided.

Regarding the first point, it should be noted that Ingarden did not simply compare literary works to biological organisms briefly, in a single work, or in a single sense; rather, his analysis of the literary work of art as an organism-like entity was something that he returned to regularly and developed in ever-greater detail in numerous works (and later revisions of works) over the course of nearly four decades.[12] This suggests the extent to which—for Ingarden—the organism-like structure and functionality of the literary work was central to its nature.

Regarding the second point, Ingarden possessed a keen and long-standing interest in theoretical biology that deeply informed his aesthetics; although the term "theoretical biology" per se only entered his consciousness after he discovered the *Theoretische Biologie* (*Theoretical Biology*) of Bertalanffy (1932) in 1943, his interest in the nature of biological organisms (and in identifying the characteristics that distinguish living organisms from non-living assemblages of elements) dates back at least as far as his article "W sprawie istoty doświadczenia wewnętrznego" (On the essence of inner experience) (Ingarden 1922) and his text "Essentiale Fragen: Ein Beitrag zum Wessensproblem" (Essential questions: A contribution to the problem of being) (Ingarden 1925).[13] Indeed, his meticulous study of Bertalanffy's theoretical biology was so significant to the development of his ontology and aesthetics that he would draw readers' attention to it on multiple occasions, carefully documenting the circumstances in which he became aware of Bertalanffy's thought.[14]

Ingarden's Account of the Life Cycle of the (Literary) Work of Art

One way in which a literary work "lives" is through the dynamics demonstrated by its concretizations over time. Every time a further human being reads a literary work, the resulting concretization will be novel and (at least somewhat) different from any that had preceded it (Ingarden 1931: 359–60). The differences between concretizations are not random; over time, they undergo an often qualitatively positive or negative development that resembles the life cycle of a psychic individual.

Just as a human being grows to reach a state of maturity and then begins to decline, so too may a particular work of art "mature"—through its growing number of concretizations and the development of its rich whole that reveals itself through many sides—until it becomes a beloved and admired focus of attention for a generation of people. But then, over time, the work will almost inevitably become more alien and incomprehensible to future generations who are no longer so fluent in the (increasingly archaic) language in which it was written; who no longer recognize the places, figures, and events that its imagery depicts; or who no longer understand the political or religious context within which it was produced. In this way, the work gradually becomes less "alive"; it falls into neglect and can no longer easily acquire new concretizations (Ingarden 1931: 364–5). Such a work becomes poorer in its quantity of concretizations (as fewer people read it) and less "plastic" and revelatory, as its language becomes ever more obsolete and no longer reveals to readers the nuances of the psychic intentions and motivations of its characters. Such a work may eventually "die a natural death, so to speak" (ger. *sozusagen eines natürlichen Todes sterben*) (Ingarden 1931: 368–9).[15] However, even an artistic work's gradual decline in popularity is (perhaps counterintuitively) a sign of its organism-like nature and "life," insofar as—for Ingarden (1937: 51)—such decline is not "accidental" but is rather a natural consequence of biological organisms' inherent structure and functioning; it is a key element of biological life.

Moreover, it is also possible for a literary work of art to be revived and to regain the life that it had (seemingly) lost: as long as it has been preserved in written form, it is always possible that even a completely incomprehensible and "dead" work (e.g., one written in some obscure ancient language) might someday come back to life; it need only await the arrival of someone who knows how to open up and "decipher" the work, to uncover meaning within it (Ingarden 1931: 369). For example, after having lain unseen and utterly forgotten in an attic for hundreds of years (and thus having experienced *no* new concretizations by the minds of human recipients during that period), the manuscript of a "lost" novel or musical score or an unfinished painting might be "rediscovered" and publicized, eventually gaining great critical acclaim and popular regard. Works of art are thus able to rise phoenix-like from the ashes of near-total societal neglect.

In the case of a literary work of art, this process of growth, development, maturity, decline, and potential death and revival—in which a work becomes popular and beloved, then neglected or disliked, and then (potentially) revived and appreciated anew (Ingarden 1931: 364–5)—may unfold over the course of years, decades, or even centuries. Ingarden argues that this pattern of sharply differentiated life-cycle phases appears especially in the case of masterworks of the highest level. A piece of low-quality kitsch, on the other hand, will not display such a characteristically dynamic and gradually developing life cycle. It will lack such naturally flowing and ordered developmental phases: any changes in its degree of appreciation by society may appear abrupt, random, and unpredictable (and thus unconnected to any internal dynamic agency or life force possessed by the work), or its degree of appreciation by society may remain static (and minimal) from the moment of its production; in that sense, it resembles a biological organism that was "stillborn" (ger. "*totgeborenen*") (Ingarden 1931: 364).[16] Having been developed by Ingarden in *Das literarische Kunstwerk* (*The Literary Work of Art*) (1931), this basic model of the organism-like life cycle of a literary work would be revisited in the original Polish edition of *O poznawaniu dzieła literackiego* (*The Cognition of the Literary Work of Art*) (1937: 51) and further refined in that work's 1968 German edition (Ingarden 1997: 84).

The Life Cycle of the Retro Game

We are now in a position to see how Ingarden's account of the life cycle of a true work of art offers support for the suggestion that 8-bit games possess artistic and aesthetic value that has thus far been weakly understood and underappreciated.

According to the "nostalgia theory," one might suppose that the 8-bit games of the 1980s were indeed terrible works of art; to the extent that they enjoyed some initial popularity in that era—especially among children—it was only because (a) they were something exciting and novel and (b) as poor as they were, they represented the best types of electronic games that could be fashioned in that era of crude computing technologies. According to that interpretation, it was only to be expected that such historical 8-bit games would be discarded once the more advanced technologies and game-design practices of the 1990s and early 2000s allowed the development of more artistically "sophisticated" games; the "natural" long-term destiny of 8-bit games was for them to be looked back on with embarrassment (or wholly forgotten) as they became supplanted by later generations of artistically superior games. According to that view, the renewed contemporary appreciation for historical 8-bit games—and the growing enthusiasm for creating new 8-bit-style games—is explained by the mental associations and emotional needs of older gamers and not by the fact that society has rediscovered some long-overlooked artistic or aesthetic value buried deep within such games.

Ingarden's thought, however, suggests an alternative explanation: that a significant proportion of 8-bit games were indeed artistic masterpieces,[17] and their renewed popularity reflects the enduring internal organic vitality that they possess as true works of art.[18] If this is true, we might expect that interest in 8-bit and 8-bit-style games will continue to be revived periodically by future generations of players who were not alive to experience such games in their original 1980s heyday. In this way, such games would take their place alongside beloved sculptures, paintings, buildings, literary works, and musical compositions fashioned by humanity over the course of millennia.

Conclusion

Here we have not tried to suggest that 8-bit games are the only good computer games—or that all 8-bit games are good. Indeed, many 8-bit and retro games are terrible, while many contemporary games with hyperrealistic 3D graphics have been recognized as incredible works of art. Rather, our aim has been to draw on Ingarden's phenomenological aesthetics—and in particular, his account of the mental concretization of a work of art—to argue that in their unique kind and degree of indeterminacy, 8-bit-style games possess a source of artistic and aesthetic value that is underappreciated by those who see simple nostalgia as the only reasonable explanation for such games' resurgent popularity. Likewise, Ingarden's account of the life cycle of works of art suggests that while critical and popular appreciation of historical 8-bit games and 8-bit-style retro games may ebb and flow over the decades, the best such games of these types will—like all great works of art—always have a place within human society as sources of meaningful aesthetic experiences, regardless of the direction in which future gaming technologies might evolve.

Notes

1 Among the most prominent devices possessing 8-bit processors were home computers like the Commodore 64 and third-generation game consoles like the Nintendo Entertainment System and Sega Master System.
2 The revival of 8-bit games and emergence of 8-bit-style imitators is discussed, for example by Camper (2008) and Wulf et al. (2018).
3 Regarding the relationship of nostalgia to the ongoing 8-bit renaissance, see, for example, Suominen (2008), Heikkilä (2010), Garda (2013), Latypova and Lenkevich (2018), and Makai (2018).
4 Analyzing the unique kind of charm or "mystique" that some works of art seem to possess is not a focus of Ingarden's aesthetics per se. It may be suggested, however, that he at least implicitly highlights the significance of such concepts through his use of terms like *magia* ("magic"), *tajemnica* ("mystery"), *tajemniczość* ("mysteriousness"), *urok* ("charm"), and *czar* ("charm" or "allure") to describe positive qualities of certain works of art and *zachwyt* ("enchantment," "delight," or "wonderment") to describe the response that they evoke. See, for example, Ingarden (1937: 122, 216, 1966c: 266, 1970a: 376, 1970c: 151). Elsewhere, Ingarden (1931: 304, 1988: 371) simultaneously critiques and suggests his appreciation for Witkacy's assertion that a work of art should produce in audiences a certain experience of the *Geheimnis* or *tajemnica* ("mystery") of being as unity in diversity; such a notion is not unrelated to that of "mystique."
5 The unique artistic qualities of such multimedial works of art are discussed, for example in Ingarden (1988: 393–400).
6 The literary theorist Zygmunt Łempicki argued in "Dzieło literackie: Moc i działanie" (1932) that Ingarden's analysis of the literary work of art as an organism-

like entity was unduly "anatomical"—focusing on a work's visible exterior "structures" while overlooking its equally important (yet invisible) internal "energy" and dynamics. Łempicki suggested that Ingarden's phenomenological "anatomical" analysis of the work of art would be beneficially complemented by a "physiological" account of the work's energy and dynamics. Ingarden welcomed Łempicki's suggestion, developing his own analysis of the literary work of art as a dual structural-functional entity in "Formy obcowania z dziełem literackiem" (Ingarden 1933); that model would later evolve into Ingarden's dual organic-structural and temporal-dynamic account of the literary work of art in "Formy poznawania dzieła literackiego" (Ingarden 1936) and his model of the literary work as an organically built hierarchical functional-structural whole in *O poznawaniu dzieła literackiego* (Ingarden 1937).

7 Of course, for Ingarden, a person viewing an opera or theatrical play is by no means "passive": indeed, it is within such a person's mind that the crucial activity of concretizing the work of art is being performed—not on the stage. Here we simply reference the fact that someone who (for example) composes, performs, *and* listens to a work fills more roles within the creative process than one who "only" listens to it.

8 Regarding concretization, see, for example, Ingarden (1931: 359–65, 1937: 52–8). The role of concretization in computer gameplay is noted in Marak et al. (2019: 9).

9 For ways in which 8-bit technologies have forced game developers to grapple with the "aesthetics of constraint," see, for example, Collins (2007) and McAlpine (2017).

10 Here an analogy exists with the fact that some persons prefer to watch film adaptations of classic literary works, while others prefer to read the less visually determinate (but more narratively determinate) texts upon which they are based; the invention of film has not rendered the novel obsolete. Similarly, the rise of more visually determinate computer games has not rendered obsolete, for example, the highly visually and narratively indeterminate game of chess.

11 See Ingarden (1931: 356, 364). He would later make a similar point in *O poznawaniu dzieła literackiego* (1937: 51–2), noting that a literary work of art cannot be a *true* "organism" because it lacks autonomous being; however, it can be understood as something that is "analogous to" or an "approximation of" an organism.

12 There are at least six texts in which Ingarden (1931, 1933, 1936, 1937, 1957, 1997) directly considers the organism-like nature of the literary work and presents new reflections on that question. The increasing clarity and sophistication of his thought on that point was intertwined with the simultaneous maturation of his thought on theoretical biology and systems theory more broadly, as reflected in works like the *Spór*, volumes I (1947) and II (1948); his substantial yet incomplete notes made in

1950–4 for the *Spór*, volume III (1974); and *Über die Verantwortung: Ihre ontischen Fundamente* (1970d).
13 See, for example, Ingarden (1922: 527–9, 1925: 196–7).
14 See, for example, Ingarden (1947: 266, 1948: 161, 1970b, 1970d: 70, 72, 78, 1997: 85). Ingarden (1997: 85) also mentions his later study of Rothschuh's *Theorie des Organismus* (1959); he does not highlight his similarly meticulous study of Uexküll's *Theoretische Biologie* (1928), although we know from the notes preserved in Ingarden's personal archive (1943) at the Archiwum Nauki PAN i PAU in Kraków that he undertook such a study in 1943.
15 Alternatively, a work may die an artificial and premature death if, for example, its author annihilates it through particular intentional acts and destroys all of the physical objects (e.g., printed texts) that might allow other human beings to concretize the work; see Ingarden (1931: 359).
16 Ingarden's account thus suggests a possible quantitative empirical approach to distinguishing masterpieces from kitsch in various artistic fields, by measuring the changes in popularity shown by a work over time to detect signs of organic "vitality."
17 Among the many remarkable games from the 1980s, titles that are frequently cited as outstanding works of art include, for example, *The Legend of Zelda*, *Metroid*, and *Ultima IV: Quest of the Avatar*.
18 The use of a (non-Ingardenian) life-cycle approach to understanding the current popularity of 8-bit and 8-bit-style games has been suggested, for example, by Swalwell (2007) and Latypova and Lenkevich (2018).

References

Bertalanffy, L. v. (1932), *Theoretische Biologie: Erster Band: Allgemeine Theorie, Physikochemie, Aufbau und Entwicklung des Organismus* (Theoretical Biology: Volume One: General Theory, Physicochemistry, Structure and Development of the Organism), Berlin: Verlag von Gebrüder Borntraeger.

Camper, B. (2008), "Retro Reflexivity: La-Mulana, an 8-Bit Period Piece," in *The Video Game Theory Reader 2*, ed. B. Perron and M. J. P. Wolf, 191–218, New York: Routledge.

Collins, K. (2007), "In the Loop: Creativity and Constraint in 8-Bit Video Game Audio," *Twentieth-Century Music* 4(2): 209–27.

Garda, M. B. (2013), "Nostalgia in Retro Game Design," in *Proceedings of the 2013 DiGRA International Conference: Defragging Game Studies*, Atlanta, August 26–29.

Heikkilä, V.-M. (2010), "Defining Computationally Minimal Art (Or Taking the '8' out of '8-Bit')." Available online: http://countercomplex.blogspot.com/2010/03/defining-computationally-minimal-art-or.html (accessed January 24, 2020).

Ingarden, R. (1922), "W sprawie istoty doświadczenia wewnętrznego" (On the essence of inner experience), *Przegląd Filozoficzny* 25(4): 512–34.

Ingarden, R. (1925), "Essentiale Fragen: Ein Beitrag zum Wessensproblem" (Essential questions: A contribution to the problem of being), *Jahrbuch für Philosophie und phänomenologische Forschung* 7: 125–304.

Ingarden, R. (1931), *Das literarische Kunstwerk* (The Literary Work of Art), Halle (Saale): Max Niemeyer Verlag.

Ingarden, R. (1933), "Formy obcowania z dziełem literackiem" (Forms of Contact with the Literary Work of Art), *Wiadomości Literackie* 10(7/478): 3.

Ingarden, R. (1936), "Formy poznawania dzieła literackiego" (Forms of Cognition of the Literary Work of Art), *Pamiętnik Literacki* 33: 163–92.

Ingarden, R. (1937), *O poznawaniu dzieła literackiego* (The Cognition of the Literary Work of Art), Lviv: Wydawnictwo Zakładu Narodowego Imienia Ossolińskich.

Ingarden, R. (1943), manuscript notes on the *Theoretische Biologie* (1928) of Jakob von Uexküll, Personal archive of Roman Ingarden, K III—26, jednostka 89/3, Archiwum Nauki PAN i PAU, Kraków, Poland, accessed May 10, 2019.

Ingarden, R. (1947), *Spór o istnienie świata* (Controversy over the Existence of the World), vol. I, Kraków: Polska Akademia Umiejętności.

Ingarden, R. (1948), *Spór o istnienie świata* (Controversy over the Existence of the World), vol. II, Kraków: Polska Akademia Umiejętności.

Ingarden, R. (1957), "O poznawaniu dzieła literackiego" (The Cognition of the Literary Work of Art) in *Studia z estetyki*, vol. 1, 1–251, Warszawa: PWN.

Ingarden, R. (1966a), "O budowie obrazu" (On the Construction of the Image) in *Studia z estetyki*, vol. 2, 5–115, Warszawa: PWN.

Ingarden, R. (1966b), "O dziele architektury," (On the Work of Architecture) in *Studia z estetyki*, vol. 2, 117–66, Warszawa: PWN.

Ingarden, R. (1966c), "Utwór muzyczny i sprawa jego tożsamości" (A Piece of Music and the Question of Its Identity) in *Studia z estetyki*, vol. 2, 167–307, Warszawa: PWN.

Ingarden, R. (1970a), "Funkcje artystyczne języka" (The Artistic Functions of the Language) in *Studia z estetyki*, vol. 3, 316–78, Warszawa: PWN.

Ingarden, R. (1970b), "O pojęciu istoty" (On the Concept of Being), lecture at a scientific meeting of the Polish Philosophical Society, April 4, Personal archive of Roman Ingarden, K III—26, jednostka 77, Archiwum Nauki PAN i PAU, Kraków, Poland. Available online: Roman Ingarden Digital Archive (accessed January 24, 2020).

Ingarden, R. (1970c), "Twórcze zachowanie autora i współtworzenie przez wirtuoza i słuchacza" (The Creative Behavior of the Author and Co-Creation by the Virtuoso and the Listener) in *Studia z estetyki*, vol. 3, 147–52, Warszawa: PWN.

Ingarden, R. (1970d), *Über die Verantwortung: Ihre ontischen Fundamente* (About Responsibility: Its Ontic Foundations), Stuttgart: Reclam.

Ingarden, R. (1974), *Über die kausale Struktur der realen Welt: Der Streit um die Existenz der Welt III* (On the Causal Structure of the Real World: The Controversy over the Existence of the World III), Tübingen: Max Niemeyer Verlag.

Ingarden, R. (1988), *O dziele literackim: Badania z pogranicza ontologii, teorii języka i filozofii literatury* (On the Literary Work of Art: Research from Ontology, Theory of Language and Philosophy of Literature), trans. M. Turowicz, Warszawa: PWN.

Ingarden, R. (1997), *Vom Erkennen des literarischen Kunstwerks. Gesammelte Werke: Band 13* (On the Cognition of the Literary Work of Art. Collected Works: Volume 13), ed. E. M. Świderski, Tübingen: Max Niemeyer Verlag.

Latypova, A. and A. Lenkevich (2018), "From the Inside of Medium: Analytics of Retro Games," in *Abstract Proceedings of the 2018 DiGRA International Conference: The Game Is the Message*, Turin, July 25–28.

Łempicki, Z. (1932), "Dzieło literackie: Moc i działanie" (The Literary Work of Art: Power and Action), *Wiadomości Literackie* 9(10/427): 3.

Makai, P. K. (2018), "Video Games as Objects and Vehicles of Nostalgia," *Humanities* 7(4): 123.

Marak, K., M. Markocki, and D. Brzostek (2019), *Gameplay, Emotions and Narrative: Independent Games Experienced*, Pittsburgh: ETC Press.

McAlpine, K. B. (2017), "Press Play on Tape: 8-Bit Composition and Musical Innovation through Technical Constraint," in *Innovation in Music 2017, London*, September 6–8.

Rothschuh, K. E. (1959), *Theorie des Organismus: Bios, Psyche, Pathos* (The Theory of the Organism: Bios, Psyche, Pathos), München: Urban & Schwarzenberg.

Suominen, J. (2008), "The Past as the Future? Nostalgia and Retrogaming in Digital Culture," *The Fibreculture Journal* 11: FCJ-075.

Swalwell, M. (2007), "The Remembering and the Forgetting of Early Digital Games: From Novelty to Detritus and Back Again," *Journal of Visual Culture* 6(2): 255–73.

Uexküll, J. v. (1928), *Theoretische Biologie* (The Theoretical Biology), Berlin: Verlag von Julius Springer.

Wulf, T., N. D. Bowman, D. Rieger, J. A. Velez, and J. Breuer (2018), "Video Games as Time Machines: Video Game Nostalgia and the Success of Retro Gaming," *Media and Communication* 2: 60–8.

7

Roman Ingarden on Aesthetic Attention

Harri Mäcklin

Introduction

Recent years have witnessed a renewed interest in aesthetic experience after several decades of bad press in philosophical literature. During the latter half of the twentieth century, the notion came under heavy criticism by those who saw it as a trivializing, decadent, or one-sidedly subjective perspective on art, or simply too vague, fleeting, and variable to merit serious attention (Shusterman 1997, 2019). Though aesthetic experience never completely disappeared from the scene, it was, as Noël Carroll (2001: 43) has it, "put on the back burner" of aesthetics. After several years of disentangling aesthetic experience from overtly simple characterizations that riddled dominant criticisms, the notion has again gained positive attention in both Anglo-American and Continental schools of thought.

In this chapter, I will take a look at one of the ongoing debates and discuss its relation to Roman Ingarden's aesthetics. This debate concerns the role of attention in aesthetic experience. Since 2015, Bence Nanay has argued in several publications that aesthetic experience is conditioned by a certain type of attention that sets it apart from other types of experience. Nanay's theory has sparked a lively discussion, which can be seen as rekindling traditional discussions regarding such notions as the aesthetic attitude and disinterestedness (Fazekas 2016; Cuccuru 2018; Westerman 2018; Irvin 2019; Schellekens 2019; cf. Nanay 2019a and 2019b for responses to Irvin and Schellekens). Though not everyone has accepted Nanay's formulation of aesthetic attention (e.g., Fazekas 2016), there seems to be a growing consensus on the claim that aesthetic experiences are indeed conditioned by a special type of attention.

My main claim in this chapter is that this debate on aesthetic attention, as it currently stands, still works with a limited understanding of the phenomenology of aesthetic experience. This is unfortunate, as thinkers like Roman Ingarden have already proposed fine-tuned descriptions of aesthetic experience and the attitude it involves. Indeed, I consider that Ingarden's oeuvre offers one of the most complex accounts of aesthetic experience we have to date. In the course of several books and essays, Ingarden fleshes out a multifaceted phenomenology that pays heed to the dynamic, temporally extended, and intentionally extremely complicated nature of aesthetic experience in a way that escapes black-and-white dichotomies such as subjectivity and objectivity, passivity and activity, or detachment and engagement. What is more, Ingarden's phenomenology includes a detailed account of the appropriate aesthetic attitude required for aesthetic experience to occur, and this, as I will claim, makes him interesting in relation to Nanay's theory of aesthetic attention. In this chapter, I would like to show how Ingarden's thinking on the aesthetic attitude in many ways prefigures, exceeds, and augments the contemporary debate on aesthetic attention.

Before I move on to elaborate my claim, a few words of caution are in order. The following comparison between Ingarden and Nanay might give the impression that they can at face value be compared. This, however, is not entirely the case. This is because their approaches to the problematics of aesthetic experience are fundamentally different. Ingarden approaches the matter through phenomenological intentional analysis, where aesthetic experience is described solely as it is given in the first-person perspective without recourse to anything that is not present in the experience in itself. Nanay, in contrast, works with a naturalistic philosophy of perception, "which is informed by recent findings in psychology and neuroscience" (Nanay 2019a: 93). The relationship between phenomenology and empirical psychology (and naturalism in general) is famously vexed (cf. Carel and Meacham 2013), and it is not altogether certain whether Ingarden and Nanay would agree on the fundamental starting points of the whole issue: Ingarden might criticize Nanay's approach for being reductive and incapable of fully appraising the constitutive role of consciousness in aesthetic experience, whereas Nanay might charge Ingarden's intentionalism with lacking objectivity and ignoring empirical findings.

Trying to find a common ground between these two approaches is, however, too complex for the scope of this chapter. Yet, even without such common ground, I think comparing Nanay's and Ingarden's theories is a valuable effort. Their theories can shed light on each other and offer possibilities that the other might have missed—possibilities whose viability can be judged from each theory's own perspective and appropriated accordingly. My approach in this chapter is mainly to point out ways in which Ingarden can help to widen the current discussion on aesthetic attention. This concentration on Ingarden's possible contribution to Nanay's theory pertains to a more general motive to show Ingarden's relevance to contemporary debates on aesthetic experience. Though I wholeheartedly welcome the recent resurgence of interest in aesthetic experience, my general concern is that contemporary debates tend to work with a rather reductive understanding of its phenomenology. I credit this to be, at least partly, based on a crude indifference to the work of Ingarden and other phenomenological aestheticians like Mikel Dufrenne, Moritz Geiger, and Nicolai Hartmann. Thus, my aim in this chapter is to push the more general point of the usefulness of phenomenology to contemporary debates by using Nanay's case as an example. I think there are many other debates besides the one on aesthetic attention that would, in my mind, benefit from a more robust understanding of the experience under discussion, but justifying this is beyond the scope of a single chapter.

In keeping with these considerations, I do not wish to claim straightforwardly that Ingarden's theory is a *corrective* to Nanay's. I will criticize Nanay's theory for being a very narrow one and claim that Ingarden's writings give us a much broader view of the complicated situation in which aesthetic attention is embedded—but this criticism is most likely one that Nanay himself would agree on.[1] Indeed, Nanay (2019b: 118) acknowledges that his theory of aesthetic attention plays first and foremost an *exemplary* role in a wider argument on the relevance of empirically informed philosophy of perception to aesthetics. His point, in my understanding, is not to develop an exhaustive theory of aesthetic attention as such but to show how naturalistic philosophy of perception can contribute to fundamental discussions in aesthetics. My point in this chapter is to do with phenomenology what Nanay does with philosophy of perception: by using aesthetic attention as an example, I aim to show how phenomenology can contribute to current issues in aesthetics.

Nanay on Aesthetic Attention

Let me first turn to Bence Nanay's theory of aesthetic attention. Nanay can be credited for bringing the notion of the aesthetic attitude—though clothed in another term—back to the agenda of aesthetic debates after decades of hostile rejection. From the early eighteenth until the mid-twentieth century, aesthetic experience was often described as being conditioned by a specific attitude adopted by the perceiver toward the aesthetic phenomenon, be it in terms of disinterestedness, psychical distance, or detached contemplation (see Bullough

1912; Stolnitz 1960, 1961). These attitude theories came under heavy criticism during the latter half of the twentieth century, most vocally by George Dickie, who in his classic article "The Myth of the Aesthetic Attitude" (1964) argued that attitude theories wrongly attribute a special mode of cognition to an experience that is simply describable in terms of attention. Furthermore, Dickie (1964) argued that there is only one form of attention, and thus there cannot be a special form of aesthetic attention that can be demarcated from other forms of attention. This criticism was enough to push the notion of the aesthetic attitude into the purgatory of suspect aesthetic theories.

Beginning with his article "Aesthetic Attention" (2015a), as well as his book *Aesthetics as Philosophy of Perception* (2015b), Bence Nanay has argued that Dickie was simply wrong in thinking that attention exists only in one form. Drawing from perceptual psychology, Nanay argues that attention comes in many forms and that there is a specific form of attention at play in aesthetic experiences. In general, Nanay argues, attention can be either *focused* or *distributed*. It is focused when it is strictly limited to a certain object or to certain properties of an object; in contrast, it is distributed when attention is spread over several objects or properties at the same time. Given that attention can be directed to both objects and their properties, Nanay (2015a: 107–8, 2015b: 23–5) claims that there are four basic types of attention:

1. *Distributed with regard to objects but focused with regard to properties.* This is the type of attention we exercise when we are searching for certain properties from a group of objects, for instance when sorting blue socks from red socks.
2. *Distributed with regard to objects and distributed with regard to properties.* This type of attention occurs when we let our mind aimlessly wander without any particular focus, for instance when waiting for an appointment at the doctor's office.
3. *Focused with regard to objects and focused with regard to properties.* This type of attention is exercised in most perceptually guided actions that require us to concentrate on the specific properties of a specific object, for example when reaching for a coffee cup on the table.
4. *Focused with regard to objects and distributed with regard to properties.* This type of attention is exercised in aesthetic experience.

So, according to Nanay, aesthetic attention is limited to a single object, but in a way that attention is distributed to several properties of the object. For example, when we look at a painting, we are engaged solely with the painting itself, and we do not attend to it as an object in a field of other objects, and in this regard our attention is focused. At the same time, we attend to the painting in such a way that attention is distributed with regard to a large number of its properties, such as colors, figures, and composition. We could certainly attend to the painting with other types of attention as well, for example when assessing whether a painting would fit our living room decor, but these types of attending would not yield an aesthetic experience (Nanay 2015a: 102–3, 2015b: 19).

Besides being focused and yet distributed, aesthetic attention has other specific features as well. First, Nanay (2015a: 109, 2015b: 26) views it as being *disinterested*, by which he means that it does not involve practical interests that would focus the attention to just certain relevant aspects of the object; on the contrary, aesthetic attention is independent of ulterior motives and thus free to wander over several properties of the object. This does not mean that aesthetic attention lacks interest, but rather that this interest is motivated by the object's properties for their own sake. Second, Nanay (2015a: 101, 112–13, 2015b: 16–17) claims that aesthetic attention is not necessarily the result of the perceiver's active assumption, but rather something that can occur *uncontrollably* in the face of some aesthetic objects. Third, Nanay (2015a: 101, 2015b: 17) argues that aesthetic attention differs from other attentional types in that it has a peculiar *lingering effect*, by which he means that we keep on perceiving our environment in an aesthetic manner for a while even after the experience itself has dissipated. Fourth, Nanay (2015a: 103, 2015b: 19) is careful to point out that his notion of aesthetic attention is not limited solely to artworks but also applies to other objects of aesthetic experience, such as natural or ordinary objects.

This is Nanay's theory in a nutshell. Though I do think that Nanay is fundamentally on the right track, I still consider his theory to be phenomenologically insufficient. To his credit, as I already mentioned, it must be noted that he does not present his theory as an exhaustive account of aesthetic experience. Nanay (2015a: 96–8, 2015b: 13) is clear in pointing out that aesthetic experiences come in many shapes and sizes, and this type of attention only applies to some, albeit paradigmatic aesthetic experiences, and even in their case it only brings up a certain central aspect of the experience. Yet I think that even if we limit ourselves to the role of attention in aesthetic experience, Nanay's account leaves several aspects untouched. Indeed, Nanay's theory has generated a lively set of responses, some pointing to its shortcomings, some augmenting them. Instead of reviewing these contemporary responses, I would next like to show how Ingarden could help us flesh out a more robust phenomenology of aesthetic attention.

Ingarden on Aesthetic Attention

Ingarden's descriptions of the aesthetic attitude form a central part of his phenomenology of aesthetic experience, dispersed in several works, most notably *Das literarische Kunstwerk* (*The Literary Work of Art*) (1931), *Untersuchungen zur Ontologie der Kunst* (*Ontology of the Work of Art*) (1962), and *Vom Erkennen des literarischen Kunstwerks* (*The Cognition of the Literary Work of Art*) (1968). I will here mostly draw from the last of the mentioned books, where Ingarden summarizes his view of aesthetic experience. First, of course, it is to be noted that Ingarden does not use the term "aesthetic attention" but opts for the more traditional term "aesthetic attitude" (ger. *ästhetische Einstellung*). Though these terms may not be extensionally identical, I think it is nevertheless clear that Ingarden understands the aesthetic attitude as involving a specific attentional stance toward an artwork. In this respect, Ingarden's and Nanay's theories can be compared with regard to their understanding of the role of attention in aesthetic experience.

By and large, Ingarden's account of the aesthetic attitude is consonant with Nanay's theory. In short, Ingarden holds that the aesthetic attitude is essentially structured by a narrowing of consciousness to the artwork alone, but in such a way that the perceiver's attention is distributed to the schematic structures and aesthetically valent qualities of the artwork. This, on the whole, is closely reminiscent of Nanay's understanding of aesthetic attention as being focused on a single object but distributed to several of its properties. Second, Ingarden, much like Nanay, also holds that there are several attitudes one can take toward an artwork, but that the aesthetic attitude is a necessary condition for an aesthetic experience to occur (Ingarden 1973: 171–4, 1968: 177–80).[2] Third, Ingarden (1973: 172–4, 1968: 178–80) also considers aesthetic attention to be essentially disinterested in the sense that it is cut off from practical interests and is sustained by an interest in the artwork for its own sake. Fourth, Ingarden (1973: 189, 1968: 196) too holds that aesthetic attention is assumed passively and uncontrollably, and not actively. The limitation of Ingarden's theory of the aesthetic attitude with regard to Nanay's account is that Ingarden limits himself to considering only artworks, and the extensional adequacy of his theory with respect to nonartistic phenomena remains unexplained.

However, Ingarden's discussion of the aesthetic attitude also brings out many aspects that Nanay does not. In this chapter I would like to raise six of them. First of all, and perhaps most importantly, it could be questioned whether

Nanay's definition of aesthetic attention as being focused-yet-distributed is enough to account for the *aesthetic* character of the experience. This problem can be approached by pointing out that Nanay does not specify if focused-yet-distributed attention is always aesthetic, or if there are also nonaesthetic instances of such attention. Regardless of the answer, Nanay's account seems to have certain problems. First, if Nanay claims that focused-yet-distributed attention is a unique characteristic of aesthetic attention, the following problem can be posed. Ingarden points out that the perceiver can engage with an artwork with attitudes that are non-practically oriented toward the work's properties without them adding up to an aesthetic experience. Ingarden (1973: 233–329, 1968: 242–342) calls these *pre-aesthetic* (ger. *vor-ästhetisch*) and *reflective attitudes*; the pre-aesthetic attitude is dedicated to investigating the work's schematic structure without actualizing its aesthetic value, whereas the reflective attitude contemplates the actualized aesthetic object after the aesthetic experience itself has dissipated. These attitudes are arguably also focused-yet-distributed, but Ingarden would reject the conclusion that they are aesthetic attitudes in the proper sense; the former precedes the aesthetic attitude, whereas the latter retrospectively reflects on the accomplishments of the aesthetic attitude. So, following Ingarden, it could be argued that aesthetic attention is not the only form of focused-yet-distributed attention. However, if Nanay concedes that there are nonaesthetic instances of focused-yet-distributed attention, this begs the question what precisely makes aesthetic attention *aesthetic*? In my opinion, Nanay does not provide a clear answer. Ingarden, on the other hand, would argue that the focus-yet-distributed character of aesthetic attention does not give a sufficient account of aesthetic experience, but it is only one aspect of a much more complicated set of mental acts.

Second, Nanay does not explain how the transition from one attentional stance to another takes place. In §24 of *Vom Erkennen des literarischen Kunstwerks* (*The Cognition of the Literary Work of Art*), Ingarden, in contrast, lays out a detailed phenomenology of the transition from the natural attitude to the aesthetic one. According to Ingarden, the transition in attitudes is a passive process, brought about by some quality in an object that catches our attention. This quality "strikes us, forces itself upon us, grips us," producing what Ingarden calls an *original emotion* (ger. *Ursprungsemotion*) in the perceiver (Ingarden 1973: 189, 1968: 196). This emotion is not be understood with the feeling of pleasure often identified as a mark of an aesthetic experience—indeed Ingarden is careful to point out that the notion of pleasure is much too vague and trivializing to account for the complicated dynamics of affects and emotions at play in aesthetic experience (Ingarden 1973: 190–1, 1968: 197–8). Rather than simple pleasure, the original emotion is to be understood as *excitement* (ger. *Erregtsein*), where the aesthetic quality "touches, rouses, or excites us" (Ingarden 1973: 189, 1968: 196). At this stage, there is no thematic consciousness of the arresting quality but merely an affective relation that manifests itself as the initial interest that draws the perceiver toward the aesthetic phenomenon. Being arrested by this interesting object, the perceiver begins to apprehend its aesthetic qualities more distinctly and adopts the aesthetic attitude. If the object is aesthetically valent, this investigation produces a new wave of emotions by "delighting" (ger. *berauschen*) and "intoxicating" (ger. *entzücken*) the perceiver, feeding into the desire to investigate the object even further (Ingarden 1973: 197, 1968: 204). In this way, the aesthetic phenomenon keeps perceivers in its hold, nourishing them with an ever-increasing hunger to experience the phenomenon more fully. This desire is only appeased by the constitution of the aesthetic object and the recognition of its aesthetic value. It is this desire, then, which accounts for the transition between the natural and the aesthetic attitude, and which sustains the aesthetic experience from start to finish.

The third shortcoming in Nanay's theory is that it does not specify the intentional character of aesthetic attention carefully enough. In Husserlian terms, every experience has an *intentional quality* (the *how* of the act), *intentional matter* (the *what* of the act), and a *doxic modality* (the belief regarding the existence or nonexistence of the intentional object). Nanay's account only stipulates that the intentional quality of aesthetic attention is one of focused but distributed attention, and the matter is made of the properties of the object; concerning the doxic modality he has nothing to say. However, this is not enough to separate aesthetic attention from nonaesthetic attention: for example, Richard Westerman (2018) has argued that we can look at a map with focused but distributed attention while maintaining a practical attitude, and this experience is markedly different looking at the map aesthetically. Again, we can find a more robust description from Ingarden. Summarizing his phenomenological aesthetics, it could be said that the intentional quality of aesthetic attention is non-practical and dedicated to actualizing the aesthetic value inherent to the artwork by synthesizing the work's various schemata and aesthetic valent qualities into a harmonious whole. Second, the intentional matter is made up of the schematic structures and aesthetically valent properties of the artwork, whereas aesthetically nonrelevant qualities are pushed aside. Finally, Ingarden points out that there is a peculiar doxic character to the intentional acts of aesthetic attention. The aesthetic object is not acknowledged to exist in the way an actual object exists, and yet it is not intended as a non-being either; the question of the object's existence is "forced to the periphery of our consciousness" (Ingarden 1973: 195, 1968: 202). In other words, the experience of an aesthetic object does not include a belief regarding the existence or nonexistence of the object.

The fourth shortcoming in Nanay's account, closely related to the third one, is that it does not sufficiently recognize that the concentration on a single object has the accompanying effect of pushing other objects into the non-thematic periphery of consciousness. Ingarden (1973: 192, 1968: 199) notes that the aesthetic qualities of the artwork produce a *check* (ger. *Hemmung*) in the perceiver. What Ingarden means is that the aesthetic quality consumes the perceiver's attention to the extent that "a narrowing of the field of consciousness" occurs, where the perceiver's relationship to actual experience is momentarily altered. What happens is that the perceiver's awareness of the actual world recedes to the non-thematic periphery of consciousness, so that the perceiver is no longer aware of the actual surroundings in which the encounter with the aesthetic phenomenon is had. This forgetting of the world has the result that the aesthetic phenomenon is experienced as being a self-contained unit, sufficient in itself, set apart from the world surrounding it. The "worldly" actual character of the object is also forgotten, and, as Ingarden says, we begin to "overlook" (ger. *übersehen*) certain qualities of the object in favor of other, aesthetically more relevant qualities—for example, when aesthetically perceiving the *Venus de Milo*, we overlook the blemishes on the marble and missing arms, and instead devote our gaze to the elegant figure of the statue (Ingarden 1973: 178–85, 1968: 183–92).

The fifth shortcoming in Nanay's theory is that he does not specify how attention is distributed between properties in aesthetic attention. This leaves an impression that aesthetic attention involves an *equal* distribution of attention to several properties simultaneously. This, however, does not seem to be the case. From Ingarden's point of view, it is true that the aesthetic attitude involves synthesizing several aspects of the work into a whole, but still, only some aspects are thematically intended at a given moment, whereas other properties are present only peripherally. For example, when I read a novel, I imagine what the characters look like, what kind of clothes they are wearing, and what the environment looks like, and yet these aspects can recede into the non-thematic background if my attention is more focused on, say, the characters' dialogue or emotions. This does not mean that these non-thematic aspects cease to play a part in the aesthetic experience, but only that the attention that sustains the experience is not evenly distributed to all relevant aspects at the same time.

Finally, sixth, Nanay seems to describe aesthetic attention as a matter of merely attending to properties that are already there in the object. One of the central claims of Ingarden's aesthetics is that aesthetic experience is not an outcome of a passive process of merely identifying properties but an active, co-creative process, where the perceiver concretizes the schematic structures and aesthetically valent qualities of the artwork. The artwork contains all sorts of *places of indeterminacy* (ger. *Unbestimmtheitsstellen*) that the perceiver needs to fill out for the artwork to become an aesthetic object—for example, the color of Consul Buddenbrook's eyes is nowhere mentioned in Mann's novel (Ingarden 1973: 50, 1968: 49), but it is something the reader must nevertheless envisage. The artwork, to paraphrase Ingarden, is only a skeleton that needs the creative acts of the perceiver in order to turn it into something living. Thus, the aesthetic attitude is not merely a question of recording aesthetically relevant qualities but also one of creating them in the engagement with the artwork.

There would, surely, be a lot more to say about Nanay's account and Ingarden's possible contribution to it, but even these six remarks are sufficient to point out that Ingarden's notion of aesthetic attention not only prefigures but also exceeds Nanay's notion of aesthetic attention. There are surely elements in Nanay's account that do not appear in Ingarden, such as observations on the lingering effect of aesthetic experience. Such observations, however, do not make up for the fact that the contemporary debate—which so far has largely circulated around Nanay's theory—misses central elements of aesthetic attention, and these shortcomings can be at least identified through the lens of Ingarden's phenomenology.

Conclusions

In this chapter, I have briefly surveyed one prominent contemporary account on aesthetic experience and pointed out how Ingarden's phenomenology could be of value in taking it further. Though my indications have been superficial at best, I hope to have shown that the debate on aesthetic attention would greatly benefit from a more robust understanding of the phenomenology of aesthetic experience—and this is precisely what we can find in Ingarden's oeuvre. As I mentioned at the beginning, I consider this to be only one example of Ingarden's relevance to contemporary aesthetics. Showing how Ingarden could contribute to other debates—such as the analytic battle between the externalists and the internalists regarding the sufficient conditions of aesthetic experience (cf. Carroll 2012; Dura-Vilà 2016; Cuccuru 2018)—is a matter for another occasion. Such comparisons surely raise the thorny issue of fundamental disagreements on philosophical methodology, but even without being able to build my case here, I remain optimistic in claiming that different schools of thought can learn from each other's accomplishments despite their disagreements. The moral of my argument is that Ingarden's work offers a robust model of aesthetic experience—certainly more robust than most contemporary accounts—and ignoring it would be a crass mistake. This is, of course, not to suggest that Ingarden's phenomenology is some sort of a forgotten philosopher's stone that can turn the baser arguments of contemporary debates into gold. There are surely several shortcomings to Ingarden's phenomenology, and it cannot be taken straightforwardly to give conclusive answers to all questions we might have regarding aesthetic experience. This should not put us off, but merely indicate that a lot of work still remains to be done. What I wish to have shown, however tentatively, is that this work would greatly benefit from a closer understanding of Ingarden's detailed phenomenology of aesthetic experience. Sometimes an old dog can teach us new tricks.

Notes

1 This claim on narrowness could even be pushed from the side of naturalistic aesthetics, as Jean-Marie Schaeffer has shown in his *L'Expérience esthétique* (The Aesthetic Experience) (2015) how aesthetic attention (which Schaeffer formulates in fundamentally the same way as Nanay) must be understood as being part and parcel with a more complex set of psychological processes that together make up aesthetic experience.
2 In the following, I will provide the page numbers of both the English translation (1973) and the German original (1968).

References

Carel, H. and D. Meacham, eds. (2013), *Phenomenology and Naturalism*, Cambridge: Cambridge University Press.

Carroll, N. (2001), *Beyond Aesthetics: Philosophical Essays*, Cambridge: Cambridge University Press.

Carroll, N. (2012), "Recent Approaches to Aesthetic Experience," *Journal of Aesthetics and Art Criticism* 70(2): 165–77.

Cuccuru, K. (2018), "Aesthetic Attention: A Proposal to Pay It More Attention," *Estetika: The Central European Journal for Aesthetics* 55(2): 155–79.

Dickie, G. (1964), "The Myth of the Aesthetic Attitude," *American Philosophical Quarterly* 1(1): 56–65.

Durà-Vilà, V. (2016), "Attending to Works of Art for Their Own Sake in Art Evaluation and Analysis: Carroll and Stecker on Aesthetic Experience," *British Journal of Aesthetics* 56(1): 83–99.

Fazekas, P. (2016), "Attention and Aesthetic Experience," *Journal of Consciousness Studies* 23(9–10): 66–87.

Ingarden, R. (1968), *Vom Erkennen des literarischen Kunstwerks* (The Cognition of the Literary Work of Art), Tübingen: Max Niemeyer.

Ingarden, R. (1973), *The Cognition of the Literary Work of Art*, trans. R. A. Crowley and K. R. Olson, Evanston: Northwestern University Press.

Irvin, S. (2019), "The Nature of Aesthetic Experience and the Role of the Sciences in Aesthetic Theorizing: Remarks on the Work of Nanay and Smith," *Estetika: The Central European Journal for Aesthetics* 56(1): 100–9.

Nanay, B. (2015a), "Aesthetic Attention," *Journal of Consciousness Studies* 22(5–6): 96–118.

Nanay, B. (2015b), *Aesthetics as Philosophy of Perception*, Oxford: Oxford University Press.

Nanay, B. (2019a), "Aesthetic as Philosophy of Perception: A Précis," *Estetika: The Central European Journal for Aesthetics* 56(1): 91–4.

Nanay, B. (2019b), "Responses to Irvin and Schellekens," *Estetika: The Central European Journal for Aesthetics* 56(1): 118–24.

Schaeffer, J.-M. (2015), *L'Expérience esthétique* (The Aesthetic Experience), Paris: Gallimard.

Schellekens, E. (2019), "Psychologizing Aesthetic Attention," *Estetika: The Central European Journal for Aesthetics* 56(1): 110–17.

Shusterman, R. (1997), "The End of Aesthetic Experience," *The Journal of Aesthetics and Art Criticism* 55(1): 29–41.

Shusterman, R. (2019), "Aesthetic Experience and the Powers of Possession," *The Journal of Aesthetic Education* 53(4): 1–23.

Stolnitz, J. (1960), *Aesthetics and Philosophy of Art Criticism*, Boston: Houghton Mifflin.

Stolnitz, J. (1961), "On the Origins of *Aesthetic Disinterestedness*," *The Journal of Aesthetics and Art Criticism* 20(2): 131–43.

Westerman, R. (2018), "Intentionality and Aesthetic Attention," *British Journal of Aesthetics* 58(3): 287–302.

Bullough, E. (1912), "'Psychical Distance' as a Factor in Art and an Aesthetic Principle," *British Journal of Psychology* 5(2): 87–118.

8

Roman Ingarden on Fictional Times

Charlene Elsby

Roman Ingarden says in the *Controversy over the Existence of the World* that "The time represented in the literary work of art is completely different from the time in which the happenings of the real world transpire" (Ingarden 2013: 282). But of course he is being hyperbolic. He writes immediately following this quotation that the time represented in the literary work of art is indeed an analogue of the time in which the happenings of the real world transpire. There are similarities all over the place, between the times that I will abbreviate as "literary time" and "real time." There is a present, past, and future to the represented objectivities of a literary work, just as there is to material objects. There is a sequentiality in the events, processes, and temporal objects of both realms. The idea that literary time is "completely different" from real time stems from their diverging ontologies; literary time, as a represented object in the literary work of art, has a purely intentional being, whereas real time is real. We know this mainly through the differing experiences we have of the present of the literary work, in comparison to the present of the real world. Ingarden quotes himself in *O dziele literackim* (On the Literary Work of Art):

> Confined strictly to what is contained in the literary work, the represented present does not have the privileged status of the genuine present vis-à-vis the represented past and future. Consequently, there is a certain leveling [*Angleichung*] of all temporal instants, similarly to the way this also occurs relative to the erstwhile now-instants of actual time that "already" belong to the past. (Ingarden 1960: 283)

This concept of literary time is strikingly similar to the theory of time presented by early 1900s 4d spacetime theorists, who argue for a de-privileging of the present.[1] In what follows, I will argue that the active nature of the present (the distinguishing feature of real time) acts as a limitation on real time that does not apply to literary time. Thus, literary time exemplifies a malleability that real time does not, because it embraces a "neutral" present (in a sense to be defined). I will examine the malleability of literary time with reference to a literary work of art which aims to represent a temporality with a de-privileged present—Kurt Vonnegut's *Slaughterhouse Five*. Through this analysis, I will demonstrate: (1) the specific difference between real and literary presents; (2) how Ingarden's concept of real time negates the trend of the 4d spacetime theorists in their attempt to remove temporality from time; and (3) how Vonnegut's representation of atemporal presents is made comprehensible by Roman Ingarden's concept of literary time. By its disordered representation of time, this example serves only to strengthen the case for Ingarden's view that temporal order is essential to both the literary work of art and its concretization as an aesthetic object.

The Present and the Neutral Present

In the act of concretizing a literary work of art, its represented objectivities become *present* to the reader. They come to be contemporaneous with the act of consciousness that lends them intentional being. But the present in which the represented objectivities exist is not the reader's present; the literary present does not have the autonomy nor the efficacy of the real present. The time of the work is portrayed as if it is real when it is not. Compare Ingarden's description of Hamlet from the *Controversy*:

> For the time being, it may perhaps suffice to show by way of example that Hamlet, say—as a character portrayed in a Shakespearean drama—is a purely intentional entity that is directly specified via the meanings of the sentences and sentence-complexes that occur in the drama, but indirectly via the intentions [*Intentionen*] of the writer's creative acts. As such, Hamlet is a heteronomous object. Nevertheless, as Hamlet, as a Danish prince who performs such and such deeds at the king's court, he is intended and portrayed as if he were a real man. On the other hand, the spirit of his father—which, as a constituent of the stratum of represented entities that goes into constituting the drama, is also heteronomous—is at the same time heteronomous as a phantom, as a figment (or more precisely: as object) of his son's, of Hamlet's imagination. This example illustrates that what comprises the *content* of a purely intentional act can appear in altogether different *modis existentiae*, whereas the purely intentional objects are always heteronomous in their intentional structure. (Ingarden 2013: 159)

That is to say, although the time of the work of art is fictional, it is posited as real within the context of the literary work of art. It is real within the reality of the work. The present of the literary work differs from the present of the reader according to its mode of being, but it nevertheless appears as *a* present—just as Hamlet appears as a man, in contrast to the phantom of his father. But where the present of the reader appears as active and effective, the present of the literary work does not. Rather, it appears as a sort of neutral present—a neutralized present—the sort of which I am familiar with not only through reading fiction but through other forms of experience as well, like the recollection of a past present, or in the described experiences of other people. It is a non-primordial present, to borrow a word from Edith Stein.[2] Ingarden specifies in the *Cognition* that

> To the extent that the reader submits to the demands of the work, he is under the influence of the temporal perspectives predetermined by the text and comprehends the portrayed events and processes under these perspectives. (Ingarden 1973a: 125)

Further on that page, Ingarden refers to the present of the work as a "special present." Vast periods of time become present with a mere mention; for instance, the bombing of Dresden that Vonnegut will write about. Ingarden introduces the notion of "temporal distance" to describe how far from the present of the work the described events are conceived of as occurring. In *Slaughterhouse Five*, sometimes Billy Pilgrim is in Dresden, sometimes he remembers it, and sometimes it has not yet happened. For the reader, the bombing is in one way conceived of as always past, but as an element of the literary work it has a varying temporal distance from the work's special present.

Significantly, the time of the work appears as variegated. Although Ingarden speaks in the *Controversy* of the "leveling" of temporal instants of the literary work, we should not take this to mean that all of the events of the work seem to happen at the same time, or in the same neutral present. That is to say, represented objectivities do not escape temporality by existing intentionally. They appear as if in time, and various intentional times appear analogously to various real times. Although the times of the literary work are all ontologically the same—heteronomous structures dependent on the author's creative activity for their realization and on the reader's consciousness for their concretization—they are nevertheless conceived of as past, present, or future, relative to the occurrences of the fictional world:

> For—true or not!—the real world as we grasp it in pre-philosophical, everyday experience appears to be organized in such a peculiar fashion that anything and

everything that occurs within its unity is somehow temporal, or is at least bound up with time. (Ingarden 2013: 227)

In sum, the "leveling" of the times represented within a literary work does not constitute an atemporality. While 4d spacetime theorists often ask us to imagine events as if they were not arranged temporally but instead appear in some other kind of sequence—like chapters in a book!—we shall find that the ordering of the chapters does, in fact, very much matter and that this order does signify a temporality. In the next section, I will provide a brief summary of how Ingarden's concept of time negates the 4d spacetime theorists' account by providing for meaningful distinctions to be made between the past, present, and future.

On the Significant Difference Between the Past and the Future

Ingarden discusses the significant differences between the ontology of the past and the ontology of the future in the section on processes in *Controversy*. The past, as a past present, is distinguishable because it is a *no longer active* present. But Ingarden disagrees with the notion that the past is in any way dependent on the present. While the present is autonomous, the past does not lose its autonomy by becoming no longer present. The past is to be distinguished from the present, rather, because it is no longer active or efficacious. He writes:

> What is past on the other hand, which was autonomous in some bygone present, precisely because it was not yet something past, does not and cannot lose its autonomy owing to the transition into the past—only its activeness. Otherwise it would prove itself to be something illusory. (Ingarden 2013: 240)

The future, on the other hand, does not yet have the autonomy lent to moments of time that are present. The future is an as-yet *unfulfilled* present. It is heteronomous until it is fulfilled (i.e., becomes present):

> The present is the fulfillment, the completion of what is future—which had only intimated itself heretofore. This fulfillment comes about, on the one hand, because what in the future (before it realized itself) was only heteronomous attains autonomy in the present owing to the immanence of the qualities determining it; on the other hand, it comes about owing to the moment of a peculiar "plenitude of being [*Seinsfülle*]," the moment of being's efficaciousness [*Effektivität des Seins*], and indeed [the efficaciousness] of both what it is and how it is. (Ingarden 2013: 241)

Three phases of time are thereby distinguished, for Ingarden. The present is the active, efficacious, and autonomous temporal phase. The past is no longer active or efficacious but retains its autonomy. The future is none of these things. It's a heteronomous temporal phase of possibilities held in readiness.

The 4d spacetime theorists aim to negate all of these distinctions by setting all times equal. On this conception, the privileging of any moment over any other can be dismissed as an illusion formed by human subjectivity. Such a theory of time would be convenient for scientific endeavors, as it would undergird the notion that any physical process described mathematically is in principle reversible. (It would be very inconvenient to the mathematicians to insist on the unidirectionality of time, that is, to point out that some of the equations used to describe physical processes work only if some particular values are plugged into those equations—and that if other values were used, they would not.) Regardless of how reality works, its mathematical description must allow for the reversibility of time. (And the same reasoning demands that we allow for the theoretical possibility of other phenomena that are never to be experienced by a living subject, like negative mass.)

That is to say, the introduction of time as the fourth dimension in early twentieth-century science demanded that we treat it similarly to the other three dimensions in space, where directionality does not matter. Philosophers have attempted in many ways to reconcile the idea with the impossibility of ever experiencing it, often introducing a God or alien capable of conceiving of four dimensions and declaring the fault to be our own.[3] And Vonnegut's Tralfamadorians from *Slaughterhouse Five* are an example of such beings.

In *Slaughterhouse Five*, Vonnegut represents a man whose experience of time is altered by experiments conducted by an alien race, the Tralfamadorians. The man's name is Billy Pilgrim. The narrator, who is not the protagonist, is an author and Earthling who says that "As an Earthling, I had to believe whatever clocks said—and calendars" (Vonnegut 1980: 22). Throughout the book, the narrator gives the reader indications of where to place the events relative to an objective time—specific times and dates. The work as a whole revolves around Billy Pilgrim's experience of the bombing of Dresden, which in real time took place February 13–15, 1945. But this is a work of fiction, and thus the Dresden it presents is a fictional Dresden, with its own fictional bombing. The narrator specifies at the beginning of the work that he has long been working on a book about Dresden, that he knew it would include the unfortunate tale of Edgar Derby, who was killed by a firing squad for stealing a teapot, and that the novel would end with a *Poo-tee-weet*. This is the sound that the birds make when all the children who were fighting the war on behalf of all of the countries are now dead.

Poo-tee-weet signifies finality. Billy Pilgrim's experience of time is implied to be an attempt to escape this finality by making all times equal (including so many deaths, which Billy dismisses with the recurring phrase, "So it goes"). Nevertheless, finality intervenes by negating the existence of the person who would attempt to experience time in this way. While a consequence of the 4d spacetime theorists' concept of time, conceived optimistically, can be interpreted to mean that anything that has lived at all is and always will be alive,[4] it is less often noted that according to the same theory, the very same things are, always have been, and always will be dead.[5]

Billy Pilgrim was born, went to war, and died, in that order. The problem is, if that order isn't temporal, what is it? Under Ingarden's conception, the order or sequence of a work of art is or becomes temporal; there's no other way to describe it.

Time and Order in the Literary Work of Art—*Slaughterhouse Five*

In this section, I'll discuss the order of the work of art and its implied temporality. But first we must distinguish between real time, the time of the work as a temporal object (as something that was created, endures, and may die, that is, a subset of real time), and the time represented by the work of art—whether that time is related explicitly or not, whether it refers to any real time or not. I posit that there is a relation between the ordering of the sentences and time as it is represented in the work.

Ingarden distinguishes between the time of the work and the ordering of the work (its words, sentences, and represented events) in the *Literary Work of Art*, noting how we do in fact refer to parts of the work in temporal terms. That is, despite the fact that the parts of the work of art exist simultaneously (in terms of real time), we distinguish them using terms like "earlier" and "later." In these cases, we are referring to the ordering of the parts of the work of art and that ordering is not necessarily temporal. Ingarden writes,

> And yet we do speak, not without reason, of a "beginning" and of "earlier" and "later" parts of the *work* while thinking, not of its concretizations or of the beginning or the later phases of events represented in the work, but rather of

> the individual parts of the *entire work*, taken together in *all* its strata. Only this "earlier" and "later," this "beginning" and "end," are *not* to be understood in a *temporal* sense. The question then is, in what sense? That is the problem. Here we confront a specific structure of the work, a structure which is grounded in the *order* of the parts of a work and which, for want of a better expression, we shall call the "order of sequence." (Ingarden 1973b: 306)

But a cursory comparison between the ordering of the work and its temporal determinations reveals that these are not interchangeable. All we need to offer as evidence of this is the fact that events that are revealed later in the work in fact might happen earlier in time, and vice versa. Ingarden writes a few pages later:

> In order to remove possible misunderstandings, we must stress that the order of sequences of phrases of a work should not be confused with either the world corepresented in the object stratum or the time in which the literary work itself exists. We will speak about the latter somewhat later (see Chap. 13). With reference to the former, however, the following should be noted: that one should distinguish between them follows already from the fact that a "later" phase of a literary work frequently represents a situation *which is earlier in time* (that is, in represented time) than another, "already" present situation, as, for example, when we learn from the narration of a represented person the "prehistory" of the situation just then being represented. The temporal order of what is represented and the "order of sequence" of individual phases of the work are, within broad limits, independent of each other, though it would require special investigation to establish whether this independence is total or whether it is limited and, if so, to what extent. To be sure, represented time shows various significant modifications in comparison with time in the real world, but it is still a time in which the basic structures of present, past, and future, even if modified, are present. In contrast, these basic structures have no meaning in the sequence of the phases of a work. (Ingarden 1973b: 312)

And this is all well and good, as long as the work is not read. That is to say, if we are discussing the ontology of the work of art, then it is appropriate to say that its ordering is not a temporal ordering. And here I take as my example the events presented in *Slaughterhouse Five* by Kurt Vonnegut, which take place in many times, out of order relative to their temporality. The fact that this can be done is nothing revolutionary. What we should note, however, is that the order of the work and its deliberate manipulation by the author in order to present a series of events out of sequence determines how the literary work of art will be concretized as an aesthetic object.

In *Cognition*, Ingarden relates the order of the work to the temporality of its reading. A book is something that is necessarily experienced over time, and the author arranges its parts in a nontemporal order that becomes temporal as it is read. And when the order of the events changes, so does the reader's cognition of it. This is an aspect of the aesthetic object (which is necessarily temporal) which is determined by the author when they present the events of the novel in an order. The events, too, have an associated temporality. In *Slaughterhouse Five*, the narrative is organized around Dresden. Vonnegut relates other events in a temporal order relative to that. The order of sequence is jumbled; nevertheless, the reader can construct a linear narrative of the life of Billy Pilgrim with the information given.

The fact that we do this (conceptually organize events in a fashion analogous to real time) is a result of the represented time's being an analogue of real time—we use our experience of real time to understand the narrative's temporality and especially when the events represented in the book have real correlates in history. But note that this does not necessitate that the order of the book become temporal. Rather, it emphasizes how it is possible for the author to play with time and its presentation by representing certain later times before earlier times, relying on the reader's concretization of the work to note *not only* that the events represented are temporal but that the order in which they are presented does not correspond to their temporal order.

Rather, the nontemporal ordering of the work of art determines how the work of art will be concretized—how the reader will go about ordering the disorder in a reading of the work which takes place in time. Thus, we have already identified temporal and nontemporal aspects of the content of the work of art, plus another temporal aspect relative to its cognition. As a literary work of art, its represented objectivities are temporal entities presented in a nontemporal order and then concretized in a temporal experience as an aesthetic object. Ingarden specifies that the order of sequence becomes temporal in its concretization in *Cognition*.

> But as soon as the order of the sequence of parts is determined in the work, that dictates to the reader the order in which he has to read those parts. In reading, the order of sequence of parts in the work itself becomes the temporal sequence of the phases of reading, as well as the temporal sequence of the parts of the concretization. The reading must be performed in a process that has temporal extension. (Ingarden 1973a: 96)

The order of the work of art and how it is to be associated with the work's temporality is all the more evident if we look to a particular example. In

Slaughterhouse Five, Vonnegut presents us with an experience of temporal disordering, as Billy Pilgrim watches a film about the Second World War. I'll provide the scene here in its entirety:

> American planes, full of holes and wounded men and corpses took off backwards from an airfield in England. Over France, a few German fighter planes flew at them backwards, sucked bullets and shell fragments from some of the planes and crewmen. They did the same for wrecked American bombers on the ground, and those planes flew up backwards to join the formation. The formation flew backwards over a German city that was in flames. The bombers opened their bomb bay doors, exerted a miraculous magnetism which shrunk the fires, gathered them into cylindrical steel containers, and lifted the containers into the bellies of the planes. The containers were stored neatly in racks. The Germans below had miraculous devices of their own, which were long steel tubes. They used them to suck more fragments from the crewmen and planes. But there were still a few wounded Americans, though, and some of the bombers were in bad repair. Over France, though, German fighters came up again, made everything and everybody as good as new. When the bombers got back to their base, the steel cylinders were taken from the racks and shipped back to the United States of America, where factories were operating night and day, dismantling the cylinders, separating the dangerous contents into minerals. Touchingly, it was mainly women who did this work. The minerals were then shipped to specialists in remote areas. It was their business to put them into the ground, to hide them cleverly, so they would never hurt anybody ever again. The American fliers turned in their uniforms, became high school kids. And Hitler turned into a baby, Billy Pilgrim supposed. That wasn't in the movie. Billy was extrapolating. Everybody turned into a baby, and all of humanity, without exception, conspired biologically to produce two perfect people named Adam and Eve, he supposed. (Vonnegut 1980: 46)

What we have is an example of a character in a novel experiencing a temporal object in a non-standard manner, presented in a nontemporal order, which becomes temporal as we read through the paragraphs. Vonnegut's presentation of the events of the Second World War, here presented in a reverse temporal order, demonstrates how temporality is essential to the experience of a series of events. Rather than a depressing story about how for a while, fascism reigned and millions of people died for no good goddamn reason, we experience with Billy Pilgrim the reverse process, according to which the dead come alive, wounded people are healed, and everyone works together to heal the destruction.[6]

The example is something Ingarden anticipated—that in a cinematic presentation, events could be reversed for any number of aesthetic reasons. The fact that the events are reversible does not mean that the ordering of the work of art is reversed. And it is not the case that the events presented by Vonnegut in Billy Pilgrim's watching a film running backward has reversed the order of the work of art. Rather, they must necessarily be presented in that fashion in order to be cognized according to the author's intention, when the author put them in that order. Note also that, in Vonnegut's report on the backward film, he reports events with very different significance than how the events would appear if they were presented according to the temporality of their actual occurrence. As Billy watches the film, he infers the intentions of the people he is watching do the work, as they dismantle the bombs and hide the minerals, "so they would never hurt anybody ever again." This element is *introduced* in the telling, which would not be there if the events were presented in their proper order.

Ingarden admits that this disordering of events is possible with the cinematic work of art, and he gives some examples on the effects to which this disorder could be used in a footnote in the *Literary Work of Art*. Nevertheless, the disorder of a cinematographic presentation and the disorder of a literary work are two very different things. As he writes:

> The idea of such an inversion is not new. I am acquainted with it from the novel *Der Zauberlehring*, by H. H. Evers, though there, to be sure, it is applied to a cinematographic representation. Here the inversion produces many comical situations and in many cases changes the content of what is represented. Eating, when shown cinematically in a reversed sequence, looks like vomiting; descending a ladder is changed into climbing it. Lighting and smoking a cigarette become an almost incomprehensible happening. But since in cinematography, as we shall see, finished instantaneous aspects of total situations which depict things are reconstructed, and since the individual images on the film strip are not destroyed by the inversion, things as they appear are still given to us in the inversion, and thus absurdity need not be transformed into nonsense. The situation is quite different with literary works. (Ingarden 1973b: 306)

The ordering of a novel is not the ordering of its events, on the other hand. The "order of sequence" still has nothing to do with the temporal order of the events presented by the novel, though it does determine the temporality of the reading. Vonnegut's novel is an extreme case of how the represented objectivities of a work can be presented with their temporalities disordered, but its order of sequence is still very much determined by the fact that it still presents as a literary work. That is to say, in film, the reverse of "Hitler turned into a baby," would be "Hitler grew up." But if we were instead to take this sentence as a miniature literary work of art and mess with Ingarden's "order of sequence" instead of the temporality of the represented objectivities, the result is instead, "Baby a into turned Hitler" or even, "ybab a otni denrut reltiH" or some other such nonsense.

This is the case Ingarden presents as a so-called backward reading, which emphasizes how essential the order of sequence is to the literary work of art, and he posits that not only does the inversion of a literary work change the essence of that work (such that a very different picture is presented), but the inversion of the order of sequence could prevent us from classifying the resulting jumble of words or letters as any kind of literary work:

> In order to show that such an order, still to be detailed, exists at all, let us try mentally to reverse or remove the order of parts in a given work. Let us try, for example, to read a given novel, e.g., *Buddenbrooks,* "backwards." This can be done in various ways: with only the sentence order being reversed, but with every sentence being read "forwards," or with the order of the word sequence simultaneously inverted, or, finally, with only the second and not the first being inverted, etc. Let us do this consistently from the "end" to the "beginning" and think, not of the course of the concrete reading, but of what is constituted by this "backward" reading. In each case we obtain, in comparison with the original work, *new* formations, which, depending on the kind of inversion, differ from it to a greater or lesser degree. Indeed, in a "work" read in this way, all of the same words, without exception, appear as in one that is read "forwards"; the inversion, however, has changed, if not everything, at any rate so much that it is no longer a question of whether we are still dealing with "the same" work but whether, ultimately, the formation we obtain is still a literary work at all. (Ingarden 1973b: 306–7)

That is to say, the material stratum of a work of art already determines, by its nature (the nature of words to be presented in orders), that the literary work of art is formed of letters combined into syllables, combined into words, which combine into sentences, which tend to be grammatical. And this order of sequence continues at the paragraph and chapter levels, such that the ordered presentation of its parts is essential to its identity.

This is all to say that, were we to unjumble Vonnegut's paragraphs in order to arrange them in a linear fashion, we would have a different book. If, on the other hand, we were to take every sentence and reverse it, we might not have a book at all. The nontemporal order of sequence functions at every strata of the literary work of art and determines how it will (or will not be) concretized as an aesthetic object.

Conclusion

Fictional times are malleable in the sense that it is possible to manipulate the order of sequence of a literary work of art in a way that presents its represented objectivities in a nonlinear fashion. Nevertheless, the represented objectivities are cognized as temporal in a sort of neutral present, and the order of sequence determines how they will function in the reader's concretization which, too, is temporal.

That is to say, the possibility of presenting a "disordered" order of sequence within the represented times of a literary work does not mean that we have escaped the limitations of real time. The specification of a neutral present in the literary work does not blur the distinction between past and future times. The order of sequence which, in a literary work of art, is nontemporal, becomes temporal in the literary work's concretization as an aesthetic object (that is to say, as a possible object of cognition). Ingarden's analyses of the literary work of art, its cognition, and more generally the controversy over the existence of the world serve to demonstrate how it is possible for 4d spacetime theorists to consider an alternative view of time, where the present isn't privileged and the past isn't necessary, but they also show how these appear to us only from within a decidedly temporal experience.

Notes

1 The view is inspired by Minkowski spacetime, which was interpreted by those who interpret things to be a dimension now similar to space. Like space, time is imagined as a construct with no privileged positions, a dimension on which it is possible to move in any direction. Thus came the ideas of time travel, along with the unfortunate consequence that scholars still working on the metaphysics of time believe this view to be the more scientific one to hold. In essence, the 4d spacetime position is that there is no essential difference between the past, present, and future—and that consequently, time itself, which is reduced to these differences, is illusory, or an artifact of our limited vantage point as finite beings. In fact, the view has existed for as long as religious philosophers have attempted to conceive of how God views time (i.e., from outside of time). In contemporary literature, it's more fashionable to use aliens, like the Tralfamadorians in Vonnegut's novel. Ingarden, following Aristotle, thinks there are differences between the past, present, and future—except perhaps in the fictional times represented in a literary work of art.

2   I compare it to the neutral present which Edith Stein describes as the present of phantasy: "The fantasized experiences are in contrast with memory because they are not given as a representation of actual experiences but as the non-primordial form of present experiences. This 'present' does not indicate a present of objective time by an experienced present which in this case can only be objectified in a 'neutral' present of fantasized time" (Stein 1989).

3   Dummett, for instance, conceives of the problem of backwards causality as having something to do with epistemology—the past has the quality of being in-principle knowable, and this is why we conceive of the past as not being changeable. We have no problem conceiving of natural processes occurring in a reversed temporal order. See Dummett 1964.

4   For an explicit relation between disordered representations of time in literature and the concept of immortality, see Mitscherling 1996.

5   Vonnegut notes, for instance, "If what Billy Pilgrim learned from the Tralfamadorians is true, that we will all live forever, no matter how dead we may sometimes seem to be, I am not overjoyed" (Vonnegut 1980).

6   I speculate that Vonnegut did this to emphasize how final the events of the war really are. Fitting with the *Poo-tee-weet* with which he ends the novel, this reversed presentation of the events of the war, being presented out of order, only serves to emphasize its irreversibility. The fact that we can't go back. It's the point Ingarden made in the *Controversy* about the past and its distinction from the future. The past is done.

References

Dummett, M. (1964), "Bringing about the Past," *The Philosophical Review* 73: 338–59.

Ingarden, R. (1960), *O dziele literackim* (On the Literary Work of Art), Warszawa: PWN.

Ingarden, R. (1973a), *The Cognition of the Literary Work of Art*, trans. R. A. Crowley and K. R. Olson, Evanston: Northwestern University Press.

Ingarden, R. (1973b), *The Literary Work of Art*, trans. G. G. Grabowicz, Evanston: Northwestern University Press.

Ingarden, R. (2013), *Controversy of the Existence of the World*, vol. I, trans. A. Szylewicz, Frankfurt am Main: Peter Lang.

Mitscherling, J. (1996), "The Metaphysics of Early Postmodern Fiction and the Human Ideal of a Meaningful Existence," *Dialogue and Universalism* 6(7): np.

Stein, E. (1989), *On the Problem of Empathy*, trans. W. Stein, Washington: ICS Publications.

Vonnegut, K. (1980), *Slaughterhouse Five*, New York: R. R. Donnelley & Sons.

Contributors

Giuditta Corbella recently obtained her Ph.D. in Philosophy at Università Cattolica del Sacro Cuore, Milano. Her research interests focus on the multidirectional use of modalities among phenomenologists, the history of phenomenology—with a focus on Heidegger and Ingarden—and the theory of questions. Her recent essays include "Necessity, Contingency, and Metaphysical Mysteries in Roman Ingarden," "Heidegger and Ingarden on Kant's Hundred Thalers," and "The Destruction of 'Possible' and 'Real' in the Early Heidegger".

Charlene Elsby is a Ph.D. and specializes in Aristotle and realist phenomenology. She is the vice president of the North American Society for Early Phenomenology, the president of the North American Roman Ingarden Society, and the general editor of *Phenomenological Investigations*. She edited the volume *Essays on Aesthetic Genesis*, and her recent essays include "The Origin of Theoretical Knowledge in the Organization of Nature," "Kill Metaphor: Kafka's Becoming-Animal and the Deterritorialization of Language as a Rejection of Stasis," "Time and Its Indeterminacy in Roman Ingarden's Concept of the Literary Work of Art," and "Gregor Samsa's Spots of Indeterminacy: Kafka as Phenomenologist." Her fictional works include *Hexis*, *Affect*, *Psychros*, and *Musos*.

Matthew E. Gladden is a member of the research team of the Center for Artificial Intelligence and Cybercommunication Research (CAICR) of the Faculty of Management of the University of Łódź and a data scientist at BRAD Consulting in Warsaw. His research seeks to analyze the ongoing "technological posthumanization" of society through the lens of phenomenology. He previously taught philosophy at Purdue University and served as Associate Director of the Woodstock Theological Center at Georgetown University. He is also an award-winning computer game designer and the author of *Phenomenology of the Gameworld: A Philosophical Toolbox for Video Game Developers* (2019).

Harri Mäcklin is an Associate Professor of Aesthetics at the University of Helsinki. His research interests focus on aesthetic experience, phenomenological aesthetics, and the history of modern aesthetics. His work has especially focused on topics related to aesthetic immersion. He is also an art critic at the Finnish newspaper *Helsingin Sanomat*.

Natalia Anna Michna is an assistant professor at the Institute of Philosophy, at the Jagiellonian University in Kraków. She is the main researcher of the project "The Roman Ingarden Digital Archive." She is the deputy editor-in-chief of *The Polish Journal of Aesthetics*. Michna is the author of *Women and Culture. The Problem of Experience in Feminist Philosophy* (2018). Her research interests concern Roman Ingarden's philosophy of art, feminist philosophy, contemporary art, and women's history.

Jeff Mitscherling is Emeritus Professor of Philosophy at the University of Guelph, Ontario, Canada. His publications include *Roman Ingarden's Ontology and Aesthetics* (1997), *The Author's Intention* (2004, with T. DiTommaso and A. Nayed), *The Image of a Second Sun: Plato on Poetry, Rhetoric, and the Technē of Mimēsis* (2009), *Aesthetic Genesis: The Origin of Consciousness in the Intentional Being of Nature* (2010), and *Artistic Creation: A Phenomenological Account* (2019, with P. Fairfield).

Peter Simons is a former professor of philosophy at Trinity College Dublin, where he held the Chair of Moral Philosophy, established in 1837. He has researched philosophy since 1972 in the UK, Austria, and Ireland. Now retired, he lives in West Sussex, but he continues to teach intermittently at Salzburg and is a visiting professor at the MAP—the research master in Metaphysics and Mind in Lugano.

Leszek Sosnowski is a full professor at the Institute of Philosophy, at the Jagiellonian University in Kraków. He is the director of the project "The Roman Ingarden Digital Archive." He is a founder and editor-in-chief of *The Polish Journal of Aesthetics*. He is the coauthor of the *Dictionary of the Philosophical Concepts of Roman Ingarden* (2001), which he intends to translate into English. His fields of interests are Roman Ingarden's philosophy, aesthetics theories of the twentieth century, and Arthur Danto's philosophy.

Edward M. Świderski is Professor Emeritus of the Philosophy of Culture and Aesthetics at the University of Fribourg, Switzerland. His areas of competence are Russian and Soviet thought as well as twentieth-century Polish philosophy. He was editor-in-chief (1988–2018) of *Studies in Soviet Thought* (as of 1992 *Studies in East European Thought*). His publications include, among others, research in

Soviet aesthetics and post-Soviet social and cultural theory, Ingarden's ontology and aesthetics, Polish Marxism (Brzozowski; Kołakowski; the Poznań School), and J.M. Bocheński's moral philosophy.

Jan Woleński is Professor Emeritus at the Jagiellonian University in Kraków, Poland, and Professor at the University of Technology, Information in Management in Rzeszów, Poland. He is also the member of Polish Academy of Sciences, Polish Academy of Arts and Sciences, International Institute of Philosophy in Paris, Brazilian Academy of Philosophy, Academia Europea, and dr hc of Łódź University in Poland. He was awarded the Prize of the Fund for Polish Science (called "Polish Nobel"). His fields of interests are logic, epistemology, legal philosophy, and the history of philosophy. He published 36 books (10 in foreign languages) and 950 papers (425 in foreign languages).

Index

8-bit game   22–3, 121–33
   2D perspective   123
   artistic crudeness of   122–3
   audio hardware of   123
   constituent literary work of art, indeterminacy of   125–7
   Ingarden's account of concretization   124–5
   and life cycle of work of art   129–32
   nostalgia   122, 132–3
   overview   121–2
   revival of   122
   as sophisticated organic whole   123–4
   storylines   123
   technical limitations of   125–7
   visual depiction of objects, indeterminacy of   127–9
   visual elements   122–3
8-bit processors   133 n.1

Absolute   38
aesthetic apprehension   88, 91–2, 95, 96–7 n.8
aesthetic attention   24–5, 105–6, 143–7
   Ingarden on   143–7
   Nanay's theory of   138–42
aesthetic attitude   16–17, 24–5, 106, 138–41, 143–5
aesthetic experience   19–25, 91, 94, 97 n.14, 103–17
   attention role in   138
   Carroll, Noël   138
   consciousness in   139
   Ingarden's views on   139
   traits of structure of   104
aesthetic reality   104, 115
aesthetic research   17–18
aesthetics as cognition of work of art   2, 17–28
   aesthetic experience   19–22

art/attitude/experience   23–5
   of computer games   22–3
   Elsby on   25–8
   empathy and   19–22, 103, 107, 115
   Gladden on   22–3
   Mäcklin on   23–5
   Mitscherling on   19–22
   and time   25–8, 150–61
aesthetic situation   19
aesthetic values   18–19, 23, 103, 107–12, 122, 132–3, 144–5
Ajdukiewicz's theory of question   70, 81 n.5
Alexander, Samuel   33
analytical philosophy   7–8
   existential   7
   formal   7
   material   7
Annecy Lake (Cezanne)   125
Aristotelian logic   53
Aristotle   6, 35, 38, 39, 48
artistic values   19
astronomers   47
attention   24–5, 105–6, 143–7
attitudes   16–17, 24–5
Augustus, Sigismund   52
autonomous objects   36

Bacchante couchée (Moreau)   22
Barcan formula   52
basic modal logic (BML)   53, 56–7, 66 n.5
Behauptungsfunktion (assertoric function)   72
Bergson, Henri   4
BML; *see* basic modal logic
Bullough, Edward   107

Carroll, Noël   138
Cartesian system   8
categories   48
characters   39
cladistic taxonomy   39

cognition 2
    general idea of 9
    of mental states 21
    object of 9
    theory of 9
Cognition of the Literary Work of Art
    (Ingarden) 103–4, 114, 131,
    143–4
complete empathy 105–6
computer games, aesthetics of 22–3; *see also* 8-bit game
concept lattice 42–3
concretization 124–5
Conrad-Martius, Hedwig 73
consciousness 9, 73–4, 110
Controversy over the Existence of the World
    (Ingarden) 6–7, 11–12, 14–15,
    26–7, 33
copula 72
Corbella, Giuditta 14–15

Das literarische Kunstwerk (Ingarden) 7,
    23, 26, 37, 129, 131, 143
de dicto modalities 52
De Interpretatione 4 (Aristotle) 75
de re modalities 52
derivatives 37
Descartes, R. 8
Dickie, George 24
disinterestedness 138
double intentionality 90, 98 n.19
Dufrenne, Mikel 140
durable objects 38

Einfühlung (Ingarden) 20
Elsby, Charlene 25–8
emotions 105
empathy 19–22, 103–7, 115
    complete 105–6
    Ingarden on empathy to emotional
        coexperience 112–17
    levels 116
    Lipps's view of 104–7
    operation of 104
    positive 105
    Stein, Edith on 107–12
Empedocles 39–40
epistemological conventionalism
    77–8
epistemology 7–8

Erickson, Richard 28
erotetics 68–79, 80 n.4
essence 68–71, 76–9
Essentiale Fragen (Ingarden) 10, 14–15,
    68–74, 76–7, 79, 92–3, 130
essentialities 68–71, 76–9
ethics 9
events 46
existential moments *vs.* moments of
    being 57–8
existential ontologies of Ingarden 11–14,
    34–6, 51–66
    absolute (transient) 11
    ideal (non-temporal) 11
    intentional (purely intentional) 12
    modes 11–12
    ontic autonomy (self-existence) 12
    ontic dependence 12
    ontic derivativeness 12
    ontic heteronomy (non-self-
        existence) 12
    ontic independence 12
    ontic originality 12
    ontic self-sufficiency 12
    real (temporal) 12

factored classification 38–40
falsehood 57
FCA; *see* formal concept analysis
formal concept analysis (FCA) 40–2, 45
formal ontology 34

Geiger, Moritz 140
Georg August University 2
Gestalt theory 93, 98 n.21
Gierulanka, Danuta 25
Gladden, Matthew 22–3
God 51
Göttingen circle 2–4

Hamlet 36–7
Harmonies 17, 90
Harry Potter 36–7
Hartmann, Nicolai 140
hearing 17
hearing sounds 90
Hennig, Willi 39
heteronomous objects 36–7, 42
hierarchical (dendritic, tree-like)
    classification 39

Index

Hinbeziehungsfunktion (connective function) 72
Husserl, Edmund 2–6, 33–4, 37, 48, 107–8
  critique of Bolzano 75–6
  erotetic theory 75
  Ideas 75
  ideation 87, 92
  Logical Investigations 37, 75, 92
  Species 87, 92

ideal 106–7
Ideas (Husserl) 75
ideation 87, 92
imitation 104–7
indecision 73, 76
(in)dependence 36–7
indeterminacy 73, 76
individuality 110
Ingarden, Roman Witold 1–28, 80 n.3, 98 n.20
  on aesthetic attention 24–5, 105–6, 143–7
  on aesthetic experience 103–17
  aesthetics and theoretical biology, efforts to connect 129–30
  aesthetics as cognition of work of art 2, 17–28
  background 2–3
  Cognition of the Literary Work of Art 103–4, 114, 131, 143–4
  computer games, aesthetics of 22–3, 121–33
  considerations 5–8
  Controversy over the Existence of the World 6–7, 11–12, 14–15, 26–7, 33
  creativity, concept of 17
  Das literarische Kunstwerk 7, 23, 26, 37, 129, 131, 143
  doctoral thesis 3
  eidetic-ontological intentions 15
  empathy to emotional coexperience, move from 112–17
  Essentiale Fragen 10, 14–15, 68–74, 76–7, 79, 92–3, 130
  existential moments *vs.* moments of being 57–8
  existential ontology 11–14, 34–6, 51–66

  extra-aesthetic approach 1–2
  Husserl, E. and 2–5, 75
  language of 5–6
  life cycle of (literary) work of art 130–1
  literary time, concept of 25–8, 150–61
  Literary Work of Art, The 69, 106–7, 129, 131, 143
  Man and Value 9
  metaphysical qualities, concept of 17, 19
  modes of being 35–48, 57–8
  musical aesthetics 15–17, 84–96
  ontology 5–17, 33–49
  overview 1–28
  philosophy 1–4, 7–8
  studies 2–4
  style of inquiry 5–6
  theory of erotetic 71–6
  theory of questions 14–15, 68–80
  Z teorii języka i filozoficznych podstaw logiki 10
instrumental sounds 89
intentional consciousness 89
intentionality 90

judgment 72

Leibniz axiom 57, 66 n.4
Leitfaden der Psychologie (Lipps) 104, 108
Levinson, Jerrold 15–16, 86–90, 94, 95
Life in a Jewish Family (Stein) 107–9
"life" of work of art 1
Lipps, Theodor 20–1, 103, 115
  on empathy 104–7
  ideal, use of 106–7
  on imitation 104–7
  Leitfaden der Psychologie 104, 108
  on projection 105–6
literary criticism 18
literary time 25–8, 150–61
  metaphysics of 27–8
  neutral present 151–3, 162 n.2
  past *vs.* future 153–5
  present 151–3
  real 27, 150
  in work 27, 155–60
  of work of art as physical object 27

literary work of art 112
    indeterminacy, spots of 113–14
    represented objects 113
    schematized aspects 113–14
    strata 112–13
    stratified structure 112
Literary Work of Art, The (Ingarden) 69, 106–7, 129, 131, 143
Logical Investigations (Husserl) 37, 75, 92
Logic of Pfänder 75
Lord of the Rings (Tolkien) 113
Lowe, Jonathan 35, 47–8

McCormick, Peter 17
Mäcklin, Harri 23–5
Man and Value (Ingarden) 9
material ontology 34
metaphysical commitment 76–80
metaphysical fantasy 86
metaphysical qualities 19
metaphysics *vs.* ontology 34
Minkowski spacetime 161 n.1
Mitscherling, Jeff 19–22
modal logic 51–66
    de dicto 52, 55
    de re 52, 55
    existential quantifier 52
    monadic modal operators 53
    ontology and 51–66
    rationalistic 57
    T-scheme 56
modes of being 35–6, 57–8
    absolute 38
    accidentality 58–60
    actuality 56–9, 63–5
    autonomy *vs.* heteronomy 58–9
    empirically possible 38
    ideal 38
    impossibility as 58
    independence *vs.* dependence 58–9
    intentional objects 38
    necessity as 58–9
    originality *vs.* derivativeness 58–62
    possibility 58–9
    real 38
    self-sufficiency *vs.* non-self-sufficiency 58–9

moments 48
monadic modal operators 53
Moreau, Augustin 22
music, ontologies of 15–17, 84–96
musical aesthetics 15–17, 84–96
    Ingarden on 86–96
    Scruton's work in 87–95
    sound 15–17, 86–95
    tones 15–17, 86–90, 95
    work identity 94–5
musical experience 84–6
    acousmatic experience 90
    cultural context 90
    double intentionality 90, 98 n.19
    externalist perspective on 86
    imagination 90
    Ingarden on 86–96
    metaphorical hearing and description 90
    Scruton on 86–96
    sounds/tones 90
musical frisson 17, 88, 97 n.14
musical imagination 17
musical organization 84

Nanay, Bence 24–5, 138–40
    theory of aesthetic attention 140–2
Nash, Suzie 28
neutral present 151–3, 162 n.2
non-fissurated objects 38, 42
non-self-sufficient objects 37, 42
notochord 39

objective aesthetics 19
objects 37–8
    absolute 37–8
    durable 38
    non-fissurated 38
    non-self-sufficient 37
    self-sufficient 37
objectum formale (OF) 71–2, 76
    and indecision 76–7
objectum materiale (OM) 71
obligation 56
occurrence table 40, 42
    concept lattice 42–3
    formal concept analysis (FCA) 40–2, 45
On the Problem of Empathy (Stein) 28 n.2, 109–10

ontologies of Ingarden   5–17, 33–49,
       66 n.2
    analytical philosophy   7–8
    for anthropological research   9
    Cartesian system   8
    concerns   45–7
    in considerations of language   9–10
    Corbella on   14–15
    for ethical research   9
    existential   11–14, 34–6, 51–66
    as existential judgments   7
    factored classification   38–40
    formal   34
    material   34
    vs. metaphysics   34
    methodological aspect   6
    modal logic and   51–66
    moments and their families   36–8
    of music   15–17, 84–96
    objective aspect   6
    other factored   47–8
    particular   8–11
    a priori analysis   6
    a priori science   6
    pure ideal qualities *vs.* pure
       possibilities   7
    reality, questions/problem of   14–15,
       68–80
    Simons's reflections on   11–14
    of sounds   15–17
    Świderski on   15–17
    taxonomy   40–5
    of tones   15–17
    Woleński's reflections on   11–14
Osloer Vorlesung (Oslo Lecture)   73

particular ontologies   8–11
perception   139
permission   56
permission-not   56
phenomenology   3, 86
philosophy   1–4
    of aesthetics   18
    analytical   7–8
    of art   18
    of literature   18
    of perception   139
*Philosophy of Psychology and the
    Humanities* (Stein)   111
pitches   90

Plato   35
*Political Cartoons in 18th Century
    England*   38–9
polyphonic harmony   112
power of concentration   25
present   151–3
prohibition   56
projection   105–7
psychical distance   107

quasi-relative property   78

Ranganathan, S. R.   39
real   38
real time   27, 150
real transcendence   73
reality   104–7
Reinach, Adolf   4
relative beings   58
represented objects   113
rhythm   17, 90
Ryle, G.   68–9, 71

schematicity   1
Scruton, Roger   15–16, 86–96
    acousmatic experience   88–9
    Levinson disputes with   87–90
    phenomenology   87–8
    work in musical aesthetics   87–95
self-sufficient objects   37
Simons, Peter   11–14
Slaughterhouse-Five (Vonnegut)   27, 151,
    154–60
solipsism   20
sounds   15–17
    as acoustic phenomena   90
    hearing   90
    instrumental   89
    vs. music   89–90
    ontologies of   15–17, 85–96
    vs. tones   85–6, 95
Spezie   87, 92
Stein, Edith   20–2, 103, 118 n.7
    criticisms of Lipps   108–9
    on empathy   107–12
    expression of experiences   105
    Life in a Jewish Family   107–9
    PhD dissertation   108
    *Philosophy of Psychology and the
       Humanities*   111

On the Problem of Empathy 28 n.2, 109–10
   on recognition of value 107–12
study of literature 18
subjective aesthetics 19
Świderski, Edward M. 15–17

Tatarkiewicz, Władysław 5
Teardrop 44–5
tempi 90
theoretical biology 129–30
theory of erotetic 71–9
theory of questions 14–15, 68–79
   Ajdukiewicz's 70, 81 n.5
   Behauptungsfunktion (assertoric function) 72
   copula 72
   epistemological conventionalism 77–8
   erotetics 68–71, 80 n.4
   Hinbeziehungsfunktion (connective function) 72
   indecision 73
   judgment 72
   metaphysical commitment 76–80
   negative cognitive component 76
   objectum formale (OF) 71–2, 76
   objectum materiale (OM) 71
   ontological erotetics 76–80
   positive cognitive component 76
   status quaestionis 70–1
   subjects 74–5
   triadic scheme 76
   volitional component 76
timbre 17
time 25–8, 150–61
   literary 27, 150–61
   metaphysics of 27–8
   neutral present 151–3, 162 n.2
   past *vs.* future 153–5
   present 151–3
   real 27, 150
   in work 27, 155–60

of work of art as physical object 27
Tolkien, J. R. R. 113
tones 15–17, 86–90, 95
   experience 86–7
   formations 87, 92–3
   nature of 86
   patterns 94–5
   properties of 90
   pure 93, 95
   qualities 87–8, 93
   Scruton's obsession with 87–95
   vs. sounds 85–6, 95
transcendence 73
   consciousness 73–4
   epistemological 73
   ontic-metaphysical 73
   ontic-ontological 73
   semantics of 74
trans-logical commitment 77
truth-value gaps 56
T-scheme 56
Twain, Mark 113
Twardowski, Kazimierz 2–3

University of Lviv 2–3

Vischer, Friedrich 20
Volkelt, Johannes 20
Vonnegut, Kurt 27, 151, 154–60, 162 n.6
Whitehead, Alfred North 33
Wille, Rudolf 40–2
Williams, Donald Cary 33
Wind in the Willows, The (Grahame) 125
Woleński, Jan 11–14, 51
work of art, life of 1

Zahavi, Dan 118 n.2
Z teorii języka i filozoficznych podstaw logiki (Ingarden) 10
Zur Ontologie und Erscheinungslehre der realen Aussenwelt (Conrad-Martius) 73

www.ingramcontent.com/pod-product-compliance
Lightning Source LLC
Chambersburg PA
CBHW052126300426
44116CB00010B/1801